D0773416

THE NEW INVESTMENT SUPERSTARS

13 GREAT INVESTORS AND THEIR STRATEGIES FOR SUPERIOR RETURNS

LOIS PELTZ

JOHN WILEY & SONS, INC.

New York • Chichester • Weinheim • Brisbane • Singapore • Toronto

Copyright © 2001 by Lois Peltz. All rights reserved.

Published by John Wiley & Sons, Inc.
Published simultaneously in Canada.

This publication is designed to provide accurate and authoritative information in regard to the subject matter covered. It is sold with the understanding that the publisher is not engaged in rendering legal, accounting, or other professional services. If professional advice or other expert assistance is required, the services of a competent professional person should be sought.

Illustrations by Ralph Butler.

Library of Congress Cataloging-in-Publication Data:

Peltz, Lois, 1956–
    The new investment superstars : 13 great investors and their strategies for
superior returns / Lois Peltz.
      p.   cm.
    Includes bibliographical references.
    ISBN 0-471-40313-X (cloth : alk. paper)
    1. Capitalists and financiers—United States—Biography.   2. Investment
analysis.   I. Title.
HG4910 .P424   2001
332.6'092'273—dc21
[B]   00-054559

Printed in the United States of America.

10   9   8   7   6   5   4   3   2   1

To the hedge fund community and the unique qualities it embodies: talent, intellect, entrepreneurship, and energy

To Jerry, for his love and support

And to my parents

Contents

     Based in Dallas, this $6 billion-plus classic long/short
     hedge fund manager is known for his intensive fundamental
     research and bottom-up approach to stock selection. The
     focus is on medium- and large-capitalized U.S. equities.
     Ainslie's hedged equity strategy has not yet experienced a
     down performance year.

     Known for his U.S. stock-picking ability, this manager is
     intensive and demanding of himself, his employees, and the
     companies that he follows. He is an energetic and active
     portfolio investor who takes a value approach to investing.

Introduction

Investors and market watchers have long been captivated by star traders—those who have the most spectacular returns on a consistent basis for a number of years. These include the likes of mutual fund manager Peter Lynch or investment manager Warren Buffett.

In most recent years, hedge fund managers have become the superstar investors. They have more flexibility than the typical mutual fund manager. Because many are not regulated by the Securities and Exchange Commission (SEC), they can use more leverage, short markets to a greater extent, and explore for opportunities around the world in many different markets using a variety of investment vehicles. While this strategy has its advantages, it can also be dangerous. We have seen a number of giants stumble in the past few years.

However, a new breed of hedge fund manager has evolved. Some are relatively young—in their 30s, such as Lee Ainslie, Ken Griffin, or Daniel Och; or 40s, such as Raj Rajaratnam, Brian Stark, David Tepper, or Bruce Wilcox. Others are in their 50s and have been around a bit longer, such as Leon Cooperman, John Henry, Mark Kingdon, Bruce Kovner, Paul Singer, and S. Donald Sussman. While their trading strategies may differ, this new breed is characterized not only by generating superior returns on a consistent basis and in different market environments but also by managing the downside risk and reducing volatility. They have been able to embrace change and profit from it rather than fight it. During their relatively long track records, they have gone through rocky periods. But they persevered and survived.

Institutions are now allocating to this new breed in record amounts. Recent studies show 104 endowments are allocating on average 2.3 percent of their overall portfolios to hedge funds, and each year those numbers grow. U.S. pension funds such as California Public Employees Retirement System (CalPERS), Public School Teachers' Pension and Retirement Fund of Chicago, and Oklahoma Firefighters' Retirement System are following the lead of the endowments. Institutions around the world are allocating to hedge funds—increasingly in Europe and Japan.

Investors—individual and institutional—can learn a great deal from this new breed. The key characteristics of these managers transcend age and generation as well as trading strategy. They love what they do, are motivated by the intellectual and emotional challenge, have the primary objective of delivering superior performance in various market conditions (not having the largest fund regarding assets under management), are the largest investors in their funds, and have a very large percentage of their own net worth in their funds. They have developed a culture consistent with their personalities. They are attempting to institutionalize the business. They have built an organization that consists of specialists and teams. While they have gone through difficult periods in the market, they learned from the experience. They have the ability to acknowledge and learn from their mistakes. Managing risk and volatility, as well as information technology are common threads.

Some characteristics are not universal but appear frequently. Most became involved with investing during their teen years. Most have Ivy League backgrounds and/or MBA degrees. Most take an opportunistic approach to the markets traded; fundamental research is the dominant approach. Most have seen their roles evolve into those of coordinator/overseer. Investment committees are a way to instill culture. Some selectively make allocations to other hedge fund managers. Minimum investments are significantly higher and lock-up of assets tends to be longer than with the typical fund. The superstar managers generally lead balanced lives—sports is a common free-time activity. Most of the organizations are located in New York.

On a number of characteristics, no agreement exists. Trading strategies differ. The amount of allocation to U.S. markets, global macro strategy, technology, and private equity varies. Little consensus exists on the degree of exposure to the stock market and the managers' choices of hedging technique. Different criteria exist on which trades are selected. Number of investors and geographic breakdown vary. The amount and frequency of information given to the investor vary considerably, as does the number of people in the firm.

Three major challenges exist for the hedge fund manager: determining when the optimal asset size has been reached; surviving challenging markets; and developing organizations that can last from generation to generation.

The natural tendency is for a manager to let the fund grow as large as possible. The larger the fund, the more fees the manager collects. Yet as a fund gets to a certain size, which varies depending on the number and type of strategies used, performance starts to deteriorate. Another problem is that managers may not be able to get out of a wrong idea quickly. Furthermore, areas of core competency sometimes are not adequate for growing funds, motivating the manager to stray into new areas that may not be related to the manager's specialty. This may necessitate hiring subportfolio managers.

Another major challenge for the hedge fund is its ability to survive in difficult markets. The bull market in stocks helped many managers post excellent returns. Now that the markets are choppier and more difficult, risk management and hedging play a larger role. The short side of the equation becomes more important.

Except for Cumberland Associates, no elite hedge fund management firm has yet been successful in creating continuity from one generation to another. It remains to be seen whether the superstar managers will be able to succeed at this. A number have made attempts through creating specialist teams, developing a culture, and emphasizing the importance of career development. Many of the 60-something hedge fund managers had started their hedge fund careers after a successful investment career and did not consider succession or exit value in their initial business plans.

MAP

There are four sections of the book. Part One looks at the past. These chapters highlight what has happened and what has changed. Chapter 1 explores the historic watershed events of the year 2000—the retirement of Julian Robertson of Tiger Management and George Soros's reorganization of Soros Fund Management. Other notable hedge fund managers who recently retired include Michael Steinhardt and Jack Nash/Leon Levy of Odyssey Partners. Chapter 2 gives reasons for retiring or diluting a fund as well as the implications the events of 2000 have on the hedge fund community going forward.

While Robertson and Soros were having trouble, the hedge fund community was prospering and proliferating; it was not uncommon to find managers in their 20s and 30s, and many were generating excellent returns. Chapter 3 provides a snapshot of the hedge fund community today—an overview of the industry, its size and growth, and types of strategies used. The chapter also looks into recent debacles and regulatory initiatives to prevent abuses.

Part Two of the book focuses on today's stars—the new breed of manager. The common and not-so-common threads among the superstar managers are explored in Chapter 4.

Individual chapters are then provided on Lee Ainslie, Leon Cooperman, Ken Griffin, John Henry, Mark Kingdon, Bruce Kovner, Daniel Och, Raj Rajaratnam, Paul Singer, Brian Stark, S. Donald Sussman, David Tepper, and Bruce Wilcox. Each manager has a chapter devoted to his investment style, his background, his influences, and his motivations. I was interested in capturing the essence of the person as well as the manager. Each manager brings his own personal skills, style, and personality into his organization. The interviews were conducted May through September 2000.

To qualify for this elite circle, each manager had to be managing at least $1 billion in assets; possess at least a seven-year track record of his own of consistently strong performance in varying market conditions, with average annualized returns at least as good as the

Table I.1 The Forbes 400: America's Richest People—Money Managers ($M)

	2000	1999	1998	1997	1996	1995	1994	1993
George Soros	5,000	5,000	4,000	3,500	3,500	1,000	1,200	785
Julian Robertson	1,000	1,000	1,700	1,000	1,000	330	N/A	N/A
Bruce Kovner	900	900	850	650	650	450	450	300
Stanley Druckenmiller	1,000	1,000	850	800	800	350	N/A	N/A
Leon Levy	750	675	600	550	475	340	310	N/A

Source: Forbes, October 9, 2000; October 11, 1999; October 12, 1998; October 13, 1997; October 14, 1996; October 16, 1995; October 17, 1994; October 18, 1993.

Table I.2   Hedge Fund Managers among *Financial World*'s Top 100 Wall
Street Earners

1991

Manager	Rank	Minimum Earnings ($M)	Company
George Soros	1	117	Soros Fund Management
Julian Robertson	2	65	Tiger Management
Paul Tudor Jones	3	60	Tudor Investment Corp.
Bruce Kovner	4	60	Caxton Corp.
Michael Steinhardt	5	55	Steinhardt Partners
John Henry	6	50	John W. Henry & Co.
Philip Hempelman	12	30	Ardsley Advisory Partners
Stanley Druckenmiller	13	30	Soros Fund Management
George Weiss	14	25	George Weiss Associates
Louis Bacon	17	20	Moore Capital Management
Leon Levy	20	20	Odyssey Partners
Jack Nash	21	20	Odyssey Partners
Malcolm Wiener	23	20	Millburn
Martin Zweig	24	20	Zweig-DiMenna Associates
Douglas Floren	35	14	Ardsley Advisory Partners
Joseph DiMenna	40	12	Zweig-DiMenna Associates
Larry Hite	47	10	Mint Investment Management
Peter Matthews	48	10	Mint Investment Management
Mark Strome	52	8	Kayne Anderson
Mark Dickstein	58	7 to 9	Dickstein Partners
Glenn Dushay	60	7	Ardsley Advisory Partners
Lang Gerhard	61	7	West Highland Capital
John Lattanzio	63	7	Steinhardt Partners
Joseph McNay	64	7	Essex Investment Mgt.
Monroe Trout	68	7	Trout Trading
Patrick Duff	87	5 to 6	Tiger Management
John Griffin	89	5 to 6	Tiger Management
Stephen Mandel	92	5 to 6	Tiger Management
Michael Delman	96	5	Mint Investment Management
J. O. Patterson	98	5	Falcon Partners

Source: Financial World, July 21, 1992, page 40.

1992

Manager	Rank	Minimum Earnings ($M)	Company
George Soros	1	650	Soros Fund Management
Michael Steinhardt	2	250	Steinhardt Partners
Julian Robertson	4	120	Tiger Management
Stanley Druckenmiller	5	110	Soros Fund Management
Bruce Kovner	6	100	Caxton Corp.

(Continued)

Table I.2   Continued

1992

Manager	Rank	Minimum Earnings ($M)	Company
Paul Tudor Jones	7	85	Tudor Investment Corp.
Louis Bacon	8	35	Moore Capital Management
S. Donald Sussman	15	25	Paloma Partners
George Weiss	16	24.5	George Weiss Association
Neil Weisman	23	19	Chilmark Capital
Martin Zweig	28	16	Zweig-DiMenna Associates
Monroe Trout	32	15	Trout Trading
Charles Davidson	37	12 to 15	Steinhardt Partners
John Lattanzio	38	12 to 15	Steinhardt Partners
Kenneth Lipper	40	12	Lipper & Co.
Gerard Manolovici	41	12	Soros Fund Management
Robert Raiff	42	10	Soros Fund Management
Leon Cooperman	50	10	Omega Advisors
Joseph DiMenna	51	10	Zweig-DiMenna Associates
Philip Hempelman	54	10	Ardsley Advisory Partners
Leon Levy	56	10	Odyssey Partners
Jack Nash	58	10	Odyssey Partners
Elizabeth Larson	68	8	Soros Fund Management
Dale Precoda	70	8	Soros Fund Management
Lief Rosenblatt	72	8	Soros Fund Management
Harvey Sandler	73	8	Sandler Capital Management
Patrick Duff	74	7	Tiger Management
John Griffin	84	7	Tiger Management
Stephen Mandel	85	7	Tiger Management
Gary Fragin	95	6	Steinhardt Partners
Shimon Torpor	100	6	Steinhardt Partners

Source: Financial World, July 6, 1993, page 38.

1993

Manager	Rank	Minimum Earnings ($M)	Company
George Soros	1	1,100	Soros Fund Management
Julian Robertson	2	500	Tiger Management
Michael Steinhardt	3	475	Steinhardt Partners
Stanley Druckenmiller	4	210	Soros Fund Management
Bruce Kovner	5	200	Caxton Corp.
Paul Kazarian	6	148	Japonica Partners
Mark Strome	8	90	Kayne Anderson
Leon Cooperman	9	85	Omega Advisors
Louis Bacon	13	55	Moore Capital Management
Leon Levy	15	50	Odyssey Partners
Jack Nash	16	50	Odyssey Partners
George Weiss	17	50	George Weiss Associates

Table I.2 Continued

1993 Manager	Rank	Minimum Earnings ($M)	Company
George Noble	20	43	Noble Partners
Philip Hempelman	22	40	Ardsley Advisory Partners
R. Jerry Parker	25	35	Chesapeake Capital
John Henry	28	30	John W. Henry & Co.
Gerard Manolovici	30	30	Soros Fund Management
Robert Raiff	31	30	Soros Fund Management
S. Donald Sussman	32	30	Paloma Partners
Martin Zweig	33	29	Zweig-DiMenna Associates
Sam Wyly	35	25-30	Maverick Capital
Charles Davidson	36	25	Steinhardt Partners
James Harpel	37	25	Harpel Advisory
Mark Kingdon	38	25	Kingdon Capital Management
John Lattanzio	39	25	Steinhardt Partners
Kenneth Lipper	40	25	Lipper & Co.
Monroe Trout	43	23	Trout Trading
Joseph DiMenna	46	22	Zweig-DiMenna Associates
Scott Bessent	47	20	Soros Fund Management
Walter Burlock	48	20	Soros Fund Management
Dale Precoda	50	20	Soros Fund Management
Leif Rosenblatt	51	20	Soros Fund Management
Harvey Sandler	52	18	Sandler Capital Management
Douglas Floren	55	16	Ardsley Advisory Partners
Stanley Shopkorn	56	16	Ethos Capital Management
Patrick Duff	60	15	Tiger Management
John Griffin	61	15	Tiger Management
Stephen Mandel	62	15	Tiger Management
Thomas Niedermeyer	64	15	Noble Partners
Gregory Panayis	65	15	Strome, Susskind
Morris Mark	73	14	Mark Asset Management
Mark Dickstein	77	12	Dickstein Partners
Glenn Doshay	95	10	Ardsley Advisory Partners
Gary Gladstein	97	10	Soros Fund Management
Elizabeth Larson	99	10	Soros Fund Management

Source: Financial World, July 5, 1994, page 40.

1994 Manager	Rank	Minimum Earnings ($M)	Company
George Soros	2	70	Soros Fund Management
Paul Tudor Jones	6	45	Tudor Investment Corp.
Monroe Trout	8	31	Trout Trading
James Simons	13	22	Renaissance Technologies

(Continued)

Table I.2   Continued

1994

Manager	Rank	Minimum Earnings ($M)	Company
Steven Cohen	17	20	SAC Capital Management
Martin Zweig	21	20	Zweig-DiMenna Associates
Peter Gruber	23	19	Globalvest Management
R. Jerry Parker	28	17	Chesapeake Capital
Stanley Druckenmiller	35	15	Soros Fund Management
Joseph DiMenna	73	7	Zweig-DiMenna Associates
Mark Dickstein	83	6	Dickstein Partners

Source: Financial World, July 4, 1995, page 40.

1995

Manager	Rank	Minimum Earnings ($M)	Company
George Soros	1	1,500	Soros Fund Management
Stanley Druckenmiller	2	350	Soros Fund Management
Michael Steinhardt	3	115	Steinhardt Partners
Julian Robertston	6	90	Tiger Management
Nick Roditi	9	75	N. Roditi & Co.
Bruce Kovner	10	70	Caxton Corp.
Paul Tudor Jones	11	60	Tudor Investment Corp.
Scott Bessent	15	50	Soros Fund Management
Lief Rosenblatt	18	50	Soros Fund Management
John Henry	19	40	John W. Henry & Co.
James Simons	20	40	Renaissance Technologies
Steven Cohen	23	35	SAC Capital Management
R. Jerry Parker	25	35	Chesapeake Capital
Robert Raiff	26	35	Centurion Investment Group
Mark Kingdon	32	28	Kingdon Capital Management
Louis Bacon	35	26	Moore Capital Management
Larry Feinberg	38	25	Oracle Management
Monroe Trout	41	25	Trout Trading
Martin Zweig	43	25	Zweig-DiMenna Associates
Walter Burlock	47	20	Soros Fund Management
Gary Gladstein	49	20	Soros Fund Management
Elizabeth Larson	50	20	Soros Fund Management
Dale Precoda	51	20	Soros Fund Management
John Tozzi	52	19	Cambridge Investments
Leon Levy	55	18	Odyssey Partners
Jack Nash	56	18	Odyssey Partners
Joshua Nash	57	18	Odyssey Partners
Jeffrey Gendell	64	15	Odyssey Partners
Lang Gerhard	65	15	West Highland Capital
Joseph DiMenna	81	12	Zweig-DiMenna Associates
John Griffin	92	10	Tiger Management

Source: Financial World, October 21, 1996, page 58.

Table I.2 Continued

1996

Manager	Rank	Minimum Earnings ($M)	Company
George Soros	1	800	Soros Fund Management
Julian Robertson	2	300	Tiger Management
Stanley Druckenmiller	5	200	Soros Fund Management
Nick Roditi	9	125	Soros Fund Management
David Tepper	12	90	Appaloosa Mgt.
Bruce Kovner	13	85	Caxton Corp.
Michael Steinhardt	14	75	Steinhardt Partners
Steven Cohen	16	70	SAC Capital Management
James Simon	17	70	Renaissance Technologies
Louis Bacon	19	65	Moore Capital Management
Leon Cooperman	23	55	Omega Advisors
John Henry	25	50	John W. Henry & Co.
John Tozzi	29	50	Cambridge Investments
Paul Tudor Jones	36	40	Tudor Investment Corp.
R. Jerry Parker	41	35	Chesapeake Capital
Monroe Trout	43	35	Trout Trading
Sam Wyly	46	32	Maverick Capital
Mark Kingdon	48	31	Kingdon Capital Management
Philip Hempelman	51	30	Ardsley Advisory Partners
John Meriwether	52	30	Long-Term Capital Mgt.
Robert Raiff	53	30	Centurion Investment Group
Kenneth Lipper	61	25	Lipper & Co.
Martin Zweig	63	25	Zweig-DiMenna Associates
Jeffrey Gendell	64	23	Tontine Partners
Leon Levy	69	20	Odyssey Partners
Jack Nash	70	20	Odyssey Partners
Joshua Nash	71	20	Odyssey Partners
Thomas Steiger	72	20	Farallon Capital Mgt.
Lang Gerhard	82	17	West Highland Capital
Joseph DiMenna	92	14	Zweig-DiMenna Associates

Source: Financial World, July 17, 1997, page 44.

1998

Manager	Rank	Minimum Earnings ($M)	Company
Steve Cohen	5	200	SAC Capital Management
Joseph DiMenna	7	150	Zweig-DiMenna Associates
Jeffrey Vinik	11	120	Vinik Asset Management
Louis Bacon	13	103	Moore Capital Management
Larry Bowman	19	70	Bowman Capital
Martin Zweig	21	70	Zweig-DiMenna Associates
Paul Tudor Jones	23	60	Tudor Investment Corp.

(Continued)

Table I.2 Continued

1998 Manager	Rank	Minimum Earnings ($M)	Company
Bruce Kovner	27	50	Caxton Corp.
Robert Raiff	28	50	Centurion Investment Group
Brenda Earl	32	45	Zweig-DiMenna Associates
Kenneth Lipper	33	45	Lipper & Co.
Lee Ainslie	36	40	Maverick Capital
Richard Perry	42	34	Perry Corp.
James Pallotta	48	30	Tudor Investment Corp.
Mark Kingdon	50	28	Kingdon Capital Management
Raj Rajaratnam	54	25	Galleon Group
Morris Mark	59	20	Mark Asset Management

Source: *Ticker*, October 1999.

Standard & Poor's 500 (S&P 500); include a strong sampling of institutional investors; and be recognized by peers and the investment industry as being among the elite. These criteria are reflected in the fact that many have been on the Forbes 400 list and/or *Financial World*'s Top 100 Wall Street Earners list year after year (see Tables, I.1 and I.2). And finally, transparency is important to these managers. By agreeing to be interviewed, they have demonstrated their willingness to share information on their investment philosophies and organizations.

Part Three is designed to give a reverse look at the hedge fund superstars. By interviewing institutions—CalPERS, a large Japanese institution, and Swiss Life Insurance Company—as well as several endowments—The University of North Carolina, Stanford University, Vassar College, and Wesleyan University—I wanted to get the end users' perspectives of these superstar managers and the hedge fund industry in general. Were the institutions' goals achieved? Were they satisfied with their hedge fund experiences? Did they see growth in the hedge fund community?

Part Four presents my thoughts on where the hedge fund community is headed.

PART ONE

Snapshot of the Hedge Fund Industry

1

THE WATERSHED EVENTS OF 2000

Julian Robertson of Tiger Management and George Soros of Soros Fund Management had long been recognized as the great hedge fund managers. For many years, Soros had been the largest hedge fund manager as determined by assets under management; but in 1998, Robertson's assets overtook Soros's. At their peaks, both had assets of about $22 billion.

Both men had long and successful track records. Soros started his fund in 1969 and Robertson in 1980. Both evolved into global macro managers—those managers who take advantage of opportunities around the world and invest in a variety of instruments including stocks, bonds, commodities, currencies, and futures, and typically take large leveraged positions.

By midyear 2000, the situation had changed drastically. Robertson had retired and Soros had significantly changed his organization and fund objectives.

TIGER UNRAVELS

I met Julian H. Robertson Jr. for the first time in August 1998. We had breakfast in his office on the top floor of 101 Park Avenue. He fit the image of the Southern gentleman that I had heard about so often. During the breakfast, he mentioned the problems that he had with *Business*

Week. (*Business Week* wrote an April 1996 cover piece on him called "The Fall of the Wizard of Wall Street." It focused on his results in 1994 and 1995. The following March, Robertson initiated a libel lawsuit in New York State courts against *Business Week*; McGraw-Hill, the publisher of the magazine; Gary Weiss, the author of the story; and Stephen Shepherd, the editor of *Business Week*, seeking to recover $1 billion in damages. The suit was dropped in December 1997 after the magazine ran an editor's note saying its predictions about Tiger's future performance were not borne out by subsequent results. No payment was made.) It was still obviously a point of contention.

At our breakfast, Robertson had agreed to speak via satellite broadcast to a conference to be held in Bermuda on October 12, 1998. As it turned out, on October 7, a few days before the scheduled speaking engagement, Robertson suffered a $2 billion loss on the surge of the Japanese yen against the U.S. dollar. Despite this setback and the gloomy atmosphere that prevailed in the markets, Robertson held to his promise and spoke to the conference via satellite. This was a man of integrity. I knew this speaking engagement was not the most important thing to him at the moment. Nevertheless, he had promised and he kept his word. Many other managers would have canceled without a second thought.

Most of the satellite broadcast was questions and answers. The audience—mostly managers and other industry professionals—had been shaken by the recent events of the Russian government bond default in August and Long-Term Capital Management's bailout in late September. Robertson did not provide too many details in his answers, but his answers were telling in the events that eventually unfolded. He also provided a sense of security and comfort to the industry.

He talked honestly and openly. "I feel very much like a batter who hasn't had a hit at the last 15 to 20 times at bat. . . . You worry about a slump even if you have confidence in yourself." He discussed heavy industry redemptions in general due to the somber atmosphere caused by recent events.[1]

He alluded to his lack of knowledge in technology—this was not an area in which he was strong. In response to a question on the proliferation of hedge fund information on the Internet, he said he was totally computer illiterate and couldn't get into the Internet if he tried. While he didn't provide details at that time, it was later released in press reports that the next year, 1999, he had short positions in telecommunications equipment and technology—Lucent Technology and Micron Technology.[2] He was highly skeptical of most Internet valuations. He eventually hired Thomas Kurlak, a former Merrill Lynch semiconductor analyst, in February 1999. As a managing director of technology research, Kurlak had been at Merrill Lynch for about 20 years.

I was particularly struck by his answer to the question on what motivates him. "Unlike Wall Street this week, this is really a fun business. I think most of us in it would almost work for free. That's the big motivation in it. I like to compete in it. These are the things that make it fun for me. Reflecting on my colleagues and competitors, they are a fine group of people in the business, and it's fun to be associated with all of them."[3]

One of the last questions concerned his stock picks. He mentioned US Airways as well as a number of financial stocks which he found attractive, such as Bear Stearns, Wells Fargo, Morgan Stanley, and Bank of America.

North Carolina Beginnings

Robertson was born in Salisbury, North Carolina. His father was a role model who passed on his fascination with investments to his children. At 90, Julian Sr. was still active running a textile mill for the Erlanger family of New York City. One of his hobbies was stocks, and he was an active investor after the Crash of 1929. When the Erlangers were convinced that the markets would recover, they lent Julian Sr. money to invest.[5]

"I still remember the first time I ever heard of stocks. My parents went away on a trip and a great aunt stayed with me. She showed me in the paper a company called United Corp., which was trading on the Big Board and selling for about $1.25. And I realized that I could even save up enough to buy the shares. I watched it. Sort of gradually stimulated my interest." He was six at the time.[6]

After graduating from the University of North Carolina with a degree in business administration, Robertson had a stint in the Navy and afterward joined Kidder Peabody, where he stayed for 20 years. For most of those years he was a stockbroker and then he headed up Webster Management, the money management unit.

He started Tiger Management in May 1980 with $8 million—$2 million of his own money and $6 million from outside investors. By 1991, the firm approached $1 billion in assets under management. At its peak in October 1998, Tiger assets reached $22.8 billion, making it the largest-ever hedge fund.

There were six funds in total—all named after cats: Tiger was a fund for U.S. investors, while Jaguar was for non-U.S. investors, plus tax-exempt U.S. foundations and institutions. Ocelot, a deal Tiger did with Donaldson, Lufkin & Jenrette (DLJ), had a 4 percent up-front fee, a five-year lock-up, and a $1 million minimum investment. About $2 billion in assets were raised with assets locked up through July 2002. Lion, a relatively new fund, was a clone of Tiger. Panther investors who were not qualified persons could gain access through Lion. Panther was dissolved in June 1997. Puma was for U.S. investors, as was Panther.

Investment Strategy

Robertson bought and sold stock on fundamentals. He used short selling and index put options to hedge. To manage risk and diversify, he had a large number of positions.

His investment credo was summed up well in a 1990 *Business Week* article.[7] First, stick to the fundamentals. Buy stock as if you were buying the company. Get to know its products and management. Second, put away the crystal ball. Don't try to time the market—but stay hedged through shorting stock and options to guard against a market downturn. Third, don't stop at the border. Keep a global perspective. Overseas stocks are areas of boundless opportunity on the long and short side. Fourth, if you're wrong, sell. Keep losses to a minimum. Sell before the losses become excessive. Fifth, short frogs if the public thinks they're princes. Sell a stock short if it is overpriced and public has a misconception of it.

Robertson was the one who made the investment decisions at Tiger. He has always been known for his stock-picking skill. His team of analysts gave him qualitative and quantitative information, but he was the main decision maker. At its peak, Tiger had about 30 analysts/portfolio managers providing recommendations. They were located in London, Tokyo, and Washington, DC, as well as the New York City office.

Succession Planning

In 1991, Robertson talked to bankers about selling a stake of Tiger.[8] Nothing developed. In 1997, he again was considering selling an equity stake to a strategic partner. Other possibilities were issuing preferred stock or selling participation in Tiger's stream of revenue that might include a payment method.[9]

In 1998, Robertson hired Philip Duff, a former Morgan Stanley chief financial officer, as chief operating officer. One of Duff's objectives was to help map out a succession plan and give the firm more structure.

In August 1998, Tiger lost $600 million when Russia defaulted on its debt. Tiger also got hit with a $2 billion loss on the Japanese yen later in 1998. Robertson refocused from the global macro mode to the strategy he did best—stock picking. Robertson followed a value approach—buying stocks at low prices and with good earnings prospects. Undervalued stocks included airline, automobile, and paper stocks of the Old Economy.

While the firm owned stock in Microsoft and Samsung Electronics, it steered clear of high-flying Internet stocks without earnings. According to SEC filings, at the end of 1999 Tiger owned a 24.8 percent stake in US Airways, 14.8 percent of United Asset Management, 7.2 percent of Sealed Air, and 3.7 percent of Bear Stearns. As Robertson stuck by Old Economy stocks, his performance lagged soaring technology stocks that attracted younger managers.

Redemptions were hurting; he had to sell holdings from his portfolio to meet redemptions. A vicious circle was created. Selling holdings hurt performance, which led to more redemptions, and so on. Between August 1998 and April 2000, $7.65 billion had been withdrawn.[10] In October 1999, Tiger announced that it would no longer redeem assets on a quarterly basis, but starting in March 31, 2000, it would allow redemptions twice a year.

Tiger had approximately 180 employees. While Robertson lost about 25 analysts in 1999/2000, he hired 15. By that time, some structure existed. There was a core of 12 senior analysts who comprised 10 industry teams, a currency and bond team, and a commodity team.

At Tiger's annual meeting in October 1999, when these key changes were announced, Robertson also revealed that he had lowered the amount he borrowed in stocks from 2.8 times capital to 1.4 times.

But on March 31, 2000, Robertson announced he was retiring; he was 67 years old. By that time, assets in the six hedge funds had dwindled to $6 billion, of which $1.5 billion was his own. He wrote to investors: "There is no point in subjecting our investors to risk in a market which I frankly do not understand. . . . After thorough consideration, I have decided to return all capital to our investors, effectively bringing down the curtain on the Tiger funds."[11] At the time of the announcement, the funds were down about 14 percent. For 1999 as a whole, Tiger funds fell 19 percent. Tiger's average annual performance since it began trading through 2000 was about 25 percent.

Investors received about 75 percent of their money in cash and 5 percent in shares still held by Tiger. The remaining 20 percent came in cash as Robertson gradually sold his five largest holdings—US Airways, United Asset Management, Xtra Corp., Normandy Mining Management, and Gtech Holdings.

Robertson is still managing his own money, approximately $1.5 billion to $2 billion.

Robertson remains an avid skier, tennis player, and golfer. He recently set up a new golf course at Kauri Cliffs in New Zealand. He has devoted considerable time and resources to charity. Robertson launched the Tiger Foundation in 1989 with the goal to support nonprofit organizations serving disadvantaged youth and families in New York City. He also set up a charitable foundation named for his father in Salisbury, North Carolina, in which $3.5 million was donated to educational community development health programs. Both Duke University and the University of North Carolina received a $25 million gift. He also donated $25 million for Lincoln Center's fountain in honor of his wife, Josie.

Net Performance [%] Tiger Management	
1980	56.30
1981	19.40
1982	42.40
1983	46.70
1984	20.20
1985	51.40
1986	16.20
1987	−1.40
1988	21.60
1989	49.90
1990	20.50
1991	45.60
1992	26.90
1993	64.40
1994	−9.30
1995	16.00
1996	38.00
1997	70.00
1998	−4.00
1999	−19.00
2000*	−14.00
Compound average annual return	**24.84**
*Through first quarter.	

THE SOROS SAGA

Soros's Quantum empire also started to unravel in 2000.* Soros Fund Management had massive losses in March/early April 2000. Quantum, the flagship fund, was down 32 percent. In contrast, Quantum had generated an annual average return of 36 percent since inception.

While it did not close as Robertson's did, it underwent tremendous change. A number of key people left. Stanley Druckenmiller, 47, who had been the chief investment officer for the Quantum Fund for 12 years, and Nicholas Roditi, 54, who had managed the Quota Fund, left. The retirement announcement for both came on April 28, 2000. When Soros announced the reorganization of his then $14 billion fund group, the flagship Quantum Fund was down 20 percent for 2000. Investors redeemed about $3 billion when Druckenmiller announced his departure.

Soon after the retirement announcement, other key employees decided to leave: Duncan Hennes, chief executive officer, and Peter Streinger, chief financial officer, announced their departures. Scott Bessent, a 10-year veteran who managed the $1.5 billion of non-U.S. stocks in London, left on June 30, 2000, to form Bessent Capital. Walter Burlock, who had been a managing director since 1990, left to start Origin Capital Management. Carson Levit joined Pequot Capital and Michael Karsh formed Karsh Capital, while David Kovitz and Sheldon Kasowitz set up Indus Capital Management.

Soros's reason for the reorganization was that the fund had become too large. Furthermore, the objectives of the Soros funds changed. Going forward, Quantum would use lower-risk strategies. Soros instituted a more conservative approach to trading. "In my old age, I have become more conservative. Using less leverage is what I want. . . . It's less risk. I'm looking for 15 percent returns, not 30 percent returns."[12]

On July 1, Soros merged Quantum Fund and Quantum Emerging Growth Fund into a new, $6.5 billion fund, Quantum Endowment Fund. The fund allocates about half to less volatile macro and arbitrage

*This profile has been written from information gleaned from Soros's several books and interviews reported in the press over the year.

strategies, and the other half of the assets are devoted to stock picking on the long and short side. The fund uses less leverage and aims for more stable returns of about 15 percent. Leverage is now only about 33 percent compared with as much as 100 percent of equity previously.

About 60 percent of the Quantum Endowment Fund is Soros's own money. Some assets are managed inside the firm and some managed outside. When Bessent started his firm with about $1 billion, it was reported that $150 million came from Soros.[13] Other managers receiving Soros allocations include Darren Davy, a Bermuda-based manager, who is overseeing the global macro strategy. Sources report he is managing about $2 billion, or one-third of Soros Fund Management assets. Davy's Nexus Fund operation became exclusively affiliated with Soros in October 1999 when it was allocated $500 million.[14]

Robert Soros, George's 36-year-old son, is acting as coordinator in the transition. In 1994, he had previously managed private equity and real estate at the firm. He also helped run the Quantum Industrial Holdings Fund in 1996.

Brief Sabbatical for Druckenmiller

Druckenmiller said he had been discussing his departure with Soros since the end of 1998. But the Quantum Fund fell 20 percent in early 1999 and he didn't want to leave with the fund down that much.

During the first part of 1999, the Quantum Fund was positioned against Internet stocks. Druckenmiller, who managed the $8.2 billion Quantum Fund, hired Carson Levit, a Silicon Valley money manager. By the middle of 1999, the Soros Funds were buying technology stocks and selling short some Old Economy stocks. Positions included DoubleClick Inc., JDS Uniphase Corporation, and Qualcomm Inc. The strategy worked; the Quantum Fund finished 1999 up 35 percent.[15]

When the technology sell-off began in mid-March 2000, Soros Fund Management was still loaded with high-technology and biotechnology stocks. The Nasdaq Composite Index plunged 124 points on March 15, 2000, while the Dow Jones Industrial Average soared 320 points. In the next five days, Quantum's 2 percent year-to-date gain plunged to an 11 percent loss.[16]

As detailed in the *Wall Street Journal*, dissension between Druckenmiller and Soros came to a head over VeriSign, an Internet-security company. At Druckenmiller's behest, they doubled their position in March to $600 million. They had bought the stock at $50 a share in 1999 and rode it to $258 by late February. The stock had fallen to $135 by early April and further to $96 later in April.[17]

Druckenmiller resigned on April 18, and the announcement was made on April 28. He took the summer off and said he would decide what to do—but it was unlikely that he would run a large public fund. He continues to manage Duquesne Capital Management, which he started in 1981 with $1 million in assets. Duquesne investors include his alma mater Bowdoin College, Berea College, and Denison University. Returns have been comparable to Quantum since 1989 when Druckenmiller took over its management—about 30 percent per year. Duquesne assets under management are currently estimated at $2 to $3 billion.

Investing Background Edge

Soros was born in Budapest, Hungary, in 1930. He made his way to London in 1947 and graduated from the London School of Economics in 1952. In 1956, he came to the United States. From 1956 to 1959 he had a job as an arbitrageur at F. M. Mayer in New York. He developed a new form of arbitrage—internal arbitrage—where common stocks, warrants, and bonds were separately traded before they could be officially detached from each other.[18] Then he went to Wertheim & Co. (1959–1963) and on to Arnhold & S. Bleichroder (1963–1973).

Soros had a competitive edge over his colleagues. He had knowledge of European financial markets.[19] People on Wall Street had little experience in understanding European markets, and only a handful arbitraged London and New York. From the moment he arrived in the United States, Soros was tagged an expert in the field.

Soros persuaded management at Arnhold & S. Bleichroder to set up two offshore funds and let him oversee them. First Eagle, a long-only fund, was started in 1967. Double Eagle, a hedge fund, was started in 1969. He started the first fund with $250,000 of his own money, and another $6 million poured in from Europeans who knew him. The offshore funds were based in Curaçao but he operated them from New York.

In 1970, Soros and Jim Rogers teamed up. Generally, Rogers did the investigating and Soros did the investing.

When brokerage firm regulations were imposed that meant Rogers and Soros would not be able to get a percentage of the profits from their company's stock trades, they left to start their own firm. In 1973, they set up Soros Fund Management.[20]

The Double Eagle Fund became the Soros Fund in 1973 and was renamed the Quantum Fund in 1979—in tribute to Werner Heisenberg's uncertainty principle in quantum mechanics. That principle asserts that it is impossible to predict the behavior of subatomic particles in quantum mechanics. The fund did so well that it charged a premium based on the supply and demand for its shares.[21] The premium/discount reflects shareholder sentiment.

When they parted in 1980, Rogers left the firm taking his 20 percent interest valued at $14 million. Soros's 80 percent was worth $56 million.[22] The fund went through what Soros described as a boom/bust cycle from 1979 to 1981. A brief interregnum followed during which he carved out portions of the fund to other managers. Then he conducted a real-time experiment where he used the financial markets to test his theories, which became the basis for his book *The Alchemy of Finance*. This was followed by the crash of 1987—another boom/bust sequence. The reign of Stanley Druckenmiller as chief investment strategist of the Quantum Fund began in 1989 and lasted until April 2000.[23]

In 1991–1992, Soros expanded his operation. Quasar Fund was started in 1991 with money allocated to 15 outside managers. Quantum Emerging Growth Fund, begun in 1992, focused on emerging-market stock markets. And Quota Fund, a fund of funds allocating assets to 10 outside managers, was started in 1992.

Survival Skills

To Soros, the key to his investment success has been his skill at surviving. In *Soros on Soros*, George recalls that 1944 was the happiest year of his life. "This is a strange, almost offensive thing to say because 1944 was the year of the Holocaust. . . . For a 14-year-old boy, it was the most exciting adventure that one could ever ask for. It had a formative effect because I learned the art of survival from a grand master. That has had a certain relevance to my investment career."[24]

"I was fortunate enough to have a father who was highly skilled in the art of survival, having lived through the Russian revolution as an escaped prisoner of war."[25] His father, Tivadar, was on the run in Siberia during the civil war years, hoping to survive. He was an Austro-Hungarian prisoner in World War I. Whatever he had to do to survive, he did, no matter how unpleasant. Survival became a noble virtue in George Soros's life.[26]

Soros's father made arrangements for the family to get false identity papers, and he found places for them to live or to hide.[27] In his book *Soros*, Robert Slater details how George recalls his father paying for false identity papers so that he could pose as Janus Kis, the godson of an official of the Hungarian Agricultural Ministry responsible for confiscating Jewish properties. Soros described this as a commercial transaction. Tivadar taught George valuable lessons about the art of survival: It is all right to take risks; when taking risks, don't bet the ranch. The war taught Soros another lesson—a gap exists between perception and reality. And just as Tivadar had, George would learn that frequently it was best to search for unconventional methods to solve problems.[28]

Soros suggests that operating a hedge fund tested his training in survival to the maximum. "Using leverage can produce superior results when the going is good, but can wipe you out when events fail to conform to your expectations. One of the hardest things to judge is what level of risk is safe. There are no universally valid yardsticks. Each situation needs to be judged on its own merits. In the final analysis, you must rely on your instincts for survival."[29]

Changing Investment Character

In *Soros on Soros: Staying Ahead of the Curve*, a book that he wrote in 1995, Soros describes his lack of investment style. "I try to change my style to fit the conditions. If you look at the history of the [Quantum] funds, it has changed its character many times. For the first ten years, it used practically no macro instruments. Afterwards, macro investing became the dominant theme. But more recently we started investing in industrial assets. . . . I do not play according to a given set of rules. I look for changes in the rules of the game."[30]

Soros identified the big themes that drove the market. Druckenmiller and the analysts did the stock picking. Soros's philosophy, strategy, and tactics set the mood.[31] Specialist funds existed, but the chief investment officer could borrow the best ideas from each and use them in the Quantum Fund.

Soros also calls himself an insecurity analyst. "I recognize that I may be wrong. This makes me insecure. My sense of insecurity keeps me alert, always ready to correct my errors."[32] He explains, "I watch whether the actual course of events correspond to my expectations. If not, I realize I'm on the wrong track. When there is a discrepancy between my expectations and the actual course of events, it does not mean I dump my stock. I reexamine the thesis and try to establish what has gone wrong. . . . But I certainly don't stand still and I don't ignore the discrepancy. I start a critical examination."[33]

Reflexivity

In *The Alchemy of Finance*, Soros says the idea of reflexivity is crucial to his analysis of market behavior. The idea was to record the decision-making process—not a scientific experiment but an alchemic experiment—because he expected he was conducting an experiment to include the results.[34]

Two words sum up the concept: imperfect understanding. On one hand, reality is reflected in people's thinking—this is the cognitive function. On the other hand, people make decisions that affect reality, and these decisions are based not on reality but on people's interpretation of reality—the participating function.

Soros says those two functions work in opposite directions, and in certain circumstances they can interfere with each other. The interaction between them takes the form of a two-way reflexive feedback mechanism.[35]

Soros observes that financial markets are characterized by a discrepancy between the participants' perceptions and the actual state of affairs. At times, it is negligible.[36] In a normal situation, the discrepancy between thinking and reality is not very large and there are forces at play that tend to bring them closer together, partly because people can learn from experience and partly because people can actually change and shape social conditions. This is what Soros calls a near-equilibrium condition. Far-from-equilibrium conditions occur when people's thinking and the actual state of affairs are very far removed from each other and have no tendency to come closer together.

Dynamic disequilibrium occurs when the prevailing bias and prevailing trend reinforce each other until the gap between them becomes so

wide that it brings catastrophic collapse. Static disequilibrium is characterized by very rigid, dogmatic thinking and very rigid social conditions.

Soros puts dynamic and static disequilibrium at the two extremes,
with near-equilibrium conditions in between. In a normal state,
reflexivity is not important. When they approach or reach far-from-
equilibrium conditions, reflexivity becomes important and you have
what Soros calls a boom/bust sequence.[37]

Soros says he does not "play" (invest) with a given set of rules. "I
look for changes in the rules of the game. I look for conditions of disequilibrium. They send out certain signals that activate me."[38]

Soros says he is ahead of the curve. "I watch out for telltale signs
that a trend may be exhausted. Then I disengage from the herd and look
for a different investment thesis. Most of the time we are punished if we
go against the trend. Only at an inflection point are we rewarded."[39]

Some memorable moments in Soros's trading:

Black Wednesday

Armed with a theory that perceptions count for everything and that
faulty perceptions can trigger reflexive behavior in the marketplace,
Soros was able to identify a key misapprehension on the eve of the Exchange Rate Mechanism crisis: the false expectation that the Bundes-
bank would support the British pound under any circumstance.

In the summer of 1992, it became known that Soros funds were selling the British pound short. Other investors followed suit.

On Wednesday, September 16, 1992, Soros made close to $2 bil-
lion—$1 billion from the pound and another $1 billion out of the chaos
of the Italian and Swedish currencies and in the Tokyo Stock Exchange.
The *Financial Times* dubbed Soros "the man who broke the pound."[40]

Saint Valentine's Day Massacre

Soros suffered a $600 million loss on February 14, 1994, when he was
short $8 billion of Japanese yen. Many managers thought that the
Japanese yen would decrease in value. The thinking was that President
Clinton and Prime Minister Morihiro Hosokawa would reach a settlement on their trade dispute, and this would lead the U.S. government
to allow the Japanese yen to fall. Previously, the U.S. government had

been encouraging the Japanese yen to increase in value as a tactic to pressure Japan in trade negotiations because the rising yen makes Japanese exports more expensive and harder to sell around the world. The talks collapsed and the value of the Japanese yen rose.[41] The same thing happened again in November 1994 with a $400 to $600 million loss for Soros.

Malaysia

In August 1997, Malaysia's prime minister, Mahathir Mohamad, criticized the United States for not regarding Soros's currency speculation as a crime. "The United States does not consider Soros as a criminal because it is not a victim of his actions. We are the victims and if we keep quiet, the United States will continue to legalize his manipulations."[42]

Mahathir accused Soros of targeting the currencies of the Association of Southeast Asian Nations (ASEAN). He said Soros drove down the value of these currencies in retribution for ASEAN allowing Myanmar (formerly Burma)—which is ruled by a military dictatorship—to join. Soros runs a foundation that opposes the Myanmar military junta, but Soros said its activities have no influence over his financial dealings.

Philosopher, Not a Financier

In *Soros on Soros*, Soros acknowledges that he has made a mark as a money manager. "But can I make a mark with my ideas? Can I formulate them and communicate them properly? Are they valid? That is what matters to me most and that is where I feel most insecure. The same set of ideas has served me for making money and for giving it away. It has worked for me but that does not mean that it has universal validity."[43]

Soros viewed himself not just as a speculator but as a philosopher— and a failed one at that. "I have been less successful in communicating my ideas and getting them generally accepted. That is why I consider myself a failed philosopher."[44] He always wanted to get a hearing for his ideas, but it was only after the sterling crisis that he became a public figure; it changed his position in the world.[45]

In *Soros on Soros*, he explains, "I would say that it is the adventure of ideas that attracts me. Basically, thinking is the most important aspect of my existence . . . . I like to understand. . . . I wasted a large part of my youth regurgitating certain ideas. Then I discovered that one can learn a great deal more through action than through contemplation. So I became an active thinker where my thinking played an important role in deciding what actions to take and my actions play an important role in improving my thinking. This two-way interaction between thinking and action became the hallmark of my philosophy and the hallmark of my life."[46]

In addition to his books on his financial theories, Soros has written two about philanthropic endeavors—*Opening the Soviet System* and *Underwriting Democracy*. He also has received honorary doctoral degrees from the New School for Social Research, the University of Oxford, Budapest University of Economics, and Yale University.

Attempts to Institutionalize

Soros has made several attempts at institutionalizing his firm. In early 1998, analysts were assigned areas to cover for the first time. Prior to this, they followed

Net Performance [%] Quantum Fund NV	
1969	29.40
1970	17.50
1971	20.30
1972	42.20
1973	8.40
1974	17.50
1975	27.60
1976	61.90
1977	31.20
1978	55.10
1979	59.10
1980	102.60
1981	22.90
1982	56.90
1983	24.90
1984	9.40
1985	122.20
1986	42.10
1987	14.10
1988	10.10
1989	31.60
1990	29.60
1991	53.40
1992	68.60
1993	63.20
1994	3.90
1995	39.00
1996	1.50
1997	17.10
1998	12.40
1999	35.00
2000*	−15.50
Compound average annual return	**32.12**

*The Quantum Fund was renamed the Quantum Endowment Fund on June 30, 2000.

whatever stocks appealed to them. Analysts were given $50 million to invest in a mini account under the Quantum umbrella.[47]

On August 10, 1999, a reorganization occurred. Former Bankers Trust treasurer Duncan Hennes became the firm's first-ever chief executive officer. This was largely to free up Druckenmiller's time from administrative detail so he could focus on trading and Quantum performance. Hennes reported directly to Soros and oversaw hiring, firing, compensation, and other aspects of running a business that included 200 employees and affiliated offices in Tokyo, Hong Kong, and London.[48]

Philanthropy

Whereas many of the other superstar hedge fund managers eventually got into philanthropy after they had made millions, Soros established his first trust the year he started Soros Fund Management. George Soros Charitable Trust was founded in 1969.

When the fund reached $100 million in assets under management and his personal wealth was about $25 million in 1979, he determined that he had enough money. He came to the conclusion that what really mattered was an open society. With the aim to open up closed societies, Soros established the Open Society Fund.

In the 1980s, Soros began to build his philanthropic empire. Initially he focused on Central and Eastern Europe, spreading money to support democracy in countries struggling to break from the old Soviet orbit. Later, with Russia adrift, he spent $100 million to help Soviet science and scientists survive the transition. The network of foundations covers over 30 countries, employing about 1,300 people. The causes focus on free media, political pluralism, and defending human rights.

Soros expanded his philanthropic work in the United States in early 1996. In this country, he is concerned with the antithesis of state control—the abandonment of state responsibility. He feels the drug laws are ludicrous. He gave $15 million over five years to groups that oppose America's "war on drugs" or want to open the debate about drug policy. He says the "unintended consequences of the war, including the criminalization of a vast class of drug users, far outweigh the limited and costly success of interdiction." In 1996, he gave an extra $1 million aimed at persuading voters in California and Arizona to allow doctors to prescribe illegal drugs such as marijuana to ease suffering.[49]

Other foundations he created include the Center on Crime, Communities and Culture; and Project Death, where he committed $20 million in an attempt to improve the care of the dying.

Overall, he has doled out more than $2 billion, which entitles him to be identified as the second largest philanthropist in the United States by *Time* magazine.[50]

EARLIER RETIREMENTS: STEINHARDT AND ODYSSEY

Up until this point, there had been two other notable retirements of elite hedge fund managers. Michael Steinhardt of Steinhardt Partners retired at the end of 1995 and Odyssey Partners closed at the end of 1997.

Michael Steinhardt, Steinhardt Partners

Michael Steinhardt entered the hedge fund arena on July 10, 1967, when he was 26 years old. When it began, Steinhardt, Fine, Berkowitz & Co. had $7 million under management. In those days, the firm was primarily stock pickers. The firm became known as Steinhardt Partners after Steinhardt returned from his sabbatical in 1978.

Steinhardt was known as an aggressive, short-term trader. He made big returns in the early 1990s on interest-rate positions. He relied on variant perception—developing perceptions that he thought were at variance with the general market view.[51] An illustration of his contrarian thinking occurred in the spring of 1981. The fixed-income market was a disaster, and the prime interest rate was at 15 percent. He began buying five-year Treasury bonds. The bond market finally rallied in the fall, and he ended the year with a 97 percent gain.[52]

By the time he retired, Steinhardt had four funds—Steinhardt Partners LP, Institutional Partners LP, SP International SA, and Steinhardt Overseas Fund Ltd. He closed down his funds at the end of 1995; assets under management were at $2.6 billion. At the peak, assets were $4.4 billion. Press reports at that time indicated that Steinhardt's own holdings were $400 million. Today, at 60, he has the benefit of being retired five years and having a broad overview of the industry for the past 33 years. His insights are quite interesting.

Steinhardt finds it peculiar to talk about a "hedge fund industry." He sees hedge funds not as an industry but as part of the broader world of money management. He does not find a common investment strategy that binds these managers. During Steinhardt's heyday, hedge funds comprised a private elite club whose members provided superior performance over a long period of time. "We were looked at dubiously yet admiringly. Performance was special. . . . It was an elitist yet controversial area."

Steinhardt says the distinguishing characteristics were the manager investing his assets solely in his own fund, having a long track record, and being successful in a variety of economic climates. The manager was intense, intellectually superior, and motivated by performance—not growth of assets under management. The managers were also entrepreneurial; they lacked skill to build an organization.

Steinhardt reminisces about how he tried to institutionalize his firm but always backed out. He was on the verge of marketing a closed-end fund with Merrill Lynch—but he didn't go through with the deal. He also had received an offer from Dreyfus Corporation to buy part of his business. Rather than do that, he focused on what he had achieved—his performance record.

Today, Steinhardt notices a shift: Managers' objectives are different. He sees the industry attracting new people since the incentive fee makes it a very desirable alternative. Growth of assets and of fees is paramount to today's managers. Yet performance has become mediocre; there are many managers who are not so good. Investors may become less inclined to pay the fees as performance deteriorates. He also observes that the short part of the hedge has become a burden in buoyant stock market times.

Steinhardt has spent considerable time trying to understand the reasons for superior performance. He says that, among other things, it is an innate ability. For him it was the repetition and the continued testing of the process that created this innate sense. This was his edge. Because he was so focused on the stock market since his teen years, he was already a very experienced trader. His father gave him 100 shares each of Penn Dixie Cement and Columbia Gas System for his bar mitzvah. That became the spark motivating his interest. He graduated from the Wharton School of Finance and Commerce at 19 years old.

The motivation for him was being able to pick the moving parts and recognize the direction of stocks. He didn't think about compensation.

Reflecting on the importance of the technology sector today, Steinhardt draws an analogy to the electronics field in the 1960s. Electronic companies added "onics" to their names and went public. "The euphoria today is broader based." Steinhardt feels that the distinction between the New Economy and the Old Economy won't last and they will eventually be melded back into one economy.

When Steinhardt retired, he stopped managing other investors' money. He trades a small amount of his own capital but primarily allocates it to about 30 other managers, mostly arbitrage and other conservative styles. His goal is to maintain the capital that he's made and to earn a good return.

Steinhardt also had a four-year struggle with the government about his role in the 1991 U.S. Treasury bond auction scandal at Salomon Brothers. He eventually paid $40 million to settle it.[53]

Why did he retire? Steinhardt had taken a sabbatical in 1978—which had initially been intended as retirement. He couldn't find anything compelling to do, though, so he returned and is glad he did. At that time, his net worth was $7 million. But by 1995, his goal was to do something else—something more virtuous and more noble than being a great money manager. He tells how one investor had sent him a letter and a photo of a new boat. The investor thanked Steinhardt—it was profits in the Steinhardt fund that had enabled him to buy the boat. Steinhardt found this demeaning. He didn't want to be remembered for being a great money manager—he needed to do something else.

Since his retirement, Steinhardt has consciously developed outside interests—politics, making movies, art collecting, Jewish philanthropy, horticulture. Steinhardt is also writing a book about his life. He says what gives him the most pleasure is his 52-acre estate in Bedford, New York, with its gardens and exotic animals—camels, zebras, llamas, kangaroos, and monkeys. He is no longer involved with politics, and none of his movies have been profitable, he says.

His office is packed full with his Judaica collection—a five-foot high menorah, charity boxes, Torah mantles. Steinhardt, who is an atheist, felt that having possession of these objects would make religion more important to him. This, however, has not happened. His interest is in the advancement of Jewish education outside religious institutions.

Steinhardt is devoted to perpetuating the Jewish population—keeping American Jews Jewish. One of his main preoccupations is Makor (the Hebrew word for source), a cultural center on the West Side of New York where single Jewish people meet. In early February 2001, Steinhardt donated it to the 92nd Street Y.

Steinhardt has been the chairman of the investment committee at New York University since 1996. He says that despite the endowment having a history of being anti-stocks, it has made some movement to equities and has even made some hedge fund investments.

Odyssey Partners

Odyssey Partners, with assets of $3 billion, returned money to clients in February 1997 and closed at the end of 1997. Partners Leon Levy and Jack Nash said they had difficulties managing and investing such a huge pool of assets.[54] They had generated an average annual return of about 28 percent since inception in 1982. When they retired, Leon Levy, who had been the macro visionary of the team, was 71, and Jack Nash, who had been the trader, was 67.

The two had met at Oppenheimer & Co. in the 1950s. Nash, who became chairman of Oppenheimer, was a pioneer in leveraged buyouts. Levy was a partner, director of research, and served as chairman of the board of the Oppenheimer group of mutual funds. In 1982, Oppenheimer was sold; that year, the duo formed Odyssey Partners with $160 million, which included $50 million they received from selling Oppenheimer. The private deal-making business became the core business for Odyssey.

Levy and Nash and their families had about $480 million invested in Odyssey Partners.

2

UNOFFICIAL REASONS FOR RETIREMENT

Despite the official reasons given for retiring or reorganizing a hedge fund, there may be other unofficial underlying reasons—some conscious, others subconscious. Topping the list are the incentive fee/high-water mark issue, assets reaching a ceiling, too much focus on short-term performance, succession problems and lack of infrastructure, frustrating markets due to volatility in technology stocks, longing to be something other than a great money manager, age and/or longevity in the markets, and a difficult environment for global macro managers.

INCENTIVE FEE/HIGH-WATER MARK

Under the hedge fund incentive fee structure, when performance falls the high-water mark kicks in. If a hedge fund manager loses money in a year, the manager doesn't get any incentive fee until the losses are made up. It is the incentive fee that provides the bulk of a hedge fund manager's compensation. In 1999 and 2000, when Tiger was down 19 percent and 14 percent respectively through the end of the first quarter, Robertson would have to earn the fund at least 43.6 percent before Tiger would get back to par. Soros's Quantum Fund was down 20 percent through the end of April.

Enormous overhead compounds a bad performance year. For example, offices at Tiger Management alone were reported to have operating costs of $45 million a year.[1] Tiger had about 180 employees in its New York headquarters and worldwide. Soros had 240 employees in New York and an additional 300 worldwide in early 2000.[2]

ASSETS REACHING A CEILING

The more assets a manager has under management, the harder it is to deliver excellent returns. Some funds have grown too large. It has been suggested that $10 billion is the ceiling. Global macro funds, those that are opportunistic and global in searching for stock, bond, currency, and futures market opportunities, have been analogized to conglomerates, since they add on different businesses to increase their capacity. The less diversified the strategies in a fund, the lower the capacity.

Some critics say that Tiger was still basically an equity stock picker. It was too big and too fundamental at its peak of $22 billion in 1998. Robertson's troubles began in October 1998. Soros's assets under management also peaked at about $22 billion in August 1998.

Some analytical studies show that many hedge funds generate their best performance in the early years when there are fewer assets under management and the fund is more nimble.[3]

Too many assets are a problem for all managers—including mutual funds. In *Common Sense on Mutual Funds*, John Bogle advises investors to avoid large organizations that have no history of closing funds or that seem willing to let their funds grow to seemingly infinite size irrespective of their investment goals.[4] "Excessive size can, and probably will, kill any possibility of investment excellence. The record is clear that, for the overwhelming majority of funds, the best years come when they are small."[5]

Bogle supported this with data on funds' returns compared with the S&P 500 Index. He looked at the experience of five of the largest actively managed equity funds whose aggregate assets grew from $500 million to $37 billion during the 1978–1998 period. Uniformly their performance deteriorated. He concludes the pattern is familiar: profound reversion to the mean. From the start of 1978 to the end of 1982, these five large funds amassed a substantial performance edge over the S&P 500 index, outpacing the benchmark by 10 percentage points a year. They achieved this edge when they were relatively small with average assets of $500 million for every $1 billion of stock market capitalization. They lost the edge when they attained elephantine size. Since the start of 1994, with relative assets reaching $3.5 million for every $1 billion of stock market capitalization, these five funds lagged the S&P 500 index by more than 4 percentage points a year. As the managed funds' relative assets increased sevenfold, their relative performance suffered a net decline of more than 14 percentage points annually.[6]

Warren Buffett's experience is similar. "For the entire 1950s, my personal returns using equities with a market cap of less than $10 million were better than 60 percent annually. At our present size, I dream at night about 300 basis points."[7]

A fund becomes so large that it has difficulty finding market opportunities that fit its target return/risk criteria. Soros and Robertson were seeking value opportunities in stocks, bonds, currencies, and commodities where they had historically achieved net returns of over 25 percent.

To ensure broad diversification, managers may set limits on the maximum percentage a position may represent in the overall portfolio—for example, 5 percent. Very few firms want to hold as much as 10 percent of a company's shares, because dominant ownership positions may constrain market liquidity.

As a fund becomes very large, it also gets so closely watched on Wall Street that it hurts. A large company leaves signs that it is taking a new position in a stock. It is possible to come up with an accurate approximation of the group's holdings by looking at federal filings that managers must make if they own a certain percentage of the company. Its footprint makes it too visible in the market. Other investors watch and copy.

Soros and Tiger had been hammered because of their size, while more nimble funds managed to exit positions more easily. The problems with the Japanese yen–U.S. dollar carry trade may be illustrative of this point. This trade had made considerable profit for Soros and Robertson over the prior several years, but the trade caused problems in late 1998/early 1999. Soros had problems with the yen-dollar trade in February 1999. In October 1998, Tiger also lost about $2 billion in the trade. Investor sources say Tiger again had problems in January 1999 when it was short the yen and short Japanese stocks. The Japanese market bounced back, causing the manager severe problems.

Another concern is that as a fund increases its assets, management responsibility is diffused often to subportfolio managers. These managers may be less experienced and paid less than the well-known manager.

FOCUS ON SHORT-TERM RESULTS

And as a hedge fund gets very large, the percentage of hot money investors or turnstile investors (i.e., investors who are quick to come in and quick to go out) also grows in proportion. Tiger was forced to redeem $7.7 billion between August 1998 and April 2000 as investors wanted to get out, and Tiger had no choice but to sell favored stocks at depressed prices.

A Tiger spokesman said the main reason Robertson left the business was too much emphasis on short-term returns and quarterly results. "Many of the hot money investors left when quarterly performance was not up to snuff. Asset managers get judged quarterly."[8] Being pressured to manage for quarterly performance as a long-term manager was not something he wanted to do.

SUCCESSION/INFRASTRUCTURE

As Michael Steinhardt of Steinhardt Partners observes, the distinguishing factor of the elite manager club was entrepreneurship. None of the great managers had the ability to build organizations even though they were able to provide superior returns. It had been reported that Steinhardt had discussions at various times with Bruce Kovner, Leon Cooperman, and Jim Leitner.[9]

If a firm wants to institutionalize, it cannot revolve around one person forever.

Robertson had long been criticized for not grooming an heir. Tiger has been the training ground for a number of hedge fund managers who did well. They include Lee Ainslie (Maverick); Larry Bowman (Spinnaker Technology); Thomas Brown (Second Curve Capital); Bob Carr (JoHo Capital); David Gerstenhaber (Argonaut); John Griffin (Blue Ridge Capital); Andreas Halvorsen, Brian Olson, and David Ott (Viking Global Investors); James Lyle (Millbank Capital); Stephen Mandel (Lone Pine Capital); David Saunders (K2 Advisors); and Arnie Snider (Deerfield Management). (See Table 2.1.)

Reasons for their leaving included the desire for more authority, wanting to lead rather than follow, potential to increase earnings, wanting

Table 2.1   Sampling of Hedge Fund Manager Spin-Offs

Manager Name	Company Spun Off From	Company Formed	When
Adair, Alexander	The Palladin Group	Quattro Investors	1998
Ainslie, Lee	Tiger Mgt.	Maverick Capital	1993
Alfieri, Stephen	Chancellor	Stanfield Capital Partners	1998
Bader, Mark	Tiger Mgt.	KiCap Mgt.	2000
Bakar, Mark	Globalvest Mgt.	ValueVest	1995
Barry, Jack	Clinton Group	Beacon Hill Asset Mgt.	1997
Bausano, Barry	Tiger Mgt.	Argonaut	1993
Berman, David	Kingdon Capital	Berman Capital	1997
Bessent, Scott	Soros Fund Mgt.	Bessent Capital Mgt.	2000
Bowman, Larry	Tiger Mgt.	Spinnaker Technology	1995
Brown, Thomas	Tiger Mgt.	Second Curve Capital	2000
Brugere, Philippe	Omega Advisors	Eurovest Capital Partners	1996
Buisseret, Jean-Francois	Buchanan Partners	Concerto Research	1994
Burlock, Walter	Soros Fund Mgt.	Origin Investment Partners	2000
Capra, Jim	Moore Capital	Capra Asset Mgt.	1995
Carr, Bob	Tiger Mgt.	JoHo Capital	1995
Clark, Tim	Zweig-DiMenna Associates	Katonah International Fund	1995
Cohen, Jeffrey	Alpine Associates	Silverado Capital Mgt.	1997
Creedon, Scott	BNP/Cooper Neff	Creedon Capital Mgt.	1995
Davidson, Chuck	Steinhardt Partners	Wexford Capital	1995
de la Hey, John	Tiger Mgt.	Toscafund	2000
DeMonici, Nella	Ethos Partners	Allegiance	1995
Derchin, Michael	Tiger Mgt.	JetCap Partners	2000
Doshay, Glenn	Ardsley Advisory Partners	Palantir Capital	N/A
Earle, Patrick	Tiger Mgt.	KiCap Mgt.	2000
Ellis, Robert	Tiger Mgt.	Catequil Capital Mgt.	2000
Fournier, Alan	Appaloosa Mgt.	Pennant Capital Mgt.	2000
Gerstenhaber, David	Tiger Mgt.	Argonaut	1993
Ghose, Udayan	Omega Advisors	Eldon Capital	1995
Goodman, John	Steinhardt Partners	Concentric Capital	1995
Griffin, John	Tiger Mgt.	Blue Ridge Capital	1996
Halvorsen, Andreas	Tiger Mgt.	Viking Global Investors	1999
Hughes, Martin	Tiger Mgt.	Toscafund	2000
Irwin, John	Clinton Group	Beacon Hill Asset Mgt.	1997
Jacobson, Andrew	Columbus Circle Investor	Axiom International Investors	N/A
Jansen, Christopher	Chancellor	Stanfield Capital Partners	1998
Kaplan, Andrew	The Palladin Group	Quattro Investors	1998
Karsh, Michael	Soros Fund Mgt.	Karsh Capital Mgt.	2000
Kasowitz, Sheldon	Soros Fund Mgt.	Indus Capital Partners	2000
Kowitz, David	Soros Fund Mgt.	Indus Capital Partners	2000
Kristynik, Kris	Tiger Mgt.	KiCap Mgt.	2000
Lattanzio, John	Steinhardt Partners	Lattanzio Group	1995
Levinson, John	Lynch & Mayer	Westway Capital	1995
Lyle, James	Tiger Mgt.	Millbank Capital	1997
Macnguyen, Curtis	SC Fundamental Value	Ivory Asset Mgt.	1999
Mandel, Stephen	Tiger Mgt.	Lone Pine Capital	1998
Marshall, Ken	Covenant Capital Mgt.	Octagon International	N/A
Minella, Amy	Deltec Asset Mgt.	Cardinal Capital Mgt.	N/A

(Continued)

Table 2.1 Continued

Manager Name	Company Spun Off From	Company Formed	When
Miszkiewicz, Mark	Clinton Group	Beacon Hill Asset Mgt.	1997
Morrison, David	Tiger Mgt.	yet to be named	2000
Napoli, Louis	The Palladin Group	Quattro Investors	1998
Nechamkin, Gabe	Soros Fund Mgt.	Satellite Asset Mgt.	1999
Newburger, Barry	Kellner-DiLeo	Avery Capital	1996
Newman, Philip	Park Place Capital	Ragazzi Newman	1997
Nichols, Janice	Chancellor	Stanfield Capital Partners	1998
Niedermeyer, Thomas	Teton Partners	Liberty Square Asset Mgt.	1998
Olson, Brian	Tiger Mgt.	Viking Global Investors	1999
Ott, David	Tiger Mgt.	Viking Global Investors	1999
Ragazzi, Michele	Park Place Capital	Ragazzi Newman	1997
Raiff, Robert	Soros Fund Mgt.	Centurion Investment Group	1995
Rajaratnam, Raj	Needham & Co.	Galleon Group	1997
Rosen, Kyle	Strome Hedgecap Fund	Rosen Capital Mgt.	1999
Rosenblatt, Lief	Soros Fund Mgt.	Satellite Asset Mgt.	1999
Saunders, David	Tiger Mgt.	K2 Advisors	1994
Schultze, George	MD Sass	Schultze Asset Mgt.	1998
Selfeld, Steven	Paloma Partners	Cos Cob Partners	N/A
Snider, Arnie	Tiger Mgt.	Deerfield Partners	1993
Sonnino, Mark	Soros Fund Mgt.	Satellite Asset Mgt.	1999
Strasser, Hannah	Deltec Asset Mgt.	Cardinal Capital Mgt.	1995
Strome, Mark	Kayne Anderson	Strome, Susskind	1992
Swain, Brian	The Palladin Group	Quattro Investors	1998
Symonds, Geoffrey	Steinhardt Partners	Trace Capital	1996
Tobias, Seth	JRO Associates	Circle T	1996
Vasvani, Ashok	Appaloosa Mgt.	Skanda Fund	1998
Walton, Clare	Walton Investments	Liberty Square Asset Mgt.	2000
Werlin, Ernest	Steinhardt Partners	Highview Capital	1995*
Yobage, Anne	Deltec Asset Mgt.	Cardinal Capital Mgt.	1995

*Stopped trading.

to receive recognition for good performance, or perhaps a midlife career change. And in negative performance years, key people may have left since the high-water mark meant they probably wouldn't be getting bonuses for awhile. Some may have had a monetary incentive to jump ship.

With too much centralized decision making in one person's hands, it is hard for talented analysts or portfolio managers to be satisfied when they do not have any discretion or authority. It was not until 1999 that Robertson allowed senior analysts to manage 15 percent of the firm's capital where they had investment authority.

At the outset, Soros had no desire to give Druckenmiller a great deal of freedom, either—he had to earn it. Almost a year after he joined

Quantum, the two had their first open quarrel. Druckenmiller had taken a position in bonds.[10] Without consulting him, Soros sold the bonds. It was the first time Soros had gone behind Druckenmiller's back. Druckenmiller exploded. Eventually Soros calmed down and promised he would keep his distance.

Events took a dramatic turn in Eastern Europe. Communist regimes began to fall. The Berlin Wall tumbled. Soros was following these events on a daily basis. In the summer of 1989, Soros told Druckenmiller he must take full charge of running the fund. "I became the coach and he became the competitor."[11]

Soros succeeded temporarily on the successor front when he hired Druckenmiller in 1989 to run the Quantum Fund so he could concentrate on philanthropy. It bought Soros some time; Druckenmiller lasted for 11 years. But there had been a list of several predecessors, including Jim Marquez and Allan Raphael.

Prior to the 2000 defections, Soros had its share of spin-offs as well. Examples included Lief Rosenblatt, Mark Sonnino, and Gabe Nechamkin, who had worked at Soros Fund Management for 11 years heading up the special situations investment team; they announced their departure in mid-1999 and the formation of Satellite Asset Management.

And even though Soros had Druckenmiller on board since 1989, when push came to shove Soros brought in his son Robert during the reorganization transition to a more conservative fund. Robert is acting as the coordinator in the transition.

VOLATILITY IN THE MARKETS AND THE SHIFT TO NEW TECHNOLOGIES

For some of the hedge fund superstars, the game was no longer fun. Market conditions were frustrating. Technology stocks were difficult to fathom. The markets were too volatile, especially the technology stocks. Six times in March 2000 the Nasdaq moved more than 6 percent in one day.

The volatility, a new phenomenon, had been largely caused by a high degree of public speculation—uninformed performance chasing and momentum chasing. Stock market moves often have no connection to rationality or anything fundamental. This has caused some managers to look more skeptically at the message given by the markets. It has also made it harder to sell short.

Technology proved to be the Achilles' heel for the Old Generation. To varying degrees, both Soros and Robertson were hurt by technology stocks and their transforming effects on the markets. As a value investor, Soros got into technology too late and held on to the shares too long. Robertson missed out largely because he avoided technology stocks.

But the issue is more than trading technology stocks. It is also the ability to use technology to harness information flow coming in from a myriad of sources. The new technology has increased information dissemination, and that has eroded some of the hedge fund managers' edge.

One superstar manager suggests that some of the older hedge fund managers may not have wanted to learn new technologies, which may have led to their demise or put obstacles in their way of surviving. He observed, "The survivors will be those who are able to adapt to new markets, adapt to information technology, and instill rigorous risk control."

LONGEVITY IN THE MARKETS/SIGNIFICANCE

Being extremely wealthy, why did these managers need this aggravation? This was true for the younger Druckenmiller as well. One hedge fund superstar speculated that it may have been too heavy a load administratively for Druckenmiller to run his own business as well as Quantum. Druckenmiller was getting heat from Soros for staying too long in the technology positions. Soros was demanding. "Why do this when I can enjoy my money without aggravation? Why take it? I don't need this!" was the suggested scenario from this fellow superstar manager. Druckenmiller had indicated an interest to leave Soros Fund Management earlier in 1999.

In 2000, Robertson was 67 years old and Soros 69 years old. "I want to set up something that will outlast me," said Soros in an interview with the *Wall Street Journal*.[12] These words were echoed by Michael Steinhardt: "I don't want to be remembered for being a great money manager. I want to be remembered for something more important." Philanthropy and writing books seem to fill some of that void for both Soros and Steinhardt.

It appears that as these superstar managers get older they become more conservative—the desire grows to use less leverage and less risk. Soros talked about this: "I'm looking for 15 percent returns, not 30 percent returns."[13] Soros also allocated a considerable percent of the assets to outside managers, thus diversifying risk. Steinhardt had the same feelings. After his retirement, he no longer managed the bulk of his assets—he parceled it out to 30 managers. Most of those are conservative managers, not hedge fund managers.

MORE DIFFICULT ENVIRONMENT FOR GLOBAL MACRO

The situations of Robertson and Soros indicate that the global macro strategy has become a more difficult arena for sustainable returns.

While financial markets have changed significantly in recent years, many of the larger hedge fund managers have not. In the past, with substantial assets and significant use of leverage, global macro managers made enormous, risky investments around the globe in currencies, bonds, and stocks. Today, it is harder to find inefficiencies.

Finding obvious macro trends—the 1992 sterling crisis, 1993 Exchange Rate Mechanism (ERM) crisis, 1994–1995 Mexican debt crisis, 1997 Asian currency crisis, and 1998 Russian debt situation—is more difficult. Opportunities tend to be in the less liquid markets where size is an obstacle rather than an advantage. Liquidity premium has overshadowed second-tier opportunity, as liquidity depth outside G-10 is shallow. (G-10 countries include the United States, Japan, Germany, United Kingdom, France, Italy, Australia, Switzerland, Canada, and Spain.)

Globalization is rapidly curtailing market inefficiencies. The introduction of the euro cut trading opportunities for macro traders such as European convergence trades. International yield curve cross-currency plays had been core trades for global macro managers.

Liquidity effect will continue to plague global macro managers for some time: Brokerage firms are less willing to allow hedge fund managers to take lots of risks, which has hurt liquidity.

As bond and currency opportunities shrank, global macro managers shifted to stocks. With the Internet, hedge fund managers no longer have the edge as information in vast quantities is available to everyone. Larger mutual fund managers sometimes can get better information access than hedge fund managers.

Smaller, more specialized funds are gaining an edge. For example, among the best performers in 1999 were specialized funds such as sector funds. As a group, they were up 76 percent in 1999. Technology sector funds soared 102.9 percent in 1999.[14] They are more nimble and can take advantage of more trading opportunities. They are often specialists in a particular arena. Investors—particularly institutions and those using the fund of funds approach—want transparency. They want to know how the manager's portfolios are constructed. Investors want to understand the style. Global macro managers tend not to be as transparent as other strategies. Investors also want to understand the risk management mechanism. Many of the global macro managers do not want to disclose this information.

Global macro strategies aren't working well in the present environment. Longer-term, when economic instability (e.g., an environment of unstable interest rates and currencies) reenters the marketplace, global macro opportunities will reappear. The environment, however, will be more challenging for the global macro manager.

IMPLICATIONS FOR THE HEDGE FUND INDUSTRY

The number of hedge funds starting and growing to a healthy size contrasts with the closure and problems of the largest hedge fund managers in 2000. In fact, the more problems these large managers have, the more spin-offs will occur from those very firms. This pattern is inherent in the system and will continue in the future.

As the number of spin-offs from the large managers continues, it is expected that many of the younger managers have learned the lessons of their mentors. The new generation understands the need to have succession, infrastructure, and institutionalization of the business. As a result, most of the new organizations are not centralized star structures, but instead are team-oriented. Teams are specialized, and senior portfolio managers are held accountable for their positions and at least partially rewarded based on their performances.

The spin-offs have seen their mentors get bombarded due to their unwieldy size. As a result, many are offering multiple funds that are smaller in size and often more specialized.

Parallels can be made with the mutual fund industry as well. Many mutual funds have adopted a team approach to fund management. Don Phillips, chief executive officer of Morningstar, observes that mutual funds are also moving toward specialization. "It is hard for a manager to switch gears from a long mind-set to a short mind-set." Phillips observes how mutual funds have become more narrowly focused in the past few years. So instead of being all things to all people, a mutual fund may be packaged as growth and value. Two separate managers—not one—trade a fund; each is a specialist.

The closing/reorganizing of some of the large macro traders indicates the era of big positions on macroeconomic trends has probably come to a close temporarily. And with big hedge funds closing up, there will be more opportunities.

Portfolio allocations to technology, quantitative skills and information technology, will continue to increase in importance in a hedge fund manager's life—for stock selection and information harnessing.

CHALLENGES

A few critical challenges exist for the hedge fund community. Only one large hedge fund management firm has been successful in creating continuity from one generation to another—there have been three successions for Cumberland Associates. It remains to be seen whether the superstar managers will succeed at this. A number have made attempts through specialist teams, developing a culture, and emphasizing the importance of career development. Many of the 60-something hedge fund managers had started their hedge fund careers after a successful investment career and did not consider succession or exit value in their initial business plans.

A second issue for the hedge fund industry is the ability to survive in more challenging markets. When looking at the hedge fund industry overall—not the small elite group interviewed in the book—it is fair to say that some of the younger managers have not experienced various market cycles due to their short track records, and they have been faced with a relatively benign stock market. Depending on how it is measured, the bull stock market had been roaring for 5, 18, or 26 years. During the roaring bull market of the 1990s, the short part of the hedge became a burden.

A third challenge is for a manager to know when the fund has reached its capacity. At a certain asset size, performance starts to deteriorate. The larger a fund grows, the more motivation the manager may have to expand into areas outside the person's core competency. The more assets a fund has, the more difficult it may be to get out of wrong trades. Also, trading and decision making may become more diffuse.

A transition took place in 2000. The markets are whipsawing and unpredictable. This may mean more difficult markets for the inexperienced hedge fund manager without a long track record. The short side of the equation—where the manager may have no experience—may become more important. Furthermore, the stock market is becoming more complex with considerable variation in the market sectors. This is making the stock market more difficult to hedge.

Today, the perception is that many of the newer/younger managers are motivated by incentive fees and having considerable assets under management, rather than providing excellent returns. This attitude has negative consequences in the long run. If the markets continue to be challenging, it is quite possible that a shakeout of sorts would occur in the industry.

3

OVERVIEW OF THE HEDGE FUND INDUSTRY

Having examined the events surrounding George Soros and Julian Robertson in the first half of 2000, it is now important to look at hedge funds and the hedge fund community in general—characteristics of hedge fund managers, the impetus behind the recent growth of hedge funds, the different strategies traded, recent black eyes suffered in the industry, and recent regulatory initiatives.

MISNOMER

The term "hedge fund" is a misnomer. What are these managers? What are their common traits? In the early days of the first hedge fund, which was run by Alfred Winslow Jones in 1949, the goal was to hedge positions on securities. Today, different styles exist and some managers take larger risks. Hedging exists in varying degrees—sometimes not at all.

Many managers use hedge fund as a term of convenience while admitting it is a misnomer. Other terms used are edge funds, absolute return funds, hybrid products, alternative securities, or private investment partnerships.

Whatever they are called, the goal is absolute returns—to generate excellent performance in different market conditions. Hedge fund managers don't like comparing themselves to a benchmark; that is relative performance. Doing so is usually to placate investors who want or need some benchmark. Managing downside risk also differentiates them from other types of managers.

Between 4,500 and 6,500 hedge funds exist with combined assets of $350 billion to $450 billion. Assets in the hedge fund industry are highly concentrated. The average hedge fund size is about $130 million. There are about 55 hedge fund managers with assets of over $1 billion. (See Table 3.1.) In contrast, an estimated 200 managers have assets under $10 million.

These numbers cannot be precise since no legal definition of a hedge fund exists. While there is no universal agreement on the size of the hedge fund industry, it is generally accepted as having exhibited strong growth. Based on a narrow definition of what hedge funds are, the following estimates show the strong growth during the 1990s[1]:

1996	$100 billion
1997	$145 billion
1998	$175 billion
1999	$205 billion

Because there is no legal definition of a hedge fund, some people define hedge funds differently than others. For example, some may include managed futures or currency traders or emerging markets, while others do not. Some may include long-only funds that use considerable leverage, while others do not.

Another issue is the increasing degree of hybrid products in the alternative investment arena. For example, some hedge fund managers are adding private equity features such as longer-term lock-ups. Meanwhile, some private equity managers are adding hedge fund features.

Furthermore, there are no regulatory bodies in the United States that a hedge fund must report to. You can't go to the Securities and Exchange Commission (SEC) to find out how many hedge funds are registered in the United States. However, if a hedge fund in the United States does trade at least one futures contract, it must register with the Commodities Futures Trading Commission (CFTC).

Table 3.1   Sampling of Hedge Fund
Managers with Assets over $1 Billion as of
December 2000

Fund	Estimated Assets ($B)
Pequot Capital	13.0
Moore Capital Mgt.	8.0
Maverick Capital	6.0
Soros Fund Mgt.	5.6
Citadel Investment Group	5.0
Galleon Group	5.0
Zweig-DiMenna Associates	5.0
Caxton Corp.	4.5
Kingdon Capital Mgt.	4.4
Vinik Asset Mgt.	4.2*
Redwood Group	3.5
Och-Ziff Capital Mgt.	3.5
Marshall Wace Asset Mgt.	3.1
Duquesne Asset Mgt.	3.0
GLG	2.5
Perry Corp.	2.5
Omega Advisors	2.4
Campbell & Co.	2.2
Tiger Mgt.	2.0*
SAC Capital Mgt.	2.0
Elliott Associates	1.9
Spectrum Asset Mgt.	1.9
Carlson Capital	1.8
Orbis Investment Mgt.	1.7
Stark Investments	1.7
Paloma Partners	1.6
Weiss Peck Greer-Farber	1.6
Appaloosa Mgt.	1.6
Everest Capital	1.5
Gem Capital Mgt.	1.5
Unterman	1.5
Sloane Robinson Investment Mgt.	1.4
Highbridge Capital Mgt.	1.4
Clinton Group	1.4
First Quadrant	1.4
Alliance Capital	1.3
The Cypress Funds	1.3
Essex Investment Mgt.	1.3
Ellington Capital Mgt.	1.3

*Announced retirement.

(Continued)

Table 3.1   Continued

Fund	Estimated Assets ($B)
CDC Investments	1.2
John W. Henry & Co.	1.2
FLA (Forstman Leff Associates)	1.2
Quantitative Financial Strategies	1.2
III Associates	1.2
Arnhold & S. Bleichroder	1.1
Voltaire Asset Mgt.	1.1
Dunn Capital	1.1
INVESCO	1.1
Bill Collins	1.1
Halcyon/Slifka	1.0
Mark Asset Mgt.	1.0
Lotsoff Capital Mgt.	1.0
Egerton	1.0

Note: Not all managers release assets on any or all of their funds. Thus the table is comprised from various sources, of which some are estimates.

INCENTIVE FEE AS MOTIVATOR

The incentive fee structure is the key. Managers are compensated on performance, not just a fixed percentage of assets under management. The best and the brightest go into hedge fund management because they get a 1 percent management fee and 20 percent incentive fee, compared with mutual funds where they get a 0.5 percent management fee and no incentive fee. To understand what this means in dollar terms, assume that both managers are managing $100 million, and this is their initial equity. The hedge fund manager takes in 1 percent of $100 million or $1 million on an annual basis, regardless of performance. This is a fixed fee. The mutual fund manager, managing the same amount of assets, takes in $500,000 in management fees (i.e., one-half of 1 percent of $100 million). Now assume both managers are up 20 percent for the year. The mutual fund manager gets nothing extra. The hedge fund manager, however, gets a 20 percent incentive fee or $20 million, for a total compensation package of $21 million.

Being a hedge fund manager is also potentially profitable because the managers tend to put a large percentage of their own financial net worth in the funds alongside the investors. This is not usually true of other types of managers. So if the fund does well, the hedge fund manager personally does well.

Other features that are common among hedge fund managers—but by no means universal—are the use of leverage and the trading of multiple asset classes. Many have lock-up periods during which investors cannot withdraw their money and a high-water mark that means the manager does not get the incentive fee until any previous losses are made up. While the minimum investment for hedge funds varies considerably, a $500,000 to $1 million minimum investment is typical.

It is the incentive fee that motivates many other fund managers to enter the hedge fund world. In addition to mutual fund managers, economists and proprietary traders have entered the hedge fund arena. Banks such as Goldman Sachs, Daiwa Securities, and Swiss Bank are running in-house funds. Bankers Trust and DLJ have a fund of funds approach.

Fidelity has lost a number of mutual fund managers who defected to the hedge fund world: Jeffrey Vinik, Mary English, Michael Gordon, Mark Kaufman, Andrew Kaplan, and Matt Grech, to name a few recent examples. Erin Sullivan, who had run Fidelity Aggressive Growth Fund with assets of $17 billion and who had generated returns of 103 percent in 1999, started her own hedge fund, Spheric Capital, in early 2000.

The success story was Jeffrey Vinik, who had run Fidelity's Magellan Fund but left to start Vinik Asset Management in 1996. He quickly raised $1 billion. On October 26, 2000, with assets of $4.2 billion, he announced he was returning assets to investors by the end of the year. The reason given was that he and the other two principals—Michael Gordon and Mark Hostetter—wanted to pursue personal interests. Performance had been excellent for the five years he had traded:

1996	13%
1997	95
1998	36
1999	29
2000 (through October)	57

The advantages that mutual fund managers have are: experience running large assets, stock-picking ability, and access to initial public offerings from Wall Street relations; in addition, they are willing to cap assets realizing that larger unwieldy assets may impact performance.

While Vinik has done well, not all mutual fund managers have done so well or even stayed within the hedge fund community.

Some of the problems encountered by former mutual fund managers may be they have no shorting experience, aren't familiar with leverage, have no experience with derivatives, or don't do well when they lack the resources of a big firm. And finally, they often have a different mind-set—outperforming the S&P (mutual funds) versus absolute returns (hedge funds).

Over the years, proprietary traders at investment banking firms have been another large source for hedge fund managers. Goldman Sachs spin-offs include Robert Albertson, Cliff Asness, Andrew Boszhardt, Leon Cooperman, Roderick Jack, Marcel Jonsen, Kent McCarthy, Dan Och, Erinch Ozada, Anthony Scaramucci, and David Tepper. Morgan Stanley had been the starting point for Phillippe Burke, Richard Coons, and Peter Ogden. Salomon Brothers had been the starting point for John Meriwether of Long-Term Capital Management notoriety as well as Michael Balboa, Tim Irwin, Alistair Kerr, Praveen Mehrotra, Nicholas Stefanou, Peter Thomas, Alfredo Viegas, and Mustafa Zida. Tom O'Neill, chief investment officer at Fleet-Boston Financial Corporation is a recent example. He has decided to focus full-time on his $350 million Navigator hedge fund family. (See Table 3.2.)

The economists have also been represented. Henry Kaufman, who had been chief economist at Salomon Brothers, started a hedge fund in 1996 with Chuck Leiberman, who had been head economist at Chase Bank and previously at Chemical Bank. Strategic Investment Management eventually closed down in 1998.

Institutions are starting hedge funds in-house in an attempt to keep their best internal traders as well as to take advantage of downturns in the market and to offer a product to an audience that otherwise would not consider hedge funds. These include Alliance Capital, Bank of America, Bankers Trust, Citibank, State Street Global Advisors, Montgomery Asset Management, Sanford Bernstein, Wellington Capital Management, and most recently Driehaus Capital Management.

Table 3.2 Sampling of Hedge Fund Spin-Offs from Mutual Fund Firms and Investment Banks

Manager Name	Company Spun Off From	Company Formed	When
Mutual Funds			
Adams, Patrick	Berger Funds	Choice Capital Mgt.	2000
Boyd, Chris*	Growth Investors Fund at America Century	Leawood Capital Mgt.	1997
Brennan, John	MFS Investment Mgt.	Sirius Capital Mgt.	1999
Ellison, David	Fidelity	Friedman Billings, Ramsey	1996
English, Mary	Fidelity	Third Millennium Ventures	1997
Feinberg, Jeff	Fidelity	JLF Investments	N/A
Felipe, Chris	MFS Investment Mgt.	Sirius Capital Mgt.	1999
Felske, Derek*	Twentieth Century	Leawood Capital Mgt.	1997
Gordon, Michael	Fidelity	Vinik Asset Mgt.	1996
Grech, Matthew	Fidelity	Thomas Weisel	2000
Kaplan, Andrew	Fidelity	Pequot Capital	2000
Marcus, David	Franklin	Marcstone Capital Group	2000
O'Neill, Tom	FleetBoston	Navigator	2000
Posner, Brian	Warburg Pincus	Hygrove Partners	2000
Richardson, Kevin	Fidelity	Tudor Investment Corp.	1997
Sullivan, Erin	Fidelity	Spheric Capital	2000
Vinik, Jeffrey	Fidelity	Vinik Asset Mgt.	1996
Investment Banks			
Albertson, Robert	Goldman Sachs	Pilot Financial	1999
Ashford-Russell, Brian	Henderson Investors	yet to be named	2000
Asness, Cliff	Goldman Sachs	AQR Capital Mgt.	1998
Ault, Milton	Prudential Securities	Ault, Glazer & Co.	1998
Bakovljev, Steven	INVESCO	Rialto Capital Mgt.	1995
Balboa, Michael	Salomon Brothers	VZB Partners	1995
Balfour, Alex	ING Barings	Furinkazan Fund	1998
Bernard, Peter	J. P. Morgan	IFM	1994
Boszhardt, Andrew	Goldman Sachs	Oscar Capital Mgt.	1996
Burke, Philippe	Morgan Stanley	Apache Capital Mgt.	N/A
Chain, Paul	Lehman Brothers	Lone Wolf Asset Mgt.	1997
Cheng, Jack	J&W Seligman	yet to be named	2000
Cohen, Steven	Gruntal	SAC Capital Mgt.	1992
Coons, Richard	Morgan Stanley	Skanda Fund	1998
Cooperman, Leon	Goldman Sachs	Omega Advisors	1992
Cotton, Robert	Credit Suisse First Boston	Soss & Cotton	1994
Covo, Mario	Merrill Lynch	Columbus Advisors	1995
Czitron, Thomas	Royal Bank Investment Mgt.	Blackberry Capital Mgt.	2000
Daniel, Joe	Dresdner Bank	Critical Infrastructure Fund	1998
English, Chris	Merrill Lynch	IFM	1994
Flynn, Clare	Deutsche Asset Mgt.	yet to be named	2000
Fraker, Paul	Brown Brothers Harriman	yet to be named	2000
Frommer, Jeremy	Bankers Trust	Guard Hill Capital	1995

*No longer trading.

(Continued)

Table 3.2 Continued

Manager Name	Company Spun Off From	Company Formed	When
Gordon, Stephen	Sandler O'Neill & Partners	Genesis Financial Partners	1995
Guan, Raymond	J. P. Morgan	Relative Value Asset Mgt.	1998
Herrmann, Jeremy	J. P. Morgan	Ferox Capital Mgt.	2000
Hutchinson, Robert	Schroder Investment Mgt.	Hutchinson Vecchini Asset Mgt.	2000
Irwin, Tim	Salomon Smith Barney	Irwin Mgt.	1999
Jack, Roderick	Goldman Sachs	Adelphi Capital	1997
Jonsen, Marcel	Goldman Sachs	Adelphi Capital	1997
Keller, Scott	Bankers Trust	Guard Hill Capital	1995
Kerr, Alistair	Salomon Brothers	Beaver Creek	1998
Lamar, Emilio	Merrill Lynch	Columbus Advisors	1995
Machado, Dean	Bankers Trust	Guard Hill Capital	1995
McCarthy, Kent	Goldman Sachs	KCM Capital	1995
Megiris, Constantine	J. P. Morgan	Relative Value Asset Mgt.	1998
Mehrotra, Praveen	Salomon Brothers	Crest Capital Mgt.	1995
Meriwether, John	Salomon Brothers	Long-Term Capital Mgt./JWM	1993
Mezzacappa, Damon	Lazard Frères	Mezzacappa Berens	1999
Mobbs, Steve	Deutsche Morgan Grenfell	Medici Capital	1997
Och, Daniel	Goldman Sachs	Och-Ziff Capital Mgt.	1994
Ogden, Peter	Morgan Stanley	MC Organization	N/A
Ozada, Erinch	Goldman Sachs	Pharos Fund	1996
Penn, Laurence	Lehman Brothers	Ellington Capital Mgt.	1995
Rossi, Vincent	First Boston	Turnberry Capital	1996
Rudloff, Hans-Jorg	Credit Suisse First Boston	MC Organization	N/A
Sandell, Thomas	Bear Stearns	Sandell Asset Mgt.	1997
Scaramucci, Anthony	Goldman Sachs	Oscar Capital Mgt.	1996
Soss, Neal	Credit Suisse First Boston	Soss & Cotton	1994
Stefanou, Nicholas	Salomon Brothers	Beaver Creek	1998
Sweeney, Joe	Salomon Brothers	Cascade Partners	1995
Tepper, David	Goldman Sachs	Appaloosa Mgt.	1993
Thomas, Peter	Salomon Brothers	Crest Capital Mgt.	1995
Tolchinsky, Gabriel	Merrill Lynch	Columbus Advisors	1995
Van Kipnis, Greg*	Jefferies & Co.	Invictus Partners	1998
Vecchini, Vanni	Schroder Investment Mgt.	Hutchinson Vecchini Asset Mgt.	2000
Viegas, Alfredo	Salomon Brothers	VZB Partners	1995
Vranos, Michael	Kidder Peabody	Ellington Capital Mgt.	1995
Waldron, Mark	J. P. Morgan	Emergent Capital Inv. Mgt.	1998
Woodcock, Martin	Smith Barney	Millbrook Capital	1997
Woolley, Tim	Henderson Investors	yet to be named	2000
Yun, Daniel	Lehman Brothers	Emergent Capital Inv. Mgt.	1998
Zida, Mustafa	Salomon Brothers	VZB Partners	1995

*No longer trading.

Another interesting case is an endowment in-house trader turned hedge fund manager. Jonathan Jacobs, who had been at Harvard Management Company, left to start his own hedge fund in 1998. When that occurred, Harvard allocated Highfields Capital $500 million.

During the roaring bull market of the mid to late 1990s and the choppy market of 2000, an amazing proliferation of hedge funds—some good, some bad—has occurred, largely due to the incentive fee structure, as well as other factors discussed in the next section.

IMPETUS FOR STRONG GROWTH, 1994–2000

Hedge fund growth has been strong due to the mystique and success of global macro managers over the years. Even when the likes of Julian Robertson and George Soros falter, it has been an impetus for key employees to spin off and form their own hedge funds. Noncorrelation to and diversification from traditional investments, attractive short- and long-term performance, expanding global markets, and fast-paced investment technology making information available on a timely basis have all contributed to the rapid growth of the hedge fund industry.

On the positive side, hedge funds have long had a mystique due to the long-term successful track records of some the global macro managers such as George Soros, Julian Robertson, and Michael Steinhardt. Their past performance has focused initial attention on the hedge fund industry. Their activity sparked other top managers from various walks of life to start hedge funds. When the performance of the top global macro managers started to falter, some key employees spun off from the large hedge fund managers to start their own hedge funds.

At the end of 1995 when Michael Steinhardt retired, a number of people who worked for him spun off and formed their own companies. Chuck Davidson formed Wexford Capital. John Lattanzio, who had been Steinhardt's head trader for 17 years, formed his own company. Ernest Werlin started Highview Capital. John Goodman found Concentric Capital. (See Table 2.1.)

In 1994, there was a large spurt in the growth of hedge funds due to the low short-term interest rate environment. This prompted investors to seek higher returns from more risky activities. The low cost of borrowed money made it easier for hedge funds to borrow cheaply, using the leverage to increase their positions and earnings. The low barriers to entry attracted entrepreneurs.

Whereas the United States—and in particular New York—had been the main center of activity, hedge funds have sprung up in other locations as well. San Francisco, Chicago, Atlanta, and Boston are homes to an increasing number of hedge fund managers.

European managers started to surface in big numbers in 1997 as long-only proprietary bank traders and fund managers left to start their own hedge funds. Contributing factors were bank consolidation in Europe, relaxation of Inland Revenue Service rules (tax laws), presence of U.S. hedge funds in London, and sophisticated European investors' appetite for locally managed alternative investments.[2] The advent of the euro, consolidation, massive growth in merger and acquisition activity, dropping of borders, an increase in entrepreneurial spirit, tax reform, deregulation, globalization, new technology leading to improved productivity, and the relative attractiveness of European stock markets are other reasons.[3]

Today, there are an estimated 300 managers in Europe representing about $50 billion in assets. Many are long/short equity managers focusing on the European markets. Some are risk arbitrage managers; they tend to use less leverage, and have local expertise. Because many investors feel managers perform better early in their life cycles and these managers tend to take a different perspective and trade different markets than U.S. managers, investor interest in the emerging European manager is strong. The European manager provides diversification to the typical U.S. investor's portfolio.

The European managers, in general, have raised assets quickly. A number now have assets over $1 billion, such as GLG, Marshall Wace, and Egerton. In addition, European hedge fund managers are raising money so quickly that a number of them have closed to new investment. Just in 2000, Charlemagne, Lansdowne European Equity Fund, and Cross Asset Management stopped taking new investment.

A number of European banks have set up hedge funds, such as Dexia Asset Management, Compagnie Parisienne de Reescompte (CPR), SEB SA, and Credit Suisse First Boston (CSFB). A number of European asset management firms have done the same, such as HongKong & Shanghai Banking Corp. (HSBC), Henderson Investments, Gartmore Investment Management, Jupiter, Schroder, and Mercury Asset Management.

OBJECTIVE

Hedge funds are also noncorrelated to traditional investments such as stocks and bonds. Noncorrelation means that there is no correlation between the two. If stocks are down, hedge funds could be up, down, or flat; there is no correlation pattern. This is not the same as negative correlation. Negative correlation means if the stock market were down, hedge funds would be up.

Thus, by putting 5 to 10 percent of an investor's portfolio into hedge funds, the investor obtains portfolio diversification. This is especially valuable when stock and bond markets are not favorable, are flat, or are choppy.

Hedge fund managers' goal is to provide superior returns under all market conditions. Hedge funds are not designed to outperform the stock market in a roaring bull market but rather to shine in flat, negative, or choppy markets. Over the past decade, we've seen a roaring bull stock market. In general, most hedge funds lagged the stock market by a few percentage points. This is because they are hedging by using either options or futures for protection against the downside. This is similar to an insurance cost they must pay during a roaring bull stock market.

However, it is the down markets or the choppy, volatile stock markets that we saw in 2000 that is the best environment for most true hedge funds.

During the roaring bull stock market of the 1990s, it was believed that some hedge fund managers, in an attempt not to get left behind in the performance game, lifted their hedges and were exposed to the stock market more than they should have been. During the periods when the stock market fell, it was possible to examine the performance of managers and see whether this was true.

For example, in February 1999, the S&P was down 3.1 percent; 78 percent of the hedge funds did better than the S&P that month, and 44 percent of the hedge funds were positive that month.[4]

Or in April 2000, the S&P was down 3 percent. About two-thirds of the hedge funds did better, and 41 percent were positive.[5]

And in November 2000, when the S&P was down 7.9 percent, 80 percent of the hedge funds outperformed the S&P.[6]

In August 1998, when the S&P fell 14.5 percent, 75 percent of the hedge funds did better than the S&P; 23 percent of the hedge funds were positive. During this brutal August 1998 period, many investors asked why hedge fund performance was not more spectacular.[7]

Time frame must be considered. While one can construct a portfolio not correlated to the stock and bond market for one month like August 1998 or April 2000, most portfolios are constructed to provide diversification for a minimum of three years. In other words, it is not smart to look at one month only to see if noncorrelation in fact exists; a longer period should be used.

PERFORMANCE

Performance for most strategies has generally been good in the short term and long term. Looking at 1994 through 1999, most hedge fund strategies have generated double-digit returns in four out of the six years. These are: event driven, market neutral, global macro, global established, and fund of funds. Global established funds' returns have been in the 20 to 30 percent range.

Looking at the short term, 2000, we also see excellent performance.[8] Short sellers, market neutral, event-driven, and fund of funds all had returns between 10 and 18 percent. No style category was down for the year.

FROM A. W. JONES–STYLE MODEL TO OTHER STYLES

Alfred Winslow Jones, a former sociologist and journalist for *Fortune* magazine, is credited with starting the first hedge fund in 1949. The company was called A. W. Jones & Co. He conceived the idea of hedging stocks by going long and short. When this idea worked correctly, the shorts did worse than the market when the market was going down and the longs did better than the market when stocks went up. His goal was to eliminate market risk by hedging long equity positions with short positions that gain in value when stock prices fall. With market risk virtually eliminated, the fund and the manager's destiny were determined by stock selection.

He combined leverage and short sales to hedge against market declines. His fund was driven by long and short stock selection, not market timing or inefficiencies. He did not invest in bonds, commodities, currencies, or derivatives. He would increase and decrease net market exposure of his portfolio based on his estimate of the strength of the market.

If there were $1,000 in capital, he might use leverage and buy shares valued at $1,100 and sell shares short valued at $400. In this example, gross investment is $1,500 ($1,100 + $400) or 150 percent of capital. Net market exposure is $700 ($1,100 − $400), making this portfolio 70 percent net long.[9]

His success during the 1960s bull market encouraged others to start hedge funds as well. During the 1960s, the small group of hedge funds tended to be long and short, following the A. W. Jones model. In the 1970s, a number of hedge funds closed during the 1973–1974 bear market. It was not until late 1989 and the early 1990s that the hedge fund concept again grew in popularity. Hedge funds have evolved to include a number of strategies with a broad range of return/risk characteristics.

Today, most hedge funds do not follow the A. W. Jones model. Different strategies have evolved; there is no uniform type of hedge fund. Because they each have different return/risk objectives, their performance patterns differ as well. Some of the different style categories are as follows.

With event-driven funds, event is the key word. An event occurs that is a special situation or creates an opportunity to capitalize from price fluctuations. There are four subcategories.

1. Risk arbitrage occurs when a manager buys stock in a company being acquired and sells stock in its acquirer. One example would be buying Time Warner and selling America Online (AOL). The principal risk is deal risk (i.e., should the deal fail to materialize). Stark Investments and Och-Ziff are managers that focus on risk arbitrage.
2. Distressed funds focus on stocks that are in bankruptcy, reorganization, or corporate restructuring. Distressed makes up a large percentage of Elliott Associates' and Citadel's portfolios.
3. Regulation D refers to investments in micro-cap and small-cap public companies that are raising money in private capital markets.
4. High yield, often called junk bonds, refers to low-grade fixed-income securities of companies that have upside potential. David Tepper's Appaloosa Management's core activity is high yield.

Fixed income strategies are based on public and private debt instruments with fixed rates and maturities and their derivatives. These strategies include long and short arbitrage.

A fund of funds strategy allocates assets among several funds usually using different strategies in order to achieve diversification. Investors have access to managers through smaller investment minimums than if they went to each manager directly. Investors are charged a fee of 1 to 3 percent on top of fees for the underlying funds.

Global emerging funds are those that invest in emerging markets such as those of Russia, China, India, and Latin America. The funds are usually either equity or fixed income oriented. Because many emerging markets do not allow short selling or offer futures or derivatives to hedge with, emerging markets often use long-only strategies. Those funds that had exposure to Russia in 1998 tended to be the worst performers. In 1999, they tended to be the best performers.

Global established funds focus on opportunities in established markets such as Japan, the United States, or Europe. One example is Maverick Capital.

Global macro managers trade opportunistically around the globe, using stocks, bonds, currencies, and other instruments and vehicles. Their positions reflect their views on overall market direction as influenced by major economic trends. They include Julian Robertson's Tiger Management and George Soros's Quantum funds.

Long/short equities are also referred to as the Jones model. The objective is not to be market neutral but rather directional. Managers shift from value to growth, from small to medium to large cap, from a net long position to a net short.

Managed futures managers invest in financial, commodity, and currency markets. Managers are either systematic (i.e., trading is based on price and market specifics) or discretionary (i.e., trading is based on judgment). John W. Henry & Co. is an example of a systematic managed futures manager.

Market neutral managers attempt to make 1 to 1.5 percent return per month as they lock out or neutralize market risk. This is accomplished by using a long/short strategy, convertible arbitrage, statistical arbitrage, and merger arbitrage. Market neutral is perceived as a conservative strategy. Industry, sector, and market capitalization are some of the exposures that managers try to control. Leverage may be used to enhance returns. Sussman's Paloma Partners concentrates on various market neutral strategies.

Sector funds focus on a specific sector such as technology, financial firms, or health care. Raj Rajaratnam's Galleon Group is an example that focuses on technology and health care.

Short sellers take a position that stock prices will go down. A hedge fund borrows stock and sells it, hoping to buy it back at a lower price.

BENCHMARKS

As institutions became more interested in hedge funds, the proliferation of benchmarks occurred. Institutions use benchmarks for judging the performance of their traditional managers, so it is only natural they would do the same for alternative investments.

Hedge fund managers, in most cases, however, perceive themselves as absolute managers rather than relative managers. For example, a manager might say, "My goal is to generate 12 to 15 percent returns each year." So independent of what the stock market is doing, this is the manager's performance goal. On the other hand, relative managers, such as mutual fund managers, compare themselves to different benchmarks.

The use of a benchmark, whichever one is used, has many inherent problems. First, it is not required that a hedge fund manager report performance numbers to any organization. Therefore, some of the largest managers—who might want to keep a low profile, or who are closed to investment—are not included in the calculated indexes. Thus, significant assets are not included in what is suppose to be a representational index. Second, most of the numbers submitted are unaudited and may be estimates. They may change down the road. There is no guarantee that the performance numbers submitted are correct. Third, some indexes may be based on gross performance numbers while others are based on net. Fourth, it is not uncommon for a manager undergoing difficult performance not to report the fund's numbers on a timely basis or at all. As a result, the benchmark may be overstating results. Survivor bias results since managers that go out of business or who are doing badly are no longer included. Finally, different degrees of leverage and different degrees of portfolio composition are used by the managers which are not reflected in the typical benchmark. Thus, the putting together of these managers may be like comparing apples and oranges.

The various available benchmarks often have different objectives and are calculated in different ways. Some may be dollar-weighted while others are equal-weighted. Some attempt to be universal while others are representational. Thus, it is best to use one benchmark and stick with it rather than use various ones in different junctures to prove different points.

Despite these drawbacks, benchmarks are useful in that they provide a guide to performance. While they should not be taken as the ultimate truth, they provide a sense of performance and comparison for those who require it. In some cases, customized benchmarks may be the answer for specific investors that take into account the particular strategies and markets they allocate to.

Several organizations are creating investable hedge funds that are intended to track their benchmarks. The benefits of such funds are the ease and convenience they bring to the investors, saved costs from the investor not having to do manager searches, circumvention of the problem of finding managers who can perform well over time, and avoidance of manager disasters and blowups. Unlike a fund of funds that attempts to select the best managers and outperform the market, the index funds are trying to deliver market returns.

VARIATIONS ON EXIT STRATEGIES

While we've seen the old generation of hedge fund manager have difficulty with succession planning, one interesting trend is the development of investment holding companies. They are similar to those set up by mutual funds in the 1960s and are viewed by some hedge fund managers as a partial exit strategy. Asset Alliance, XL Capital, Capital Z, and Value Asset Management are a few such companies.

Asset Alliance, which generally purchases about a 50 percent stake in alternative investment managers with assets of between $50 million and $500 million, has bought an interest in Beacon Hill Asset Management, Bricoleur Capital Management, JMG Capital Management, Liberty Corner Asset Management, Metropolitan Capital Managers, Milestone Global Advisors, Pacific Asset Management, Silverado Capital Management, Trust Advisors, Wessex Asset Management, and most recently in 2001, P/E Investments and Zola Capital Management.

XL Capital, a Bermuda-based insurance, reinsurance, and financial products firm, by 1999 had acquired a minority interest in MKP Capital Management, Highfields Capital Management, and Pareto Partners. In July 2000, they bought a minority stake in Agora Capital Management.

Other examples include Capital Z, a venture capital firm. Since 1998, it has raised $1.5 billion for alternative investments. Capital Z has backed five hedge funds and 11 private equity funds. The hedge funds include Galtere and Quattro Investors. Capital Z takes an equity stake ranging from 20 to 50 percent, investing between $20 million and $50 million.

Value Asset Management bought 70 percent of Grosvenor Capital in 1998. Consolidated Advisors, controlled by Imperial Bank of Wood Gundy, took a minority interest in KD Partners (Kellner-DiLeo) in June 1997.

In mid-2000, a number of acquisitions occurred in the fund of funds sector, again reflecting a variation on the exit strategy. Bank of New York had signed an agreement to buy Ivy Asset Management, a fund of funds with $2.4 billion in assets. Bank of New York attributed the deal to requests from high-net-worth and institutional clients who wanted to invest in alternative investments and hedge funds.

On August 31, 2000, Switzerland-based ED&F Man purchased Glenwood Investments, a fund of funds in Chicago. Glenwood had $570 million in U.S. assets and another $850 million in products created for its joint venture Man-Glenwood. Man paid $110 million in cash.

Halcyon/Alan B. Slifka Management Co. formed a joint venture company with Baker Nye Advisors called Halcyon Capital Management, which will oversee assets of $2 billion. Motivations were to boost distribution channels and develop product lines. A large share of Halcyon's offshore business had been from institutions, but the U.S. hedge fund has been dominated by high-net-worth investors. In the joint venture, Halcyon will provide consulting and research services to Baker Nye.

BLACK EYES

There have been several debacles in the past few years that have put hedge funds in a bad light. In order, from most recent to oldest, they are as follows.

Michael Berger's Manhattan Funds—2000

The most recent infraction occurred in January 2000 with Michael Berger's Manhattan Capital Management. This was a short-biased fund (i.e., long/short U.S. equity fund specializing in short selling). Berger misrepresented the fund's financial condition to the auditors, Deloitte & Touche. He allegedly manufactured fictitious account statements, overstated performance and assets since September 1996, and misstated assets at $426 million when they were $28 million. Berger told different parties to ignore information, that it didn't represent his entire portfolio. Deloitte & Touche were fired after they withdrew their approval of accountant's statements.

In August 2000, Berger was charged with two criminal counts of securities fraud in connection with the loss of more than $400 million by at least 300 investors. The charges mirror a civil suit filed by the SEC in January. A number of investors have also filed civil lawsuits to recover damages. Berger, who pleaded guilty to securities fraud, will be sentenced in March when he could receive up to 10 years in jail and a fine of up to $1.25 million.

Long-Term Capital Management—1998

Long-Term Capital Management, which had close to $7 billion in assets at the end of 1997 and two Nobel laureates among its advisers, Robert Merton and Myron Scholes, came close to collapse in 1998. Fourteen banks and brokerage firms orchestrated a rescue on September 22 and 23, 1998, in which $3.65 billion was raised. Problems started to surface in May when LTCM suffered a 6.7 percent loss. In June, LTCM had a 10.1 percent loss for the month, bringing the year-to-date loss to 15 percent. The losses continued to hemorrhage, and by August LTCM was down 44 percent for the month, and down 52 percent for the year. In its last five months, there was a 92 percent loss.[10]

LTCM was primarily a global arbitrage fund. An example of a global arbitrage trade is trading U.S. junk bonds versus U.S. government bonds or high-grade corporate bonds. Five-year junk bonds usually yield 2 percent over five-year Treasuries because of the higher risk. For example, a global arbitrageur would say that if the yield spread goes wider than 2 percent, it would narrow again. Similar examples of trades would be Italian government bonds versus U.S. T-bonds or U.S. mortgages versus U.S. Treasuries.

What caused the LTCM situation? LTCM's view was that the spread would narrow between various pairs of government bonds and other credit instruments. The opposite happened—spreads widened.

Spreads between bonds began to widen by June 1998, exactly opposite of what LTCM's models had forecast. LTCM, relying on historical models, bet that perceived risk would diminish; but prices were moving in the opposite way. As was later revealed, LTCM's models did not go back as far as 1992.[11] Part of the cause was Russia declaring a debt moratorium on August 17, 1998, and the fund's heavy use of leverage accelerated its troubles. Leverage at one point was 100:1, without including the derivatives positions.[12] One of the implications of the emerging markets dislocations was a global flight to liquidity. Investors wanted only the safest bonds. In July 1998, investors fled junk bonds and went into Treasuries. Yields went higher on junk bonds and lower on Treasuries. Instead of converging, they diverged. Credit spreads between Treasuries and convertible bonds widened. All over the world, investors were buying the safer lower-yielding bonds and selling the higher-yielding riskier ones, pushing the spreads wider.

This global flight to liquidity forced liquidations by other investors in their markets. The flight to liquidity led to a credit crunch; margin calls became prevalent. Highly leveraged funds near their margin-call boundary received margin calls. The banks and brokerage firms were nervous, thus requiring higher margin deposits, and changing criteria.

In reassessing LTCM, John Meriwether said in 2000 that the fund got too big and too risky. Its traders didn't see that others were making the same investments—and would turn on a dime to sell in a crisis.[13]

LTCM stopped trading at the end of 1999 and quietly liquidated in early 2000. The fund ultimately paid back $1.3 billion to investors.

Meriwether has since formed JWM Partners, a relative value opportunity fund. Meriwether, Eric Rosenfeld, and several other LTCM partners are working from LTCM's old offices in Greenwich, Connecticut. JWM had raised between $350 and $400 million as of late August 2000 despite a $1 billion goal. The same strategy is used: relative value using bonds and stocks. The fund is called the Relative Value Opportunity Fund II. It is billed as a conservative version of the former fund. Leverage is lower, at about 12:1 to 18:1, and the minimum investment is $5 million.

Victor Niederhoffer—1997

On October 27, 1997, Niederhoffer, a contrarian trader, was highly leveraged while trading S&P 500 options. He received a $50 million margin call on a large short position on S&P index futures puts from his clearing broker, Refco, when the Dow Jones Industrial Average fell 554 points on October 27. He was forced to liquidate after the market plummet.

A volatile trader, he had been down 51 percent in August, up 28 percent in September, and then out of business by the end of October. Investors in the fund had limited liability.

David Askin—1994

David Askin's Granite Funds collapsed in 1994. He traded $600 million in mortgage-backed securities. In February 1994, the Federal Reserve increased interest rates for the first time in five years. When interest rates increased, mortgage prepayments fell. This caused the value of Askin's bonds to fall. Askin used his own estimates to value the portfolio in February, indicating a 1.7 percent loss. This was later revised to a loss of 28 percent. The funds filed for bankruptcy, and Kidder Peabody and Lehman Brothers filed lawsuits. Other civil suits occurred as well.

LESSONS FOR INVESTORS

Despite these problems, investors find that the rewards outweigh the risks in hedge funds—if the managers are selected carefully.

These problems have made investors more aware of what can go wrong and have led to better due diligence efforts. This is all very good for the hedge fund industry.

Investors make a better effort to understand the strategies, to determine whether managers are trading the styles they say they are or drifting into other areas that are not their expertise. This occurred with the Russian problem in 1998. Investors found out that many managers had Russian positions even though the funds were not ostensibly emerging market funds.

Investors now try harder to determine whether managers are truly hedging or just saying so. If long-only, protection will not be provided in stock market downturns. Such long-only managers are not true hedge fund managers—they are just attempting to take advantage of the 20 percent incentive fee.

Transparency is key. Investors ask about the degree of illiquidity in a market. What instruments are traded and how liquid are they? Investors want to know how these illiquid instruments are marked to the market (i.e., priced)—it should be done by someone outside the firm, and there should be more than one source. They want to make sure the approach is consistently applied. Investors should make sure the formula in the document detailing how the process will be carried out is the one actually applied.

Investors now make an effort to quantitatively measure a manager's ability to liquidate positions. The general rule of thumb is that it takes one to two days for a long/short hedge fund; one week for a convertible arbitrage fund; three months for a distressed fund. Some investors suggest looking at the bid-offer spread as a gauge. The tighter the spread, the more liquid the stock.

Investors are now wary of funds that are near capacity, because they may have passed capacity. Long-Term Capital Management had reached close to $7 billion by the end of 1997 and gave back $3 billion to maintain good performance. It had already passed capacity. As it turned out, size was a major factor. In 1997 when asset size was at its peak, spreads were shrinking, which meant fewer trading opportunities. Spreads were shrinking because rival banks and competitors were entering the arbitrage business. Almost every investment bank on Wall Street had to some degree been getting into the game.[14] With a common European currency, the easy money on convergence in Europe had been made. With borders disappearing, the spread between Italian and German bonds had shrunk.[15]

Due to these diminishing opportunities, LTCM returned profits on money invested during 1994 and returned all money (principal and profits) invested after that date.[16] LTCM also strayed outside its area of expertise into Brazilian and Russian bonds and Danish mortgages. It made more directional bets, abandoned some of its hedging, got deeper into equities, and lost all sense of scale.[17]

Investors now make a better attempt to understand noncorrelation. An often-heard statement in 1998: "The only thing that goes down in bear markets is correlation between asset classes."[18] During severe dislocations, things that aren't usually correlated may become so. We saw this in emerging markets. The spreads between Eastern Europe, Latin America, and Asia were all pushed out of whack.

The importance of the back office has become more critical. Investors need to find out the depth/liquidity of the back office and ask about the relationships that exist between each manager and their prime broker and accountant. In some of the trouble spots, prime brokers and accountants were the first to get early warning signals of potential trouble.

Depth of management team is studied more closely. There should be more than one brilliant key person. There should be a senior management team to provide checks and balances.

Investors are also taking an interest in finding out about the other investors. They don't need the names but need to know the degree of sophistication.

Investors are also more interested in managed accounts where they have transparency and liquidity. New products generating lower volatility with lower returns in the 9 to 13 percent range are gaining more interest from investors. Investors have a chance to select from different levels of risk. Long-only funds with futures overlay or hedged by short sales are being developed, as are more guaranteed products and insurance annuity products.

REGULATORY INITIATIVES

Regulatory initiatives followed the LTCM crisis in the United States. The President's Working Group, comprised of representatives from the Federal Reserve, Treasury, SEC, and CFTC, released a document in April 1999 that urged more disclosure of hedge fund leverage and risk through quarterly reports. It didn't recommend direct regulation but instead called for greater regulatory oversight of banks and registered derivatives dealers that lend to hedge funds.

The study said the SEC doesn't have direct jurisdiction over hedge funds but that the industry needs to develop its own standards. This led to the formation of the Group of 12.

The Group of 12's standards were released in June 1999. They advocated enhanced information sharing between counterparties or dealers and their trading clients. They also called for evaluation of leverage on market liquidity and credit risk, improved credit risk estimation techniques, and more disclosure of risks to dealers and regulators.

The key point of difference between the President's Working Group and the Group of 12 was the issue of whether information should be disclosed only to regulators (Group of 12) or to the public.

The General Accounting Office criticized the President's Working Group. The GAO wanted the SEC/CFTC to have regulatory authority similar to the Federal Reserve in regulating banks.

There have also been a number of congressional regulatory proposals in the United States. The Hedge Fund Disclosure Act (HR 2924), also known as the Baker proposal, suggested that hedge funds over $3 billion in assets file quarterly reports to the Federal Reserve. These reports would detail such things as the assets of the fund, derivative positions, and leverage ratio. The issue is that this proposal would affect only the largest hedge funds. Some critics also question whether the costs of compliance and information gathering are greater than the value of the information gathered. The proposal had initially been referred to the House Agriculture Committee on September 23, 1999, and then the Subcommittee of Risk Management. There are no plans to introduce the bill into the 107th Congress.

In October 2000, the House of Representatives passed a bill designed to reduce risk in the financial markets and the banking system. The bill concentrates on preventing a domino-effect collapse in the financial system rather than on policies and practices within hedge funds. The bill focuses on the valuation methods of derivatives contracts for bankruptcy court–protected investment firms and banks. Currently the gross value of losses from derivatives trading is used. The new bill allows these parties to use the net value, which is much smaller. The proposed method will also speed up bankruptcy proceedings.

In mid-February 2000, a group of five large hedge funds—Soros Fund Management, Moore Capital Management, Tudor Investment Corporation, Caxton Corporation, and Kingdon Capital—issued their own guidelines as a response to the President's Working Group. Guidelines included establishing risk monitoring systems that are independent from portfolio managers, and having managers perform periodic stress tests to determine how changes in market conditions would affect their portfolios, develop and monitor several measures of risk, and make periodic reports to lenders and counterparties. They did not suggest mandatory limits for borrowing or ways to manage risk, and also said that some of the recommendations would not be practical for smaller funds. Managers must apply those that suit their own business model since funds vary by size, nature, complexity, strategies, and resources.

Outside the United States, initiatives have occurred as well. In January 1999, in Basel, Switzerland, the Bank for International Settlement proposed tough standards for banks such as setting loan limits, and gathering better information from funds on risks of investors. In late 1998–1999, banks became stingier with credit. They demanded transparency, greater disclosure, additional reporting requirements, efforts to monitor derivatives, and modified standards for hedge fund investors.

By January 26, 2000, the Bank for International Settlement observed that competitive pressures again had led banks to cut corners, slip in credit standards, and have mixed adoption of new standards.

PART TWO

The Superstar Managers

4

COMMON THREADS AMONG THE SUPERSTAR MANAGERS

While the hedge fund industry has moved from a private elite club to a broader and more diverse industry, the crème de la crème of hedge fund managers still have distinguishing characteristics.

These best and brightest managers have a passion for what they do and are not primarily motivated by money. It is more the intellectual and emotional challenge of figuring out the markets and the relationships that exist between various investment classes. Generating superior performance in different market climates is a key objective—not having the most assets under management. As a result, many of these managers' funds are often closed to new investment. Some will take in assets only to replace redemptions or take in strategic investors.

These managers at the time of their interviews, have assets under management of over $1 billion. They tend to be the largest investors in their own funds, have a long track record, have been successful in a variety of economic conditions, and have done as well as or better than the S&P over the long term. Inevitably, the manager has gone through rocky periods but has managed to survive and emerged stronger for it. Lessons are continually being learned. In other words, these managers know they are not smarter than the markets. Managing downside risk is a critical part of their business and determines the leverage used, percentage risked per position, degree of diversification, and number of positions in the portfolio. They also understand the importance of managing information flow to their advantage.

They have developed a business and they are attempting to institutionalize it. They are developing an infrastructure and culture. They are empowering key employees with decision-making ability. Most often, the organizations are built around specialist teams.

Many of these managers receive considerable allocations from institutions, which provide a relatively stable long-term asset base.

The common threads highlighted in this chapter are often general themes while execution, strategy, and details may be quite different for each of the managers. The degree of importance of these issues varies by manager. Thus where it seemed important and was highlighted by him, I conveyed these details. In trying to illustrate the range and variation, I present the views on a continuum.

BEST AND BRIGHTEST

After each interview, I was truly amazed at each person and his qualities. Take Ken Griffin—he started his first hedge fund while he was a sophomore at college. At 32 years old, his assets under management now total approximately $5.0 billion and he has about 350 people working for him. Another example is Leon Cooperman, who was nonstop in his search for information. He could carry on an interview with me while also talking to chief executive officers and other senior managers. Bruce Kovner analyzes information flowing in from all sources—including oil tankers he purchased as a source of intelligence. Or Raj Rajaratnam, who as quarterback of the Galleon Group was tireless and omnipresent as he managed the Galleon Technology and New Media funds, often accompanied analysts to their company meetings, met officers of about two to three companies a day, visited about 25 companies in California one week out of every month, and also made it a point to meet with investors rather than delegate it to someone else. S. Donald Sussman of Paloma was impressive and seems ahead of his time. Focusing on market neutral strategies since the early 1980s, he created an internal money management team with the risk management controlled by the investor, not the manager.

I was also impressed that three of the managers—Ainslie, Och, and Rajaratnam—had never had an annual down year in their flagship funds despite 1994 and 1998, which were generally negative years for the hedge fund industry as well as 2000, which was a negative year for the stock market. And their performance in those years had been quite strong.

Then there was Cumberland Associates with a 30-year record and into its third generation—a rare feat in the hedge fund world.

These are some of the lasting impressions that these managers left with me.

LOVE WHAT THEY DO

The first and foremost similarity the managers have is that they love what they do—that is their prime motivation. Loving what they do and being the best at it runs hand in hand. Cooperman is a prime example—working 90 hours a week. He is motivated by doing a job well and gains satisfaction in finding what others don't. He makes a total commitment. Sussman also identified pride in a job well done as well as professional respect.

Kingdon also is motivated by the love of the business—the intellectual and emotional challenge. Kovner, Singer, and Stark echoed this sentiment, all making an analogy between investing and solving a puzzle.

Griffin is motivated by the competition—whether it's investing or a tennis game. The same theme was expressed by Ainslie, Henry, Rajaratnam, and Tepper.

Many say that once they don't love what they do, it's time to exit. Robertson was 67 when he called it quits—long after many others retire and with a lot more money.

Money is not the primary motivator. As Kingdon puts it, money is just a way of keeping score. Robertson, when he was trading, said this was a fun business (except for the very difficult days) and he, and probably others, would almost work for free. Working with and being associated with smart people was something he liked. Others feel the same way. Griffin also gets tremendous satisfaction from building a team of smart people who are always challenging him. Kovner also receives great satisfaction in creating a community of smart people with whom he can have discussions at any time around the clock. Och is motivated by building the best team.

ASSETS OF AT LEAST $1 BILLION

While their views differ on what is optimal capacity and how to grow the business, all the managers, when interviewed, had assets under management of at least $1 billion. This alone attests to the fact that they are among the elite managers, since only about 55 managers on a global basis fit this category. Several of the managers cluster between $1 billion and the $2.5 billion level, including Wilcox, Henry, Tepper, Singer, Sussman, Stark, and Cooperman. At year-end Och was at the $3.5 billion level. The $4.5 billion-plus managers include Rajaratnam, Kovner, Kingdon, Ainslie, and Griffin.

CLOSED TO NEW INVESTMENT

Many of the managers are often closed to new investment. Some may take strategic investors or investors to fill investors redeeming. This indicates an acknowledgment that growth in assets is not of prime importance; maintaining superior performance during different market environments is. Being the largest hedge fund is not the main objective. As Kingdon said, asset size is a potential concern, not a goal.

Kovner said that if he felt he were at capacity, he would return assets to investors. In 1995 he returned two-thirds of assets to investors because he felt that under current conditions, the asset size was too unwieldy. Kovner says he would do the same from time to time.

Tepper made the decision in mid-2000 to shrink Appaloosa to $1 billion and go back to its core competency—distressed and high-yield bonds. He intends to return about $500,000 to investors because he feels the fund's best performance generally occurs at about the $1 billion level.

Stark feels there isn't a fixed level of capacity for his core style—convertible arbitrage. Capacity changes with the markets and the environment. At points when there isn't sufficient opportunity or concerns in the market, taking capital is not the right thing. At other times, capacity seems beyond the capital of even the largest arbitrage fund.

Throughout the years, several of the managers have taken steps to have controlled growth. This has meant entering new strategies and taking new initiatives. Increasing capacity has been the issue for Griffin, Kovner, Och, Stark, and Sussman. Kovner observed that for an organization to survive, it must change with the opportunities available. Griffin acknowledged that if you're not aware of product development, you can't survive in the long term.

In their quest to have controlled growth, some of the managers conduct studies to quantify and measure the impact of assets on performance. For example, Ainslie compares Maverick's performance each month against pro forma performance as if no trades had been executed each month. Each day they look at trade executions against the closing price and the volume-weighted average price. JWH similarly conducts slippage studies to examine the impact of position-taking on markets he is participating in.

PERCENTAGE OF THEIR OWN MONEY

The managers' personal assets in their funds are significant. This means they have strong conviction in their own talent. It also means their own net worth is highly correlated to the performance of their funds. Thus they have a huge incentive to do well. While they describe their participation differently, the result is generally the same.

Kingdon says his entire financial net worth is in his funds. Stark estimates about 95 percent of his net worth is in the funds, while Och estimates his participation at about 80 percent of his net worth.

Singer, his family, and the principals are the largest investors in his fund, while Griffin says he and Citadel's other professionals are the second largest investor in the fund.

Caxton's principals' assets are currently under 30 percent of the fund. Cooperman said 12 percent of the capital in his funds are the general partners'. The principals' assets at Paloma, Appaloosa, and Cumberland (including retired principals' assets) are about 10 percent of the respective firms' capital. Stark and his staff represent 8.3 percent of the total assets under management. Ainslie estimated that Maverick principals and related entities have over $400 million in the Maverick funds, about 7 percent of the total assets. The partners and employees of

Galleon have invested $300 million, which is about 6 percent of total assets. Henry estimates his investment at $35 million to $75 million, about 2.9 percent to 6.3 percent of the total assets.

At several firms, the policy is that employees cannot have their own personal trading accounts. This is to ensure integrity and prevent front-running. This is the case at Galleon and Elliott Associates. At Citadel, a comprehensive personal trading policy restricts employees from transacting securities in Citadel accounts or portfolios. All employee trades must be preapproved.

TRACK RECORD

Each manager has a long track record with consistently superior performance during varying market conditions. Of those interviewed, all have at least a seven-year track record of their own as a hedge fund manager. Cumberland went back to 1970. Singer's inception was 1977, Henry and Sussman both started in 1981, and Kovner and Kingdon both started in 1983.

The length of performance record translates into independent experience over various economic and business cycles including 1990, and 2000, which were negative years for the stock market (as measured by the S&P), as well as 1994, and 1998, which were difficult years for hedge funds. Over a relatively long period, these managers generated consistently superior returns.

Performance has generally been excellent over a long period and over different market conditions. The compound average annual net return ranged from about 14 percent, slightly higher than the S&P, to 34 percent per year. Due to the different styles used and the different performance objectives, it is unfair to compare the managers against each other. Some managers may use an S&P benchmark or a blended benchmark with the Russell 2000, while some absolute managers don't have a benchmark. The use of leverage and the resulting volatility also make it difficult to compare returns. Furthermore, different environments are more favorable or less favorable to certain styles.

As a guide, despite the caveats, Singer and Sussman have an average annual return of about 14 to 15 percent. Cooperman, Cumberland, Stark, Och, Kingdon, and Ainslie are in the 17 percent to 25 percent range. Tepper, Kovner, Henry, and Griffin have compound annual returns between 25 percent and 30 percent. Rajaratnam's compound average annual return is about 34 percent.

Consistency

The consistency and discipline of most of the track records is very interesting. (See Table 4.1.) Ainslie, Rajaratnam, and Och have not had a down calendar year since they started trading in 1993/1994. Singer, Stark, Griffin, and Tepper have each had only one down year since their inception of trading in 1977, 1987, 1990, and 1993 respectively.

Double-digit annual returns to the upside are commonplace among these managers.

Noncorrelation

Hedge funds are suppose to perform well even when the stock market is flat, choppy, or negative. To see whether this occurred, I looked at three such years for the S&P—1990, 1994, and 2000.

Looking at the down stock market year of 1990—when the S&P was down 3.1 percent—most of the superstar hedge fund managers came out smelling like a rose. All but one of the managers who were trading generated positive results. John Henry climbed 83.6 percent, Kovner soared 39.4 percent, Kingdon gained 20 percent, Singer was up 13.4 percent and Sussman climbed 11.3 percent, while Stark gained 6.4 percent. Cumberland was down 18.8 percent. The other managers did not yet have their own track record.

In 1994, the S&P was up only 1.3 percent. The superstar managers had mixed results, while hedge fund managers in the overall general hedge fund community did not do well. Five of the 13 managers were positive. and one was flat. Rajaratnam soared 29.3 percent, while Och climbed 28.5 percent. Tepper was up 19.0 percent, and Stark gained 10.4 percent. Ainslie was up 6.8 percent. Singer was flat.

Seven were down: Cooperman was down 24.6 percent, while Cumberland gave back 6.4 percent. Sussman dropped 5.4 percent, and Henry gave up 5.3 percent. Griffin fell 4.3 percent, while Kingdon and Kovner both lost 2.2 percent. Reasons for a poor 1994 were the credit squeeze and unusual cross-correlation of different asset

Table 4.1 Net Performance Numbers

	Ainslie Hedged Equity Strategy	Cooperman Omega Capital Partners	Griffin Longest Running Fund	Henry Financial and Metals Program	Kingdon Kingdon Capital Management	Kovner Essex Ltd	Och Och-Ziff Capital Management
1970							
1971							
1972							
1973							
1974							
1975							
1976							
1977							
1978							
1979							
1980							
1981							
1982							
1983					44.7		
1984				9.9	−18.4		
1985				20.7	101.6	17.33	
1986				61.5	5.2	56.16	
1987				252.4	0.0	92.76	
1988				4.0	23.6	−0.85	
1989				34.6	50.1	54.53	
1990				83.6	20.0	39.43	
1991			43.0	61.9	41.4	23.28	
1992		18.47	40.7	−10.9	22.5	22.89	
1993	22.57	62.96	23.5	46.8	38.3	40.41	
1994	6.82	−24.57	−4.3	−5.3	−2.2	−2.19	28.49
1995	24.47	25.68	36.3	38.5	31.1	16.24	23.53
1996	44.66	36.74	23.0	29.7	15.4	21.30	27.36
1997	20.08	26.97	27.6	15.2	28.1	36.99	26.65
1998	21.84	−5.43	30.5	7.2	7.0	17.16	11.15
1999	25.83	24.12	45.2	−18.7	37.4	24.43	18.80
2000	27.40	13.80	52.0	12.9	11.6	33.40	20.50
Compound Annual Rate of Return	23.83	17.42	30.8	29.33	22.99	29.02	22.02

Rajaratnam Galleon Technology Fund	Singer Elliott Associates	Stark Stark Investments	Sussman Paloma Partners	Tepper Appaloosa Management	Wilcox Cumberland Partners	S&P (Dividends Reinvested)
					34.7	3.93
					26.0	14.56
					10.7	18.90
					−2.2	−14.77
					4.1	−26.39
					45.2	37.16
					38.4	23.57
	6.7				13.9	−7.42
	9.9				20.2	6.38
	16.6				38.4	18.20
	22.6				40.7	32.27
	23.4		7.80		11.7	−5.01
	17.6		17.41		34.5	21.50
	22.1		18.77		29.7	22.30
	16.4		13.46		7.3	6.30
	22.5		25.09		41.7	32.10
	10.7		16.51		18.4	18.70
	6.6	22.44	25.75		−3.5	4.90
	13.4	26.78	16.69		21.0	16.60
	23.8	15.41	20.73		26.4	31.80
	13.4	6.40	11.32		−18.8	−3.10
	12.4	20.22	19.31		37.5	3.05
33.2	15.1	21.63	11.01		24.1	7.61
21.1	21.6	39.75	15.45	57.62	31.1	10.08
29.3	0.0	10.36	−5.41	19.03	−6.4	1.31
56.1	18.3	42.89	11.66	42.06	21.4	37.58
34.8	19.0	27.30	19.87	78.46	17.9	22.96
6.6	12.1	19.35	17.33	29.54	32.0	33.36
30.5	−7.0	−7.88	−20.95	−29.19	−3.0	28.58
96.3	18.1	25.89	30.45	60.89	35.0	21.04
16.0	24.0	28.80	27.00	0.03	−0.5	−9.10
33.98	14.71	20.71	14.34	27.59	19.04	12.01

classes. Convertibles became undervalued during the collapse of the bond market as competitors were forced to liquidate positions due to mounting losses.

In 2000, the S&P fell 9.1 percent. Out of the 13 managers interviewed for the book, 12 were positive and one was down 0.5 percent in 2000. At the high end, seven had returns over 20 percent: Griffin's fund was up 52 percent, Kovner 33.4 percent, Stark 28.8 percent, Ainslie 27.4 percent, Sussman 27.0 percent, Singer 24.0 percent, and Och 20.5 percent. Rajaratnam, Cooperman, Henry, and Kingdon all generated returns between 11 and 16 percent. Tepper and Wilcox were both about flat for the year.

The year 1998 represents another interesting situation. The S&P had an excellent year; it was up 28.6 percent. In such a year, it would be expected that hedge funds would do well but trail the roaring stock market as the hedged positions would provide downside protection and have some protection cost. In 1998, seven of the 13 managers had positive results. Rajaratnam and Griffin both climbed 30.5 percent, while Ainslie soared 21.8 percent, Kovner gained 17.2 percent, Och rose 11.2 percent, Henry was up 7.2 percent, and Kingdon increased 7.0 percent.

Meanwhile, the other six managers were hurt badly. Tepper fell 29.2 percent in his main fund due to believing a sense of false liquidity existed in Russia. Sussman lost about 21 percent as he expected spreads to widen. Stark Investments was down 7.9 percent. Singer lost 7.0 percent, while Cooperman fell 5.4 percent and Cumberland dropped 3.0 percent.

Overall, Och and Rajaratnam were up double digits in 1994, 1998, and 2000. Ainslie was up in the three years but up double digits in 1998 and 2000. None of the three were trading in 1990. Seven of the other managers were up in either 1994 or 1998.

TECHNOLOGY INFORMATION

Most of these managers acknowledge the importance of technology information—being able to harness the information coming in and using it to their advantage. Rapid adoption of technology seems to give the managers an edge.

Information flow and information management are important to Och. On the front end it is harnessed for analysts, traders, and portfolio managers. In the back office, technology is harnessed for position and portfolio monitoring, as well as tracking exposure on a real-time basis. Och's view is that as the world becomes more integrated and more complex, they can focus on the more unusual complex securities where their hedging and analytical capabilities create a competitive edge.

Stark, Griffin, and Kovner devote considerable resources to this area as well. For Stark, equities, options, and convertibles are all involved, and they each have different hedge ratios. This requires powerful risk management tools and powerful screening tools.

Griffin, who has an office in Silicon Valley staffed with 125 people, also has several dozen servers providing the backup for market feeds, risk management, and data for the front office to make decisions. Nearly half of his employees in Chicago are systems or technology professionals. The quantitative research group develops and enhances proprietary mathematical models. They provide tools for portfolio management, stress testing of the trades, and stress testing of the portfolio. In addition, the information systems group writes and maintains the code to keep the systems current. The investment and trading group identifies the investment opportunity using mathematical and statistical models, proprietary valuation techniques, and fundamental analysis.

CULTURE

Most of the organizations have developed a culture. Teamwork was a common description of the culture at Caxton, Citadel, Cumberland, Elliott Associates, Galleon Group, Kingdon Capital, Maverick, Och-Ziff, and Stark Investments. While individuals may have strong personalities, they are all part of a team culture. "The team is stronger than the individual components," says Och. "The story at this firm is not about me. We have a strong and deep team which has been together for many years." This theme was echoed by many of the managers.

Cooperman, Rajaratnam, and Singer each describe his culture as one where a strong work ethic prevails. Cooperman's culture is intense, demanding, and research driven. Singer says what makes Elliott Associates different is that they apply more resources to the task. He focuses on those areas that are effort-laden—for example, where manual effort is required. Rajaratnam compares the business to getting a report card every day.

A few of the managers have a culture that emphasizes patience. They take a longer-term perspective of the market, and positions are often held for the long term. Patience was acknowledged by Kingdon, Henry, Cooperman, and Wilcox. Kingdon recalled 1990 as his most painful year. He was bearish on the market and only 1 percent invested. He was sitting still in cash. By year-end, he was up over 20 percent. Henry feels that patience during poor trading periods is the most important asset in a manager's arsenal. It is not uncommon for him to hold trades for years. Cooperman expects the majority of the portfolio to be held for at least two years.

The cultures were described in other ways as well. Griffin describes Citadel's culture as one where change is accepted. When the firm adds new strategies, new risks appear. As a result, there is a huge emphasis on learning, sharing, and teamwork. Most of the people are in their thirties.

Kingdon describes his as quiet intensity—individuals who compete with the markets, not with each other, and who take responsibility for their positions. The culture is maintained since portfolio managers have veto power over new hires.

Stark describes his culture as a cautious one. For example, they do not invest in rumor deals; they wait until a deal has been announced. They are not quick to add new strategies, and they always hedge.

Cumberland's portfolio management structure encourages give-and-take, challenge, debate, and compromise. All of the portfolio managers at Cumberland are interdependent on each other. The culture has allowed the firm to continue into its third generation. Wilcox describes it as a cumulative wisdom of the organization (i.e., the ability to keep current and retired principals nearby). Three of the seven original limited partners from 1970 are still involved.

To reinforce the company culture and help institutionalize the firm, most of the organizations are built around teams and specialists, divided by industry, region, trading strategy, and/or type of situation. This is the case with Ainslie, Cooperman, Cumberland, Griffin, Kingdon, Kovner, Och, Rajaratnam, Singer, and Stark.

Having a specialist, decentralized organization keeps talented key employees on board. They have a degree of decision-making authority and responsibility; they are not just hired hands. They have a stake in the firm as well. This environment is a healthy one for institutionalizing the firm (i.e., making sure a succession strategy is in place).

In the case of Cumberland, there are five portfolio managers; each portfolio manager directly runs about 20 percent of the firm capital. That means 80 percent of their capital is run by the other partners. They are interdependent on each other.

Tepper's group appears to have a loose organization without too much delineation of responsibility. Due to its different trading approach (computerized long-term trend following of managed futures), John W. Henry & Co. (JWH) is organized along functional lines.

At the end of the spectrum is Paloma. Sussman's culture is entrepreneurial based on independent managers. Sussman also describes it as a big family atmosphere—easygoing in both dress and demeanor. He wants an environment that makes the managers most productive.

At most firms, the overall profitability of the firm as well as the sector both determine the compensation scheme. At Kingdon Capital, portfolio managers take responsibility for their positions, but authority is shared. Each portfolio manager's reward is based on the performance of his or her positions plus a bonus pool for the entire firm based on that year's performance. At Appaloosa, profitability of the fund as well as sector performance are key.

At Maverick, sector heads have significant discretion and authority. They are rewarded on overall profitability of the fund and the contribution of their specific sectors, but more weight is given to the former.

At Galleon, compensation is based not only on profits of the firm but also, for the analysts, on the incremental research and expertise they add to the firm's knowledge.

At Citadel, Cumberland, Och-Ziff, and Stark Investments, however, the predominant source of compensation is the overall performance of the firm. Stark says that some years a certain part of the portfolio will do better than others. Yet compensation is very much the same for both sides if both are doing a great job. "You can do a great job in a tough market and still lose money."

At Caxton, individual performance is heavily weighted, but the group performance is also given some weight. At Omega, the portfolio managers and/or sector heads are highly accountable for their positions. They are compensated on the results of their profit/loss responsibility. If they don't prove their ability in two to three years, they are asked to leave. At Paloma, the managers receive an incentive fee over a specified hurdle.

SURVIVAL/HONESTY/LOSSES AND LESSONS

Survival is a key motivator. Over the long run, at various times, the managers have gone through adverse times. All have suffered losses, survived, and learned from those difficulties. Resilience, a key word for Kingdon, indicates how the manager reacts to adversity and client withdrawals. While admitting to many mistakes over the years, one situation often stands out in these managers' minds. Also key are the lessons they learned.

The year 1990 was a memorable one for Cumberland. Wilcox says they had done great analysis, but the distressed high-yield markets became illiquid. At year-end, they were faced with redemptions that had to be funded in an illiquid market. They learned to pay more attention to portfolio liquidity.

Henry lost almost 11 percent in 1992 in his longest-running program, financials and metals. That loss motivated him to tighten risk control and reduce leverage.

For Cooperman, non-U.S.–dollar bonds stood out in 1994, as did Russian fixed income in 1998. As a result, Cooperman no longer includes emerging markets or illiquid instruments in the portfolio.

For Rajaratnam, one memorable rough period was the fourth quarter of 1997 during the Asian crisis. Lessons learned were to spend more time on macro issues. Now if the fund is down 4 to 5 percent a month, they reduce exposure.

For Stark, who suffered his only annual loss in 1998, he learned you can be right on the fundamentals but short-term liquidity constraints can dominate arbitrage pricing. The year 1998 also reinforced the value of diversification—diversification by strategy and geography. More emphasis is put on the component of the portfolio derived from credit. More investment-grade product is used in all kinds of environments even if it is not as cheap as lesser-grade products. Stark has increased the extent of asset swapping and default protection.

As a result of 1998, Sussman learned never to put capital where he is not in control of what's going on.

The managers acknowledge that they can and often do make errors. Kovner, a big supporter of intellectual honesty, emphasizes that you have to be honest about what you don't know. It is not so much about being right all the time as being able to adapt and find a strategy that works. He said more often he is wrong than right. He made a wonderful analogy to a painter applying many brush strokes. No one stroke is right or wrong; they are cumulatively painting a picture. He expects losses all the time because ideas are constantly being tested. He becomes concerned, however, when losses are larger than expected or predicted, or when risk levels are exceeded.

Griffin viewed losses in the same manner—loss is a central part of the firm's day-to-day experience. It is a process-driven firm where people learn by making mistakes. Kingdon says he thinks about being wrong before he invests.

RISK MANAGEMENT

Controlling the downside risk is foremost in these managers' minds. Kingdon and Kovner were two of the five large hedge fund managers who issued guidelines in February 2000 as a response to the President's Working Group in regard to Long-Term Capital Management's bailout.

Specific risk management tools include strategy diversification, maximum allocation per position, number of positions in the portfolio, and degree of leverage, as well as stress testing, reducing allocations quickly, and other factors.

Diversification

Diversification is a main way these managers manage risk. Multiple strategies are used by Griffin, Henry, Kovner, Och, Stark, and Sussman. The managers further diversify by geography. In Sussman's case, he uses a number of managers for each strategy to provide further diversification.

Maximum Allocation per Position/Sector

In order to ensure diversification, the managers often impose trade and sector maximum allocations. The maximum allocation of any position in Och's portfolio is 1 percent. For Kovner, no more than 2 percent of the fund's equity is risked on one idea. Stark's maximum allocation to a trade is 3 percent for convertible arbitrage and 2 percent for risk arbitrage. For Rajaratnam, a situation cannot have more than 5 percent of the portfolio, although a position can grow to 7 percent before it is trimmed. For Sussman, there are no formal written rules, but generally no manager allocation is greater than 5 percent of portfolio capital.

For Ainslie, no sector has more than 20 percent of the portfolio. Net exposure in any one sector is never greater than 10 percent. No long has been greater than 5 percent of net equity, and no short has a been greater than 3 percent of net equity. Cooperman limits the percentage allocated to macro to 5 percent. Och limits the percentage of cash tender offers.

Number of Positions in the Portfolio

Positions in the portfolios range from an average of about 50 for Tepper and Henry to 2,500-plus for Sussman and thousands for Kovner. Cooperman, Cumberland, and Rajaratnam are clustered in the 90 to 100 position area, while Singer, Kingdon, and Ainslie have about 200 to 250 positions. Stark is in the 400 to 600 range. The greater the number of positions, the less dependent the portfolio is on one position.

Leverage

Leverage is borrowed money, a factor that influences the rapidity with which changes in market risk, credit risk, or liquidity risk alter the value of a portfolio. The use of leverage varies often depending on trading style. Some of the managers do not use leverage. Rajaratnam and Cumberland do not use leverage. Kingdon hasn't used much leverage in 13 years.

Ainslie uses leverage in the 2.5:1 range. Och uses leverage only in convertible arbitrage of about 3:1. Tepper's leverage is also about 3:1 in low-volatility, safe situations. At the moment, Sussman's leverage overall for the portfolio is 3.5:1. This is much lower than in 1998 when leverage was about 8:1 across the entire portfolio. Since 1996, Cooperman has reduced leverage considerably. Leverage has never exceeded 3.5:1 and has typically been less.

Stark's leverage varies within the 1.5:1 to 7:1 range for arbitrage trades. Leverage is adjusted downward when the macro environment becomes more of a concern or the degree of arbitrage mispricing diminishes. Griffin's self-described leverage is 3:1 to 7:1. Griffin feels comfortable with this because he attempts to mitigate macro risk, and rewards can be small with arbitrage. Singer feels limiting leverage is the most important risk management tool at the moment. Singer says he uses a low level of leverage, 1.3:1 to 1.5:1, in all businesses, except with fixed income arbitrage. With fixed income, Singer's leverage is 20:1, which he says is in line with his peers. His strategy has not changed over the years.

While not specifying a level, Kovner says he uses leverage cautiously.

Henry adjusts leverage; leverage can be anywhere between three and six times capital. Leverage is managed to be lower during choppy, negative periods and geared up during strong periods. Leverage in managed futures is different from that in stocks. It is the margin put up versus the value of the contract size, therefore reflecting the dollar amount the manager controls.

Other Factors

Other risk management techniques include stress testing, taking smaller positions, or reducing allocations quickly if a situation becomes unattractive.

Kovner says he takes smaller positions than do other managers, and does considerable stress testing on the portfolio daily.

Och reduces allocations quickly if a situation becomes unattractive. Liquidity of positions is always taken into account.

For Kingdon, rule number one is to cut losses. Rule number two is not to forget rule number one. Other rules are not to try to turn a loser into an investment. If you buy a stock and it is no longer valid, sell it. A technical breakdown of 15 percent from cost is sufficient reason to reverse the trade.

To lessen the impact of herding, Singer finds out who else owns the spreads and determines their motivations. If there are too many players, the position can be a trap. Singer also tries to do as much as possible that is uncorrelated to the stock market.

At Paloma, the risk manager is independent of the manager.

INSTITUTIONAL PARTICIPATION

Institutions make up a large percentage of these managers' investor bases. With a long-term time horizon, the institutions' assets make these managers' asset bases more stable.

Och-Ziff's investor base has always been institutional. Institutions represent about 40 percent of Griffin's client base. Tax-exempt entities are about 40 percent of Cooperman's clients. About one-third of Stark's clientele are institutional clients. Wilcox estimates that 25 percent of Cumberland's clients are U.S. nontaxables. While not providing specifics, Kingdon says his share of endowments is on the rise. Sussman says his core investors include insurance companies.

Because managers are generally unwilling to disclose their client names, we went to the National Association of College and University Business Officers (NACUBO) 1999 annual survey on investment allocation. We found that many of the managers receive endowment allocations.

Ainslie has allocations from Carnegie Mellon University, King's College, the University of Michigan, the University of North Carolina at Chapel Hill, Whitman College, Oberlin College, Vassar College, the University of Vermont, Southern Methodist University, and the University of Texas System. Och has allocations from Amherst College, Carnegie Mellon University, Colgate University, Middlebury College, Yeshiva University, and the University of Michigan. Kingdon receives allocations from Bowdoin College, Colby College, State University of New York—Stony Brook, Yeshiva University, and the University of the South. Cooperman has allocations from Clark University, Franklin and Marshall College, and Rensselaer Polytechnic Institute. Tepper has allocations from Middlebury College and Davidson College. Griffin has Oberlin College as an investor. Singer receives an allocation from Vassar College.

ALMOST COMMON THREADS

Some characteristics are shared by many of the interviewed managers—but not all of them. For example, most of them became interested in investing at an early age—often as a teenager. A large percentage of this elite group attended Ivy League schools and/or received MBAs.

Most tend to be opportunistic in their approach—moving freely to where investment advantages and geographic advantages exist. A few have gravitated to their core competency after having difficulty. Fundamental research is generally important to their success. Most of their roles have evolved into that of a coordinator or overseer of the organization, a risk and/or capital allocator. Many times an investment committee exists. Interestingly, some of the managers selectively make allocations to other hedge fund managers.

Most are located in New York, and if a second office exists, it is usually in London. Their minimum investment is typically higher than that of the average hedge fund manager, which is usually about $500,000. In many cases, the lock-up of assets is longer than a year.

Many look for challenges during their free time as well. Winning at sports or mastering a technique were common themes. Also mentioned were philanthropy, public issue reform, and, to a lesser degree, music and politics.

INITIAL SPARK

Several of the managers were first introduced to investing and stocks in their teenage years. Tepper says he became involved with investing at about 10 to 11 years old. Kingdon and Cooperman both received stock shares as bar mitzvah presents. Ainslie joined an investment club in high school. Stark became involved with warrant and risk arbitrage while working one summer during high school. (Risk arbitrage occurs when a manager buys a stock in a company being acquired and sells stock in its acquirer.) Griffin was motivated by an options profit he made at 17. When he realized that the market maker's profit was more than his own, he became motivated to understand options pricing strategy. Sussman got his first taste of investing at a summer job during college at a brokerage firm.

IVY LEAGUE/MBA BACKGROUNDS

Of the 13 managers interviewed, five went to Harvard University as either an undergraduate (Kovner, Griffin) or a graduate student (Singer and Stark for law and Kingdon for business).

Two went to the Wharton School of Finance and Commerce at the University of Pennsylvania—Rajaratnam (MBA) and Och (undergraduate).

In total, six received MBAs. Ainslie went to the University of Virginia and then on to graduate school at the University of North Carolina. Cooperman went to Hunter College of the University of the City of

New York and then Columbia University Graduate School of Business. Tepper went to the University of Pittsburgh and then on to Carnegie Mellon Business School. Sussman received his undergraduate and MBA degrees from New York University. As mentioned before, Kingdon received his MBA from Harvard and Rajaratnam from Wharton.

OPPORTUNISTIC VERSUS CORE COMPETENCY

Most of the managers describe their portfolio optimization as opportunistic—they allocate capital where the opportunities are. There is no predetermined commitment to a given investment category, though there are often limits to sector and position allocations. This is the case with Ainslie, Kovner, Och, Singer, Stark, Sussman, and Tepper.

These managers view the world as having rapidly shifting opportunities. Singer's initial focus was convertible arbitrage (the simultaneous purchase of convertible securities and the selling of the underlying securities of the same issuer), but after the crash of 1987 he found it too correlated to the stock market and too difficult to hedge. He now focuses on distressed securities and arbitrage while approaching convertibles in an opportunistic manner. (Distressed securities is an event-driven strategy. Managers invest in companies in financial distress or bankruptcy.) Griffin's initial focus was convertible arbitrage. He said that to survive and find opportunities as the market changed, he had to add new strategies and products. Relative value and event driven are the primary trading focus. Kovner has expanded opportunistically as well from futures, commodities, and currencies in the early days of his career.

Others have been opportunistic on a much more cautious basis. Stark originally traded convertible arbitrage and then risk arbitrage. In the past few years, he has added private placements and is incubating other arbitrage strategies including high-yield arbitrage and convertible structure arbitrage. (High-yield arbitrage refers to arbitrage between low-grade fixed-income securities of companies that have upside potential.) Similarly, Och's original core businesses were merger arbitrage, convertible arbitrage, and event-driven restructuring. He added distressed credits in 1999.

A few have stayed within a general area and move around within that category. For example, Rajaratnam's focus is technology. Within that theme, he has added biotechnology, Internet sector, communications (electronic, voice, and data), and health care (pharmaceuticals, medical devices, biotechnology, health-care information technology). Henry has stayed within managed futures and has not ventured into the stock arena for investors. But within the managed futures area, he moves where the sector and market opportunities are.

Sussman's core competency remains market neutral. But within the category he opportunistically moves to and from convertible arbitrage, merger/event arbitrage (the simultaneous purchase of stock in a company being acquired and the short sale of the acquiring company, thus making a directional bet that the deal will go through), statistical arbitrage, volatility arbitrage, and other strategies when he feels the environment changing. Sussman is currently focusing on statistical arbitrage and feels that adding a few more managers with different approaches in this area may help capacity grow.

Only a few of the managers are still doing what they did originally. They stuck to their knitting because that's what worked. An example is value stock picker Cumberland. Kingdon is primarily a global stock picker, although small interest rate, metal, and currency exposure exists.

We've seen a few of the managers gravitate back to their core competencies. For example, Tepper had moved into other areas from his core competency, distressed and junk bonds, but has decided to go back to basics and stick to his core. Cooperman also gravitated back to his core competency—developed country equity stocks (primarily U.S. and Western Europe).

FUNDAMENTAL RESEARCH/QUALITATITIVE VERSUS QUANTITATIVE

Except for Henry, a technical long-term trend follower, the managers highly value fundamental research. Henry relies exclusively on long-term trend-following computerized trading. His philosophy is based on the premise that market prices, rather than market fundamentals, are the key aggregation of information needed to make investment decisions.

Within the general context, the others value fundamental information but significant differences exist. Ainslie, Cooperman, Cumberland, Kovner, and Och are very much at the fundamental end of the spectrum. Och says computers at Och-Ziff are used only to analyze and model; they are tools. The decision making is done by people.

For Kingdon, his edge is doing solid fundamental research, yet valuations and technicals are also important. And while fundamental research is critical at Galleon, Rajaratnam says trading is as important. The firm actively trades around its core positions. A dual focus exists with equal weighting. Tepper is also a trader, trading around his positions.

While qualitative research is very important to Singer, Stark, and Griffin, quantitative skills are important as well. Singer says they have quant cleverness skills but are not a quant shop. They also know the companies, and are close to the companies. They combine quantitative and qualitative.

For Sussman, the percentage allocation is driven by opportunity. The computers spit out expected return and expected risk of each investment owned. Opportunities are analyzed and simulations done. But overlay of judgment is very important.

Stark says he fits between center and the pure black box (undefined computerized approach) end of the continuum. Models indicate where they should be, and they adjust qualitatively. They are quantitatively driven but not purely. Human inputs are used to adjust hedges and analysis. Portfolio optimization is an amalgam of qualitative and quantitative analyses. They screen strategies on a global basis for risk and expected return. In convertible arbitrage, they look at theoretical mispricing, then at creditworthiness of the convertible, and then at fundamentals of the underlying equity. Overall portfolio analysis is applied for strategy and geographic diversification, as well as balancing the risk of the position.

BOTTOM-UP VERSUS TOP-DOWN

Cooperman follows a bottom-up approach to stock selection. In determining a company's private value, he looks at over 100 different economic, monetary, and valuation data points. Ainslie, Och, Cumberland, and Rajaratnam also take a bottom-up approach—visiting companies, talking to management, analyzing cash flow. Stark describes his approach as bottom-up as well, based on credit research and knowledge of the markets. Sussman also describes his approach as bottom-up because his people are intimately familiar with specific markets and opportunities that arise. Decision making is done trade by trade.

In contrast, Kovner is top-down oriented. He makes an overall judgment of the economy/environment and then seeks out specific opportunities.

Kingdon describes his approach as top-down and bottom-up. Top-down analysis determines portfolio structure and industry concentrations, while opportunities uncovered by individual stock research (bottom-up) are important as well.

TAX EFFICIENCY

Tax efficiency did not appear to be a major priority of the managers. Most let the fundamentals determine the course of action. The managers are tax sensitive when they can be (e.g., at year-end), but tax efficiency is not the main driver. Strategies such as arbitrage are naturally not tax efficient since a significant amount of trading is going on in the portfolio.

Yet a few exceptions exist. Singer's U.S. fund achieves excellent tax optimization since its goal is long-term gains. Cooperman is planning a fund with a three-year lock-up that will be more tax sensitive. Tax efficiency is something that Ainslie considers. He says, in an average year, over half their gains are unrealized.

COORDINATOR, OVERSEER

Rather than be the one key decision maker, as may have been the case in the early days of the organization, the key person's role has often evolved as the overseer or the coordinator of the team. Often this role includes being in charge of risk management or capital allocation. In some cases, this is the key person's main function.

For example, Kingdon determines how invested the firm will be. Griffin plays the role of coordinator, strategist, risk manager, and capital allocator. Kovner spends most of his time developing strategy, risk control, and risk allocation. He spends time on how to grow the business and developing structures that work. Singer is the senior risk manager, has input on position size, and is responsible for all positions.

Ainslie's focus is on asset allocation, risk control, and being a sounding board. His input drives the size of positions. He makes sure the analysis is complete and all the relevant resources have been brought to bear.

Sussman describes his role as "chief opportunistic officer"—he is looking for the overall opportunities. Once he finds them, he then hires the person to execute the strategy. Sussman also serves as the risk manager—independent from the managers to whom he allocates assets.

In other cases, the coordinator/overseer role is done in conjunction with being active in the portfolio. Och, Rajaratnam, Stark, and Wilcox are cases in point.

Och is very involved in portfolio decisions and is focused on the investment process. He leads the arbitrage/restructuring unit. As managing member, he is also involved in broader issues such as capacity and the firm's capabilities.

Rajaratnam is the managing general partner and portfolio manager. He describes himself as the quarterback of the team. He is involved with everything in the firm and often accompanies the analysts to their company meetings. He meets with two or three companies a week. One week out of the month, he visits about 25 companies in California. He also meets personally with investors.

Stark heads up the convertible arbitrage area. For 80 to 85 percent of the time he is an investment manager. In addition, he along with his partner are responsible for overall allocation of assets. They are also sounding boards for the portfolio managers.

Wilcox estimates that he spends about 60 percent of his time interacting with management of companies, analysts, and other industry participants in carrying out his portfolio management duties. Another 20 percent is spent on management.

Cooperman's interest is more in being an investor. He is actively involved in stock selection; he is hands-on. Since Steven Einhorn had been hired as vice chairman in May 1999, Cooperman says he can delegate more to Einhorn, which allows Cooperman to visit more companies.

Tepper is also actively involved and is the key decision maker when it comes to positions of size.

Henry, who describes himself as semiretired since 1986, meaning he hasn't run the day-to-day business, spends a great deal of time researching the markets.

Many of these managers take on the role of mentor as well. This appears to be the case with Singer and Kingdon. In trying to groom their people, they delegate responsibility and decision making. Their role is to make sure the person has done the thinking correctly. Ainslie, Och, and Stark also feel they are developing excellent teams. Henry describes himself as a parent watching a child grow up. The rules and procedures are written down, and he observes that they are followed. He may call up a trader and ask, "Are we doing this?" rather than saying "Do this."

INVESTMENT COMMITTEES

A number of the superstar managers have investment committees—senior-level advisory groups broadly responsible for evaluating and overseeing trading policies. Issues include market view, liquidity, capacity, and performance cycles. These meetings are held at various frequencies; they help reinforce a culture.

Cooperman's investment committee meets weekly to discuss macro trends and find out-of-favor asset classes.

The frequency of Griffin's meetings is determined more by the volatility of the underlying stock market. For instance, in 1998 when volatility was high, the committee would meet at least once a day. In 2000, they meet less frequently—perhaps once a week.

Henry, Kingdon, Och, Stark, and Tepper also have investment committee meetings.

Ainslie, Cumberland, Kovner, Rajaratnam, Singer, and Sussman do not hold such meetings. Ainslie points to the dangers of consensus thinking—for example, the more interesting and exciting ideas get weeded out. Furthermore, he wants people focused on their individual stocks rather than looking outside their own industry.

Cumberland's management committee gives risk limits to the portfolio manager—not sector allocations.

Many of the managers hold daily meetings to discuss market movement and development. To name a few—Cooperman, Galleon, Kingdon.

ALLOCATIONS TO OTHER HEDGE FUND MANAGERS

Some of the managers say they allocate to other managers on a selective basis where other managers command an expertise. Doing so diversifies their portfolios, increases potential returns, helps find new ideas, and develops relationships. Kingdon says under 3 percent is allocated to a dozen other managers. Ainslie allocates less than 1 percent of assets to other managers. At times, he has seeded other managers and in those cases owns a small percentage of those hedge funds. Kovner has made such allocations from time to time to a few managers. But he doesn't feel it is the best way to participate with other managers, and he doesn't like the loss of control or synergy. Griffin and Cooperman make infrequent allocations.

Cumberland, Och, Rajaratnam, Singer, Stark, and Tepper do not allocate to other managers.

At the other extreme of the spectrum is Sussman, who allocates to 22 outside managers, each representing a different strategy, as the main tenet of his methodology.

In this group of 13 managers, I uncovered many interrelationships among the managers that I did not know existed when I started the project. For example, one of Sussman's earliest allocations in 1981 included Singer. Sussman was also an early backer of Stark and Kovner. The publication of Stark's book *Special Situation Investing: Hedging, Arbitrage and Liquidation* in 1983 caught the attention of both Singer and Sussman. Tepper and Och worked at Goldman Sachs at the same time.

LOCATION/VARIOUS OFFICES

Most of the managers have just one office, while a few have satellites. The New York City area was the most frequently named location. Cooperman, Kingdon, Kovner, Och, Rajaratnam, Singer, and Wilcox are located in New York City, while Sussman in Greenwich, Connecticut, and Tepper in Chatham, New Jersey, have suburban offices. Kovner has a back office in Plainsboro, New Jersey.

London was the second most common city: Griffin, Och, Singer, and Sussman have offices in London. A London office has been essential to their ability to analyze and invest in European deals. Silicon Valley was the third most frequently named location for an office. Griffin has an office in San Francisco, and Rajaratnam has one in Santa Clara, the purpose being to develop good contacts with the technology companies they follow.

The managers based in New York highlighted the convenience of meeting key players ranging from company executives to IPO (initial public offering) road shows. The free flow of ideas outweighs the dangers of groupthink, says Kingdon. New York also attracts bright, energetic people. Kovner describes it as the world's capital where you can see all kinds of people from economists to government officials.

However, Ainslie in Dallas; Griffin in Chicago; Henry in Boca Raton, Florida; and Stark in Mequon, Wisconsin, do not appear disadvantaged by not being located in the New York City area. Griffin highlighted the advantages—no other managers nearby trying to poach his key employees, and employees being more committed and long-term. Stark feels it makes the firm less influenced by herd mentality.

MINIMUM INVESTMENT

When they were open to investment, some of these superstar managers required a much higher minimum investment than the typical hedge fund manager, which is often $500,000 to $1 million. For example, Och's minimum was $10 million. Both Tepper and Sussman required a $5 million investment. Kingdon required a $5 million investment from corporations and $1 million from individuals. Ainslie's minimum was $2 million to $5 million.

LOCK-UP OF ASSETS

A number of the managers require investors' assets to be locked up for more than the typical one year—in some cases, two to three years. This helps ensure a stable investor base and a high-quality committed investor. Tepper requires a three-year lock-up. Ainslie has a three-year lock-up with a fee penalty if assets are redeemed earlier. Och generally requires a two-year lock-up.

FREE TIME

Most of the managers seem to lead balanced lives and are passionate about some outside interest. Sports is a common theme. The challenge of winning and/or the mastering of a technique is exhibited in what managers do in their free time. Griffin plays soccer; Ainslie plays basketball and golf. Kingdon has enjoyed tae kwon do for over 19 years. Och skis and golfs. In addition to golfing and swimming, Tepper coaches his children's teams. Wilcox has been a surfer for 30 years.

Rajaratnam plays tennis and squash and swims. Stark also turns to sports during his free time.

Henry has exhibited his interest in sports by owning several baseball teams over the years, including his January 1999 purchase of the Florida Marlins.

A number of managers focus on charity work. For example, Cooperman has set up an educational foundation and serves on many boards. Och is chairman of the Wall Street division of the United Jewish Appeal (UJA) and is on the board of City Harvest. Wilcox has been instrumental in bringing classical music to areas where it may not otherwise be heard such as rural North Carolina or a boys' correctional facility in Kansas. Singer runs a family foundation.

Public issue reform is important for a few of the managers. Kovner has spent time and money on educational reform. Singer's efforts are in the social policy area. Sussman's passion is the environment—preventing the paper industry from cutting down more trees in Maine. He also devotes considerable resources and efforts to pure science at the Weitzmann Institute in Israel, where he recently established a building for environmental sciences.

Politics was named less frequently. Henry and Sussman have been big Democratic campaign contributors.

Music is an outlet for a few of the managers. Kovner plays the piano daily, and Henry, who earlier in his life had been a bassist, has a recording studio. Wilcox plays rock guitar in a band.

Rajaratnam likes to travel with the stated objective of visiting two new countries per year. Kovner also collects rare books and recently provided the structure to publish the only Bible illustrated by a single artist in the twentieth century.

DIFFERENCES

On some issues, no similarities exist. Age was one. Varying styles and strategies was another. The amount of stock market exposure and the ways that is hedged differed considerably. Portfolio composition varied, including the emphasis on the U.S. markets, macro trading, technology, and private equity. The criteria required for taking a trade differed widely.

Degree of transparency as well as the number of investors and the number of people in the firm varied widely.

No consistency existed on the investment background of the elite managers and how they finally arrived in the hedge fund world. Their views on retiring differed as well.

AGE

Of the managers meeting the criteria to be interviewed, the youngest was 32 (Griffin). Of the 13 interviewed, three were in their thirties—Griffin, Ainslie, and Och. Rajaratnam, Stark, Tepper, and Wilcox were in their forties. Six were in their fifties—Cooperman, Henry, Kovner, Kingdon, Singer, and Sussman.

STYLE/NUMBER OF STRATEGIES/ALLOCATIONS

A number of the superstar managers include market neutral strategies. Stark focuses mostly on convertible arbitrage, but risk arbitrage and private placements are important. Sussman's overall focus is market neutral strategies. At the moment, his main focus is on statistical arbitrage. Convertible arbitrage and merger arbitrage receive significant allocations.

Some include event-driven strategies with or without market-neutral strategies. Singer focuses on distressed securities and arbitrage. For Griffin, it is relative value and event driven. Och focuses on merger arbitrage, convertible arbitrage, event driven, and distressed credits.

Tepper's focus is high-yield bonds and distressed.

On the stock-picking front, Cooperman and Cumberland are value stock pickers. Ainslie is an opportunistic stock picker with heavy emphasis on the United States. Kingdon is primarily a global equity long/short stock picker.

Rajaratnam is a sector trader. Kovner is more macro oriented. Henry is the only pure futures trader, not using stocks at all.

In their approaches, a few are self-described activist managers. For Singer, this means getting involved in negotiations and committee work; there is a higher unit of effort to money invested. Cooperman is also an activist. He loves to go head-to-head with companies if he thinks a problem exists.

U.S. VERSUS GLOBAL

Rajaratnam focuses completely on the United States. Most of Galleon's trades are U.S.-based or American depositary receipts (ADRs) of non-U.S. companies. Rajaratnam wants to stick to local expertise.

About 95 percent of Cumberland's trades are U.S.-based. Singer says the majority of his trades are also U.S.-based. Cooperman finds most of his opportunities in the United States as well. Usually about 75 to 80 percent of the Omega portfolio is U.S.-focused. Others at Omega focus on global and international.

The United States has always been the dominant piece of Ainslie's portfolio because this is the area he knows best, and where he finds the most consistent performance. It is the most efficient location to short stock. Current exposure to the United States is about 75 percent.

About 25 percent of Och's overall portfolio is European-focused. Within that amount, 35 percent of the merger arbitrage portfolio is European arbitrage. The majority of the convertible arbitrage portfolio is composed of Western European and Japanese bonds.

More global in nature is Kingdon's global long/short equity investing. Kingdon allocates about 35 to 50 percent of the portfolio outside the United States. Two-thirds to one-half of Griffin's portfolio is focused on the United States, with Europe and Japan playing significant roles.

Further along the continuum, Stark's historical mix has been 65 percent non-U.S. to 35 percent U.S. Japan has been a large focus at times. Stark feels the inefficiencies are greater outside the United States. Europe had historically been a small allocation, but in the past year that has changed. Historically the mix is 65 percent non-U.S., 35 percent U.S.

Tepper's opportunistic approach brings him into non-U.S. markets frequently (e.g., emerging markets, Russia, Korea). Sussman also has a global orientation.

Kovner's global macro trading and Henry's focus on global futures and currencies can be more non-U.S. oriented.

Macro trading as a percentage of the portfolio has generally shrunk over the years. For Kovner, global macro typically accounts for 30 percent to 60 percent of the portfolio; it is a smaller percentage than it had been 30 months ago.

Macro trading peaked a bit over 40 percent in 1998 for Kingdon; by year-end 1999 it was less than 5 percent. For Cooperman, due to his 1998 Russian experience, macro now has a defined risk limit of 5 percent of capital. Only liquid markets are allowed.

TECHNOLOGY ALLOCATION

Managers emphasize technology differently in their portfolios. Cooperman has had very little exposure to technology, admitting it has been a weak spot. However, he hired a technology analyst in 2000 to cover the area.

At the other extreme is Rajaratnam, whose specialization is technology and who has an office in Santa Clara, California. Griffin, with an office in San Francisco, also allocates considerably to technology. Through mergers and acquisitions, convertibles, and long/short equity positions, Citadel is significantly invested in the New Economy. Technology represents anywhere between a 5 percent and a 50 percent allocation of the portfolio.

Most of the other managers fall in between the two extremes on the continuum. Ainslie approaches technology like any other sector in the portfolio—the maximum allocation it can get is 10 percent. Kingdon's allocation varies based on valuation, as well as fundamental and technical factors, but usually ranges from 10 to 45 percent. At the time of the interviews, Kovner's and Cumberland's allocations to technology were each about 17 percent.

PRIVATE EQUITY

The managers approach private equity in different ways. (Private equity is the frequently illiquid market for closely held, usually small companies, often done under an exemption from the laws and regulations covering the transfer of publicly traded securities.) Some of the managers include private equity as a small percentage in their own funds. Kingdon has allocated to private equity for the past six years though the allocation is less than 5 percent of the assets. He says it provides him with an early window on developing technologies and sometimes offers outstanding returns. Wilcox says Cumberland's allocation to private equity is less than 5 percent. Singer views himself as doing the same as private equity managers but that his positions are smaller. Tepper says if opportunities arise in private equity, he may take them.

Some of the managers are involved with private equity through separate entities. For example, Ainslie created a strategic relationship and played an instrumental role in creating Brazos Investment Partners in late 1999. He is keeping the hedge fund separate but can benefit from the information and expertise of the other organization. He feels private equity requires someone with different skill sets than are needed in a hedge fund—someone to evaluate opportunities and negotiate. Furthermore, private equity is difficult to hedge.

Kovner has a joint venture with Fred Iseman called Caxton Iseman Fund. One of the Caxton funds has the flexibility to allocate a small percentage to illiquid investments such as private equity which an investor must hold for several years.

Paloma's investment in the Cathay Fund is less than 1 percent of Paloma's assets. Within the Cathay Fund, there are six publicly listed companies and seven private unlisted companies, so it is in part private equity.

Cooperman, Henry, Griffin, Och, and Stark generally make no allocation to private equity.

Rajaratnam does not have any plans for private equity at this time, though it has been discussed by his board of advisers.

MARKET EXPOSURE AND HOW IT IS HEDGED

Net exposure to equity markets, as a measure of risk, compares short positions to long positions. Market exposure is calculated by subtracting short exposure from long exposure. It is criticized by some as being confusing, and it may mask whether a manager is massively long or massively short. For example, if a manager has a 10 percent net long exposure, he can get there in a many ways. He could be 40 percent long and 30 percent short or he could be 100 percent long and 90 percent short. Generally, the less net exposure, the less risk in a down market; but it depends on stock selection and how long and short the components.

Net exposure varies across the board. Cumberland's and Cooperman's equity exposure averages about 65 percent. Kingdon's is currently under 50 percent but over the past five years has averaged about 56 percent. Maverick's average net exposure is 48 percent. Rajaratnam's exposure ranges between 30 percent and 40 percent. Kovner's long exposure to the stock market has always been low, in the 10 to 25 percent range. Och's exposure is less than 10 percent. Stark prefers to use a hedge ratio, but in his case, net exposure is 70 to 90 percent. Cumberland's net exposure to the market is 70 percent.

The managers use different vehicles to hedge. Ainslie's hedging strategy closely resembles that of A. W. Jones—the first hedge fund. While not perfectly hedged, it is much more hedged than the typical fund. Ainslie doesn't use futures and options as hedging tools. He feels that sophisticated investors can use futures and options to place their own hedges. His value-added is shorting stock.

Rajaratnam and Griffin also describe themselves as close in concept to the A. W. Jones model. Short positions are as important as the long positions, says Rajaratnam. Rajaratnam also prefers shorting stocks. While options are used, they tend to be more expensive. Moving to cash is another alternative he takes.

Keeping assets in cash while also using futures, options, and short selling is a technique used by Kingdon. Tepper, at the time of the interview, was heavily into cash (September 2000) because he feels the market is not going anywhere and the probabilities of a favorable outcome are not high. Besides cash, he'll use S&P futures and treasuries. Sussman moves to cash as well.

Cumberland will also hold cash. Occasionally, the firm's managers use paired securities tactics or use index- and company-specific options to effect short strategies. Shorting stock is done to make a profit rather than to hedge.

Cooperman shorts stock, index options, and futures.

Stark says the firm tries to hedge most risk and typically overhedges on a theoretical basis. He says currency exposure is fully hedged but interest rate exposure hedging is variable. Where it is possible to do an asset swap or a credit or buy default protection, they will do so. They may also short high-yield bonds, short other convertibles, or short credit derivatives.

Options volatility swaps are used by Singer and Sussman to protect the portfolio when there are large movements.

Most of what Kovner trades is not correlated to the stock market to begin with. Singer also takes the approach of doing as much as possible in distressed securities and arbitrage that is uncorrelated to the stock and bond markets. Where positions are subject to market forces, Singer hedges with short sales, indexes, options, volatility positions, volatility swaps, and derivatives.

TRADES TAKEN

Some managers look for a return objective. For example, when buying a stock, Kingdon's goal is at least a 30 percent gross return. Tepper usually looks for double the return on small caps and perhaps a 50 percent return on larger caps.

Others look for a certain risk per trade. The risk per trade Griffin looks for varies by strategy. For example, the risk taken on a fixed income arbitrage trade is much smaller than that of a risk arbitrage trade. Stark focuses on risk-adjusted returns but adjusts for portfolio considerations. He wants strategic and geographic diversification. Och also focuses on risk-adjusted returns. He avoids positions with explicit/implicit correlation to the stock market. He says the firm often focuses on more unusual and complex securities where hedging and analytical capabilities create a competitive advantage.

Both Cumberland and Cooperman, value investors, usually like to get $1 of value for 50 to 60 cents. Rajaratnam takes those trades where he feels Wall Street analysts haven't done the correct analysis and in effect arbitrages the research. Rajaratnam also describes Galleon as a thematic investor. Five to six themes are identified, and trades are placed based on those themes.

NUMBER OF PEOPLE

Several of the organizations have between 40 and 85 employees. The exceptions were Kovner's Caxton with 160 to 170 people, Sussman's Paloma with over 200, and Griffin's Citadel, which has over 350. On the smaller end were Wilcox's Cumberland, Tepper's Appaloosa, and Rajaratnam's Galleon at 22, 25, and 35 people respectively.

NUMBER/GEOGRAPHIC REPRESENTATION OF INVESTORS

The number of investors ranges from a low of 100 to 150 for Cooperman to as many as 700-plus for Ainslie.

The geographic client breakdown is also interesting; the percentage of non-U.S. investors varies considerably. Stark has investor representation from 22 countries. Non-U.S. investors represent about 60 percent of Citadel's investor base. For Cooperman, non-U.S. investors account for about 30 percent.

Henry, Och, Sussman, and Tepper have mostly U.S. investors.

Strategic investors are important at Galleon; 60 percent of U.S. investors fit in this category. Outside the United States, this is less so.

TRANSPARENCY AND INVESTOR RELATIONS

Most of the managers provide quarterly reports.

Monthly reports are the exceptions—only Cumberland, Sussman, and Henry provide them. For example, Wilcox says Cumberland investors are shown their top 30 long positions in dollar terms, as percentage of equity, and the respective gain/loss. Also, gross long and gross short positions as well as long call options and short call options, plus portfolio concentration by industry in both the long and short sides are shown.

Sussman actively discusses percentage capital allocated to strategies, balance sheet leverage on the overall portfolio and by strategy, number of trading positions overall and by strategy, average static returns and hedge ratios in the convertible book, and year-to-date profitability attribution by strategy.

Ainslie gives out most information that is requested—performance by sector or geography, long/short exposure by sector or geography, and a trading summary.

Cooperman provides clients with a report on a quarterly basis that lists the 25 positions generating the largest profits and largest losses. Current exposure is detailed as well as Omega's view of the market.

Singer provides investors with quarterly reports and annual audits. Och provides investors with a quarterly letter that lists the top positive contributors and negative performers. He also provides information on portfolio allocation and sizable positions. Stark provides quarterly information on leverage and geographic profit and loss.

Tepper gives investors the investments by category on a quarterly basis. He lists the percentage in stocks, emerging markets by country, and stock investment by category.

Kingdon provides quarterly data outlining performance by region and asset class, as well as month-end summaries of invested positions and quarterly SEC filings on long positions.

While a variety of detail is given, the most sensitive information is stock-specific short positions for a number of managers; Cooperman and Ainslie do not give out this information. Singer will not give out exact positions. In some cases, Stark will require a confidentiality agreement be signed if additional information is requested. Stark permits only on-site reviews of the portfolio. Tepper does not list individual names of companies.

The superstar managers generally tend to deal with investors from afar. The majority seem to delegate the responsibilities to others, saying that investors are long-term in nature and they don't receive many calls. The exceptions were Och, Rajaratnam, Stark, Sussman, and Wilcox, who meet with investors on a frequent and regular basis.

BACKGROUND

The managers came to the hedge fund community in a variety of ways. The 30-something managers were either spin-offs from larger hedge fund managers or investment banks, or came directly into the business. For example, Griffin started his first hedge fund while he was still in college. Ainslie had been at Tiger Management while Och had been at Goldman Sachs.

The 40-plus crowd often had Wall Street careers or worked elsewhere for awhile. Kovner was in academia before he joined Commodities Corp. Both Singer and Stark were attorneys whose hobby was investing. Kingdon started working at AT&T in the pension fund administration group, then joined a hedge fund before starting his own.

A number of managers were from brokerage firms. Rajaratnam had been at Needham & Company. Cooperman worked at Goldman Sachs for 24 years; Och had been at Goldman Sachs for 11 years, and Tepper for over seven years. Sussman had been a convertible bond arbitrageur at a brokerage firm.

Wilcox had been a portfolio manager at Central National-Gottesman.

Henry, who grew up on a farm, became a hedger, then commodity speculator, then trading adviser.

VIEWS ON RETIRING

At one extreme is Cumberland, which has successfully gone through three successions over its 30-year history. Succession is a matter of business and part of the accepted culture.

Some managers, such as Kovner, indicated that in the long term, say 10 years, he would almost not be needed—that the firm would be able to run without him or at least not require a lot of input from him. Och expects his firm will outlast his involvement. Stark similarly sees no reason why the organization can't function without him. Sussman wants to build his organization into an institutional entity yet retain his role as the person identifying the opportunities and making the capital allocations. The general feeling among these managers is that their organizations will be strong enough that they will be comfortable leaving their assets there to be managed even if they are not involved on a full-time basis.

However, others were taken aback to think of their companies continuing without some of their involvement. Cooperman had no plans to retire—only bad performance, poor health, or not enjoying the business would be reasons to leave. Henry could not think of any reason not to be involved in the firm, nor any reason to sell. Singer says he doesn't believe in retirement and can do what he is doing for the long haul.

5

LEE AINSLIE
Maverick Capital

Classic Long/Short Hedge Fund
Fundamental, Bottom-Up Manager

When people think of the new generation of hedge fund managers, they often think of Lee Ainslie. Ainslie at 36 years old runs Maverick Capital. After graduating from the University of Virginia, where he studied systems engineering, he worked as a consultant at KPMG. He then attended the University of North Carolina Business School, where he came to know Julian Robertson. He eventually worked at Tiger Management as managing director for three years and credits Robertson (and other traders at Tiger) as having an influence on his career. "He [Julian] reinforced the life lessons of integrity and how critical one's reputation is." Ainslie also felt that there were many talented traders at

Tiger as well. Ainslie recalls what a difficult decision it was to leave Tiger for Maverick. But he felt Maverick was a unique opportunity.

I first met Ainslie in 1994 when I attended Maverick Capital's annual meeting in Dallas. Sam Wyly, one of the founders of Maverick, was a successful entrepreneur. His businesses included a string of diverse public companies—University Computing, Sterling Software, Michaels Stores, and Sterling Commerce. Wyly started his own portfolio in 1990 investing family money, and with his son Evan and Ainslie founded Maverick Capital in August 1993. In October 1993, Maverick began to take outside investors. At that time, they were managing assets of $60 million. The guest of honor at Maverick's 1994 partners meeting, held at the Kimball Art Museum, was former President George Bush. That night Bush shook everyone's hand and had his photo taken with them. That was my first meeting at Maverick Capital.

By February 1995, Ainslie was running the entire portfolio. In January 1997, he bought out the majority interest of the firm. Assets have now burgeoned to $6.0 billion and Ainslie has total control of the fund. Evan Wyly is involved as a managing partner, focusing on the long-term strategic direction of the firm. As I entered their offices at The Crescent in Dallas, expansion was going on. It was their third expansion in three years at this location. Maverick Capital and its affiliates have about 60 people in their Dallas, New York, and Philadelphia offices. We met in Lee's octagonal conference room adjoining his office. Two Chinese porcelain horses greeted visitors at the entrance to the room.

Ainslie runs his hedge fund differently from many other managers. For one, he is hedged in the A. W. Jones sense of the word. While not perfectly hedged, Maverick is much more hedged than the typical hedge fund. Shorting is critical to what Maverick does. Individual securities are shorted; futures and options are not used to hedge. He feels that sophisticated investors can use futures and options on their own to hedge. "We hope to add value by shorting individual stocks that we believe will underperform the market."

INTENSIVE FUNDAMENTAL RESEARCH

Maverick takes a fundamental or bottom-up approach, visiting companies, talking to management, and analyzing cash flow. Maverick has strong relationships with the various industries and understands forces within these industries. Maverick is diversified with about 250 positions in the portfolio.

Allocations are determined by where the best ideas are at the time. The United States has always been the dominant piece of the portfolio. "This is the region we know best and where we have had the most consistent performance. It is the most efficient market to short stocks. Japan has been the best-performing, but it also has had more volatility."

Ainslie observes, "In down markets, it is more difficult for us to produce absolute returns but on a relative basis we look smart." If you look at each month the S&P was down—29 months in the past seven years—all four major U. S. indexes were down 49 to 65 percent. Maverick was up 2.9 percent. "This performance has been driven by the outperformance of the longs and the underperformance of the shorts. As a result, we have done relatively well in these periods."

Ainslie emphasizes the importance of the whole team, not just himself. The organization is one of a group of peers—not one based on the contribution of a single person. It is this environment that allows him to attract senior people. "Our edge is the experience and industry expertise of the team. All of the eight sector heads are well known, talented, and experienced in their industries. That gives us an edge on both the long and short side. Experience is especially critical on the short side." Sector heads have significant discretion and authority themselves. "They are peers, not employees." The sector heads are rewarded on both the overall profitability of the entire fund and the contribution of their specific sectors. More weight is given to the former, however.

Ainslie owns the vast majority of the firm. Several individuals are partners.

He has known most of the sector heads for years, and mutual respect exists. "The sector heads and myself make the decisions together." Ainslie also commented that because of these self-contained teams, sectors, and regions, the fund doesn't feel like $6.0 billion. Maverick is able to maintain the agility of a series of focused smaller funds.

The key to making money is the team's industry expertise. The teams focus on winners and losers in each industry. There are eight teams—retail, media and telecommunications, technology, health care, financial, cyclical, Japan and Asia, and Latin America. No sector is typically more than 20 percent of the portfolio. Net exposure is rarely more than 10 percent to any one sector. For example, when discussing technology, Ainslie said the exposure was currently 5.9 percent (September 2000). Ainslie observed that a long bias existed in every sector and in every region.

Throughout the interview, Ainslie referred often to the gap between the long positions and the short positions as driving their performance. "The gap drives profitability. Our [long/short] gap has averaged about 28.1 percent on an annualized basis."

While Maverick has averaged a 48 percent net long bias, it does not have a significant correlation to the S&P. The correlation to the stock market, referred to as R^2, has been 29 percent; anything under 40 percent is typically considered not correlated. Therefore it is more difficult to outperform in an up-bias market. Maverick's daily volatility has been roughly half the volatility of the S&P over the past four years, and monthly volatility has been about 80 percent of the S&P volatility.

Maverick maintains low net exposure to each region and industry in which it invests. It is typically 25 percent to 75 percent net long. It is net long for the entire portfolio and also within each region and industry sector in which it invests. Net exposure has averaged 48 percent, and gross exposure has averaged 211 percent.

Unlike some of the other great hedge fund managers, Ainslie acknowledges that his expertise is in picking stocks, not in market timing. Portfolio optimization begins by screening industries. It is a position-by-position process where the risk/return profile of each position is critical. The process could be described as suggested judgment.

How liquid are the markets traded? Ainslie says the median market capitalization is now $7.7 billion. Maverick invests primarily in medium-cap and large-cap U. S. equities.

Ainslie's role is as the overseer and coordinator. His focus is on asset allocation, risk control, and as a sounding board. His input drives the size of the positions. "I play devil's advocate and make sure the level of analysis has been complete and thorough and that all the relevant resources have been brought to bear."

Ainslie approaches most issues from an analytical standpoint, including business issues (e.g., determining the impact of assets on performance or how to improve returns to investors).

Ainslie spent considerable time discussing the issue of capacity—the amount of assets Maverick can comfortably manage without impacting performance. While not specifying the exact number, he said considerable effort and studies have been made to understand the advantages and disadvantages of size and growth. Maverick compares its performance each month against pro forma performance as if no trades had been executed that month. That trend has improved over time.

Ainslie attempts to find out to what degree Maverick's agility and nimbleness have been negatively impacted by size of assets under management. Maverick tracks and cares about execution of trades (i.e., does its asset size move markets?). Each day they look at the trade executions against the closing prices and the volume-weighted average prices.

Ainslie points out that the fund has consistently grown since it was set up seven years ago. There has been only one quarter with a net withdrawal and only three quarters with down performance. Those were the first quarter of 1994 when Maverick was down 6.4 percent, third quarter 1998 when it was down 4.1 percent, and the third quarter of 1999 when it was down 4.7 percent.

He discussed the potential disadvantages of being too large. At the top of that list was being forced to change investment style, which has not been an issue for Maverick. Ainslie also continuously analyzes whether agility and nimbleness have been impaired. He feels that is a long way off.

On the positive side, says Ainslie, as assets have grown more people have been hired, which has allowed them to move closer to the individual stocks. As the firm grows in size the resources and capabilities of the trading desk improve. For example, in 1993 each investment professional watched about 100 positions. Today, with 24 investment professionals, each professional has fewer than 10 positions.[1]

The bottom line is performance. For the year ending March 31, 2000, Maverick had one of its best years on a relative performance basis, absolute basis, and volatility basis, says Ainslie.

Less than 1 percent of the gross assets are allocated to other managers. While this is done infrequently, Ainslie finds it valuable. Maverick can find new ideas, develop relationships, and see other managers' portfolios, as well as increase their own expertise. Maverick has also seeded other managers, and in those cases owns a small percentage of those hedge funds.

None of Maverick's portfolio is allocated to global macro. Ainslie believes macro investing will become less significant as the macro opportunities shrink.

Ainslie says at times there is significant irrationality in the market, which creates prices that don't necessarily reflect fundamentals, and such periods don't usually last long.

No investment committee exists at Maverick. Ainslie points to two dangers: First, consensus thinking becomes the lowest common denominator; in other words, the more interesting and exciting ideas get weeded out. Second, he wants people focused on their individual stocks rather than looking outside their own industry.

LEVERAGE AND RISK MANAGEMENT

Maverick's typical gross leverage is 240 to 250 percent. Daily volatility is about half that of the S&P 500, yet the firm has outperformed the S&P. "We are comfortable with this risk/return profile." Leverage has been consistent over the years. Compared with its hedged equity peers, Ainslie says Maverick's leverage is slightly lower.

While the maximum theoretical leverage Maverick can use is 6 to 1 (i.e., 600 percent), that amount of leverage has never been used. The highest ever was 257 percent. The self-imposed limit is 300 percent.

Ainslie says Maverick can afford more financial risk and still maintain a superior risk/return profile because it has limited so many other types of risk as well, is diversified, and follows strict loss limits. By hedging, Maverick shifts the risk from macro risk to security selection risk. This allows it to add value over time through security selection.

Other managers may get into trouble if they use leverage but are not hedged, are not diversified, are too correlated, or are too concentrated.

Because Maverick is truly hedged, its macro risks are lower. It has a low net exposure within each region and industry in which it invests. It typically maintains fewer than 250 positions and has strict position limits. Therefore, one position cannot be too costly. No long has been greater than 5 percent of net equity, and no short has been greater than 3 percent of net equity. Relatively liquid stocks are traded, so if a mistake is made the position can quickly be exited.

TYPICAL DAY

Ainslie starts the day at 7:30 A.M., when he talks with the trading desk on new developments that have occurred overnight and discusses how to react. Most mornings, he does this from his office at home—which is an exact replica of the one at the Maverick office—in peace and solitude, avoiding the rest of the world.

Most of the rest of his day is spent talking to the senior team. He doesn't speak much with sell-side analysts, but he does spend time with investors who can be helpful in the investment process.

Every night, a plan of action is developed for the next day—what should be bought and what should be sold. Loss limit rules and tax planning guidelines are maintained by Maverick's systems. Ainslie is often on the phone to senior members. He also likes to see how the Japanese market opens before he leaves for the evening. This process occurs from 4:30 to 7:30 P.M. and he's usually home by 8 or 9 P.M. Another hour is often spent focusing on overnight markets.

The plan of action is distributed to each section head the next morning.

When he's not working, Ainslie likes to play basketball and golf. Besides investment literature, he likes to read historical novels.

Ainslie loves what he does. He is competitive and finds the markets to be the ultimate competition.

INVESTOR BASE

Since mid-1997, the fund has been closed to new investors to temper the growth rate. Maverick will take new money from strategic investors (e.g., institutions and senior managers of large companies). They take advantage of investors' expertise and collective brainpower. Ainslie said there are over 700 investors.

Roughly one-third are individuals and trusts; another one-third are endowments, foundations, and pensions; and the remaining investors are partners, principals, and related entities, as well as banks, corporations, insurance companies, and fund of funds entities.[2]

According to NACUBO's 1999 annual survey of endowments, those allocating to Maverick include Carnegie Mellon, King's College, the University of Michigan, the University of North Carolina, Oberlin College, Southern Methodist University, the University of Texas, Vassar College, and Whitman College.

Maverick principals and related entities have over $400 million invested in funds managed by Maverick, making them its largest investor.

When the funds were last open, the minimum investment for individuals was $2 million; it was $5 million for institutions. Maverick has a three-year lock-up of assets. If investors want to get out earlier, a fee is imposed.

PRIVATE EQUITY

Maverick has created a strategic relationship by playing an instrumental role in the creation of an entity called Brazos Investment Partners in late 1999. It is a union between two former Hicks, Muse Tate & Furst principals, an operating principal, and Maverick partners. Brazos Equity Fund looks for buyouts and recapitalizations with values of between $25 million and $150 million.

Through normal activities, Ainslie sees many private equity ideas—some companies that are about ready to go public—but so far has not been able to take advantage of those ideas. He hasn't wanted to use capital from the Maverick fund. Private equity ideas require someone with different skill sets—someone to evaluate the opportunities and negotiate. Private equity is hard to hedge, and Ainslie believes he shouldn't force significant private equity exposure on Maverick investors. Maverick investors had an opportunity to invest in Brazos but it wasn't forced on them. Brazos is located on one of the Maverick floors.

Maverick and Brazos share ideas. Maverick can coinvest without diluting its time and effort. Brazos can take advantage of Maverick's Wall Street relationships. "It is a win-win situation."

CHANGING INDUSTRY ENVIRONMENT

Implications from Julian Robertson closing and Soros unraveling are that the macro environment is less competitive today than it had been, observes Ainslie. Robertson's and Soros's assets total a significant percentage of the hedge fund asset market; collective market share of the two was huge. The unraveling of the global macro giants may also help the commodity trading adviser world, which in some respects is similar to the global macro world—currencies are heavily traded.

Another implication is that the stumbling of the global macro giants frees up assets. It is not known whether these assets will leave the hedge fund industry. Many of the top hedge fund managers are closed and won't consider taking more assets unless they are from strategic investors.

Day-trader implications? Ainslie says that volume has become a less meaningful indicator of liquidity. Day traders have also made it more difficult for brokerage firms to make markets in an efficient manner. On the positive side, however, they create price-move spreads.

Ainslie is excited about the

Net Performance (%) Hedged Equity Strategy*	
1993	22.57
1994	6.82
1995	24.47
1996	44.66
1997	20.08
1998	21.84
1999	25.83
2000	27.40
Compound average annual return	**23.83**

*Hedged equity strategy represents the performance of all assets of the equity portion of the portfolio managed by Ainslie from September 1993 through February 1995 and the entire portfolio since Ainslie became sole manager in March 1995. Most investors find this track record to be most relevant since Ainslie is the current manager and since all assets are managed in this strategy.

future of the hedge fund industry. He feels that institutions are recognizing the value of the investment category for its performance as well as its risk control. As institutions become more educated, they will make wiser decisions.

He doesn't feel that fees are an issue for institutions, because the relatively higher fees attract the best and brightest talent. Return/risk is very attractive after fees for many funds. The institutions won't take the second-rate firms simply because they have lower fees.

Regarding information given out to investors, Ainslie says Maverick gives just about anything on request except short positions. On a monthly basis, the firm provides performance by sector or by geography, long/short exposure by region or sector, as well as a trading summary.

Tax efficiency is also something that Maverick studies. Ainslie feels that investors should pay more attention to this, and that as time goes on they will. Initially, investors looked at only gross returns. Then it became net returns. Next, he expects the interest will be net after-tax returns.

LEE AINSLIE
Maverick Capital

Organization

Inception	September 1993
Assets	
Current	$6.0 billion+
Peak	$6.0 billion
Edge	Experience of team; stock picking
Office Location	Dallas, Texas
Number of People	58
Type of Organization	Team
His Role	Overseer, coordinator, sounding board
Investment Committee	No
Reward System	Profitability of the overall fund, contribution of sector, subjective element
Number of Investors	Over 700
Type of Investor	Diversified
GP/Principals' Ownership of Assets	Over $400 million
Endowments (*Source:* 1999 NACUBO)	Carnegie Mellon University King's College University of Michigan University of North Carolina Oberlin College Southern Methodist University University of Texas System Vassar College Whitman College

Methodology/ Portfolio Composition

Style	Fundamental, bottom-up
Number of Positions in Portfolio	250
Trades Taken	Hurdle return rates in conjunction with risk

Role of United States	100 percent
Role of Technology	6 percent
Role of Private Equity	Strategic relationship
Role of Macro	0 percent
Allocates to Other Managers	Less than 1 percent

Risk Management

Net Exposure	Averages 48 percent
Hedging Technique	Short stocks
Maximum Leverage	Self-imposed 3:1 Theoretical 6:1
Memorable Loss	Three losing quarters: Q1 1994, Q3 1998, Q3 1999
Risk Management	Hedged Low net exposure Diversification Position size limits Liquid positions only

Background Information

Initial Spark	High school
Professional Background	Accounting consultant
Education	University of Virginia; University of North Carolina Business School
Motivation/Satisfaction	Competitive
Age	36
Free Time	Basketball, golf, reading

LEON COOPERMAN
Omega Advisors, Inc.

U.S. Stock Picker, Active Value Investor
Eyeball-to-Eyeball

I spoke with Leon Cooperman, chairman and chief executive officer of Omega Advisors, after trading hours on May 31, 2000. It was an exciting day for him in the markets. On that day, the Dow Jones Industrial Average was down 4.8 percent. He had a long position in Aetna, going on 14 months. The day of our meeting, CNBC's David Faber came out with a rumor that ING Group was in renewed talks to buy Aetna's financial services and international business for more than $8.5 billion. This was good news for Cooperman. Aetna moved up $4 that day. I saw Cooperman in action. Unable to contain himself, he took and made many telephone calls during our time together. The calls ranged from company chief executives, other senior managers, press, and other investment managers to people on his staff.

Cooperman, a chatty, energetic man of 57, was continually on the move during our interview. I was exhausted just watching him. You could tell he thoroughly enjoyed what he was doing; this explained why he spent 90 hours a week working. The smile on his face and the twinkle in his eye were constant.

On a typical day, Cooperman arrives in his office at about 7 A.M., after a one-and-a-quarter hour commute from his Short Hills, New Jersey, home. On three out of five days he meets with his trainer, with whom he goes on a treadmill and does some stretching exercises. At 8:45 A.M., he has his team meeting. At the meeting, the analysts talk about things they've learned about the companies they are tracking. Views are exchanged on the economy. During the day, Cooperman usually speaks to about five companies. He works until about 6 P.M. seldom arriving home before 8 P.M. "I eat dinner in 15 minutes and log back onto the computer for the evening to check out the portfolio, markets in Asia, and late-breaking news. I'm an information hog; I want to know what is going on."

His motivation is not money. When he retired from Goldman Sachs, he was already a wealthy man. He is motivated by doing a job well and making a total commitment. What gives him a lot of satisfaction is seeing something that no one else does.

Cooperman says he will keep doing it as long as he is healthy, has no performance problem, and likes what he does. He has no plans to retire. At the start of the interview, Cooperman let it be known that he was a regular guy. "I went to P.S. 75, Morris High School, then Hunter College of the City University of New York, where I met and married my wife of 37 years." Perhaps Cooperman felt he had something to prove, and he has done so.

Right after Columbia Business School, he went to Goldman Sachs where he stayed for 24 years; for 15 of those he was a partner. He spent 22 years in the investment research department and for 15 years was partner-in-charge, cochairman of the investment policy committee, and chairman of the stock selection committee. He built the research department from near-scratch, from a 35-person department to 200 people. In 1989, he became chairman and chief executive officer of

Goldman Sachs Asset Management and was chief investment officer of the equity product line, including managing GS Capital Growth fund, for one and a half years. For nine consecutive years, *Institutional Investor* magazine named him the top portfolio strategist in its All-America Research Team survey.

At the end of 1991, he retired from Goldman Sachs to pursue a lifetime ambition—to manage money, including his own. It is clear that Goldman Sachs played an important part in Cooperman's life. His office, which overlooks the Brooklyn Bridge, contains many mementos from his Goldman Sachs days, including a whip. The Goldman Sachs sales force gave him the whip after accompanying him on a whirlwind schedule of out-of-town meetings with clients.

Cooperman explains his choice of the name "Omega," the Greek letter that means eternity. "This is my last venture. Likewise, I didn't want to put my name on the door. I wanted partners who felt like they were owners, not workers."

He started with approximately $500 million. A significant amount was Cooperman's own money and assets from retired Goldman Sachs partners. Over 20 of the initial investors had worked at Goldman. Today, Omega's assets total about $2.4 billion. About 12 percent of the capital in the funds today are the general partners'.

ACTIVIST U.S. STOCK PICKER

Unlike some of the other managers who take a coordinator or strategic role, Cooperman is active in the portfolio—he loves being an investor. Cooperman's reputation is, and always has been since his Goldman Sachs days, as a U.S. stock picker. His specialty is finding undervalued equities, those that have low multiple-to-growth ratios. He visits companies and is on a first-name basis with many chief executive officers and senior managers. He is actively involved with stock selection. At the time of our meeting, he was intensely involved and personally responsible for over a dozen stocks. He is ultimately responsible for all 90 to 100 stocks in the overall portfolio and has approved every one of them.

Cooperman is active and vocal with some of the companies he owns. He loves to go head-to-head with some companies where he thinks problems exist. He has been known to be extremely open about top management's performance. He actively attends annual meetings and has been highly critical of management when he believes such criticism is warranted. The press recently reported such an episode at the Warnaco annual meeting.[1]

Cooperman calls himself an investor, not a trader, because the majority of the portfolio is expected to be held for at least two years. There are exceptions, however: if his price objective has been met, if initial expectations on the company don't materialize and a decision is made to cut losses, if he finds a better idea than the one he owns, or if his view on the market changes.

In conjunction with its macroeconomic analysis, Omega pursues a bottom-up approach to stock selection. Cooperman talks about five ways to make money: first, determining market direction (i.e., forecasting the anticipated investment environment); second, spending lots of time on the asset allocation decision, which Cooperman feels is more important than being in the right stock (e.g., determining the relative attractiveness of U.S. versus non-U.S. or stocks versus fixed income); third, buying undervalued stocks; fourth, selling overvalued stocks; and fifth, nonconventional financial assets, such as currencies.

Cooperman differentiates a company's two values—public market value and private market value. Private market value reflects the price an informed buyer would pay for control of a company. Public market value is the price a marginal investor would pay for a minority position. Private market value is an imprecise concept that can only be estimated. Public market value is a precise figure published daily in the press.

Private market value, though imprecise, is stable and changes only gradually over time. Public market value, though precise, is volatile and can change in one day. Private value is determined by a company's economic prospects. He compares the current price—the public market value—of a company's stock with its private value and evaluates the potential catalysts for change.

In analyzing the investment environment, Cooperman assesses many factors. He analyzes the economic environment, monetary policy, valuation of the market and individual sectors, supply/demand patterns within markets, consumer and investor sentiment, quality of attractive investment opportunities, and technical indicators.

Omega invests in two basic classes, equities and macro. Equities are U.S., non-U.S., and special situations such as bankruptcies, reorganizations, and arbitrage. While Cooperman focuses on U.S. companies, he has hired others to do non-U.S. equities under his direction.

Omega refers to its macro investments as G-10. At Omega, G-10 includes fixed income, foreign exchange, and equities in the United States, Japan, Germany, United Kingdom, France, Italy, Australia, Switzerland, Canada, and Spain as well as other markets outside the traditional G-10 that meet Omega's investment criteria, which include an emphasis on liquidity. While macro has added significantly to Omega's returns in the past years, it has also increased their volatility. Omega has developed a clear risk management strategy that focuses on markets with perceived liquidity, which may allow a quick exit if necessary.

Before Omega makes an equity investment, the company is generally visited and a report is written. With a value bias, Cooperman likes to buy what he perceives as a $1 investment for 50 to 60 cents.

ACCOUNTABILITY

There are 41 people in the firm, of whom 15 are investment professionals. All the analysts are accountable for their positions; they are required to know their portfolio companies extremely well. Generally, each analyst will have six to ten companies in the portfolio at any one time. Typically, Cooperman gives new analysts a couple of years to prove their ability. If they are not making money in two to three years, they are asked to leave.

There are 17 partners in the firm. They are rewarded either by percentage of the firm's profit or based on their own profit and loss. The reward system is anchored around the performance of the recommendations. "If they're not a money maker, you're not doing them a favor by keeping them on board. That's the name of the game. You're not doing the investors a favor, either."

In hiring an analyst, Cooperman looks for a strong work ethic, analytic foundation, capability to easily write a several-page summary of their investment views, and a good nose for making money (i.e., knowing a good idea when they see it). In a typical year, an analyst should be able to produce at least six core-type ideas and 15 to 20 trading ideas.

Analysts must have an intensity that leads them to be fully informed about their positions and ahead of the crowd. They must have pride of ownership, a sense of loyalty, and care for Omega clients. Commitment and loyalty run through Cooperman's life. He expects the same of his staff. "You've got to be committed to this business or get out."

With these factors in mind, the culture can best be described as intense, demanding, and research-driven.

Cooperman admits that he is not technology oriented—something he shares with Warren Buffett—and that has been a blind spot. He hired a technology analyst in 2000.

Decision making is centralized. Cooperman has the final word in all investment areas. If he has people whom he trusts, they are given more discretion. For example, Cooperman hired Steven Einhorn in May 1999 for the second time. Einhorn is vice chairman of Omega. The two had worked together at Goldman Sachs for 12 years, where Cooperman had hired him as a portfolio analyst. Cooperman says the hiring of Einhorn has given him more flexibility to do things he likes, such as visiting more companies.

Cooperman, while acknowledging his disappointment over high staff turnover, feels there is a broad-based capability in the firm. "There are a number of young people coming up."

The investment policy committee includes Cooperman and Einhorn as cochairs; Raj Gupta, who is head of the macro group; and a senior equity portfolio manager who changes from time to time. "We discuss macro trends, try to identify straw hats in the winter (since most people buy straw hats in the summer), out-of-favor asset classes where the return/risk ratio is appealing." The committee meets on a weekly basis. Portfolio decisions and optimization are fundamental-based.

The total Omega portfolio typically consists of 90 to 100 stocks, of which one-third make up 50 to 65 percent of the portfolio and the other two-thirds the balance. The average company typically makes up 2 to 3 percent of the assets in the portfolio.

Cooperman likes to visit companies and go eyeball-to-eyeball with management. Accordingly, he sees their New York City office as an advantage to their investing style. "New York is the mecca, the financial center." Many companies visit New York regularly, but when necessary, Cooperman will travel to relatively remote locations to find investment opportunities. He visits about five companies a week; he is company intensive.

MISTAKES

Cooperman admits to making many mistakes over the years. One was not being more fully invested prior to and during the stock market bull run. "I've been too conservative in the last five years." Overstaying his welcome in non-U.S.-dollar bonds in 1994, and getting caught in the Russian fixed income situation of 1998 were other mistakes.

Omega's 1998 losses were macro oriented, relating to emerging market debt, in particular Russian fixed income. "It had a collateral effect on other emerging markets and limited liquidity. I was disappointed with out ability to adjust positions. In our analysis, we always factored in that Russia could devalue but not that Russia would default." Cooperman has, as a result of his 1998 experience, exited emerging markets as a dedicated business. "I do not want to be in markets where liquidity is not provided."

Cooperman has gravitated back to his core competency—the core returns have always been developed-country equity stocks—primarily U.S. and Western Europe.

RISK CONTROL

There are three elements to the management of risk. Daily reports summarize positions (these include static market exposure, upside target, and stop-loss levels), on a real-time and daily mark-to-market basis. Capital at risk methodology is used, based on stop-loss levels and options premium. When appropriate, Value-at-Risk is used.

Virtually all of the portfolio consists of freely marketable securities. Currently, nonlisted stocks or private placements total less than 0.3 percent of the portfolio. Cooperman says his net exposure tends to average about 65 percent. Leverage has never exceeded about 3.5 to 1, and has typically been significantly less. Returns are principally from the move in the asset owned, not from leverage.

Cooperman hedges by shorting stocks, index options, and futures.

Currently, the macro side is allocated about 5 percent of capital.

Day-to-day management of macro risk exposure is vested in Gupta, who reports directly to Cooperman.

INVESTOR BASE AND CAPACITY

Omega has between 100 and 150 clients. About 40 percent of clients are tax-exempt entities, 30 percent non-U.S., and 30 percent high-net-worth investors. Cooperman offers different partnerships for investors with different tax statuses. As with his portfolio of stocks, no one client dominates. According to NACUBO public documents, endowment clients include Clark University, Franklin and Marshall College and Rensselaer Polytechnic Institute.

Does tax efficiency play a role? Omega is sensitive to tax issues (e.g., tax-loss selling at year-end), but it is not the main driver. Fundamental analysis is key. Omega is considering an equity-only product that will have a three-year lock-up and be capped in the $250 million area. With the three-year lock-up, a product is a bit more tax efficient.

On a quarterly basis, Omega gives clients a listing of the 25 positions generating the largest profit and the largest loss. Current exposure is detailed, as is Omega's view of the market. The only items Omega won't give out are stock-specific short positions.

On the capacity issue, Cooperman says it is a lifestyle decision. He believes he could readily manage $5 billion, but he has no desire to grow to $10 billion. Such a capital base would be more demanding and limit investment flexibility because of size. He is comfortable with Omega's current asset base of $2.6 billion. Omega reached its peak in assets under management in 1998 at $4 billion; the 1998 losses in Russia and related redemptions reduced assets under management.

FREE TIME

While Cooperman is not one to admit to having free time, he gives a lot to charity. "Working gives you money to give to charity, Uncle Sam, or your children. I don't want to spoil my children." Cooperman is active in many charities. He has a foundation that endows scholarships at the Columbia University Graduate School of Business for a student who is a graduate of the New York City public school system. He is also on the board of St. Barnabas Hospital. He serves on the national board of trustees of the Crohn's and Colitis Foundation, is a member of the board of directors of the Cancer Research Foundation of the Damon Runyon–Walter Winchell Foundation, and is a member of the investment committee of the Museum of Modern Art.

Net Performance (%) Omega Capital Partners*	
1992	18.47
1993	62.96
1994	−24.57
1995	25.68
1996	36.74
1997	26.97
1998	−5.43
1999	24.12
2000	13.80
Compound average annual return	**17.42**

*Omega's original partnership for U.S. investors.

THE INDUSTRY TODAY AND TOMORROW

Although Cooperman says he considers the hedge fund industry "a young man's game," his work ethic continues to be intense. Interestingly, Cooperman's son, Wayne, is also a hedge fund manager.

Cooperman suggests looking at managers' core competencies. He observes that "those that do well keep with their style and don't get shaken out."

While he acknowledges that global macro managers are currently out of favor, he believes it probably means there will be excellent opportunities going forward.

Regarding day traders, he says they have impacted the stock market and made it more volatile and more of a momentum market, yet it doesn't affect him personally since he is a long-term investor.

LEON COOPERMAN
Omega Advisors, Inc.

Organization

Inception	1992
Assets	
Current	$2.4 billion
Peak	$4.0 billion
Edge	Activist; research
Office Location	New York, New York
Number of People	41
Type of Organization	Centralized
His Role	Active portfolio investor
Investment Committee	Yes
Reward System	Performance of recommendations
Number of Investors	100–150
Type of Investor	40 percent tax-exempt
	30 percent non-U.S.
	30 percent high net worth
GP/Principals' Ownership of Assets	12 percent
Endowments (*Source:* 1999 NACUBO)	Clark University
	Franklin and Marshall College
	Rensselaer Polytechnic Institute

Methodology/ Portfolio Composition

Style	Value investor; activist investor
Number of Positions in Portfolio	90–100
Trades Taken	If he can get a $1 of value for 50 to 60 cents
Role of United States	100 percent
Role of Technology	Limited
Role of Private Equity	Limited
Role of Macro	5 percent
Allocates to Other Managers	Yes

Risk Management

Net Exposure	65 percent
Hedging Technique	Stocks, options, futures
Maximum Leverage	3.5:1
Memorable Loss	Non-U.S. dollar bonds—1994; Russian/fixed income situation—1998
Risk Management	All marketable securities, low leverage, hedge, 5 percent maximum allocation to global macro

Background Information

Initial Spark	Bar Mitzvah
Professional Background	Goldman, Sachs & Co.
Education	Hunter College, Columbia University MBA
Motivation/Satisfaction	Job well done; finding what others don't
Age	57
Free Time	Philanthropy

7

KEN GRIFFIN
Citadel Investment Group

Relative Value/Event-Driven Arbitrage
Dynamic Portfolio Assessing New Strategies

Visiting Ken Griffin and Citadel Investment Group, L.L.C., in Chicago was quite an experience. Of the managers I visited, Griffin has the largest organization and infrastructure. Citadel occupies five floors at its headquarters in Chicago. It currently employs approximately 350 people in offices in Chicago as well as San Francisco; Greenwich, Connecticut; and through affiliates, in London and Tokyo. One floor alone was devoted to several dozen servers that provided the backup for market feeds, risk management, and data for the front office to make decisions. Nearly half the employees in Chicago are systems and technology professionals.

Griffin, like a number of the other managers interviewed, was educated at Harvard University as an undergraduate. One thing differentiates him, however—his age. He is only 32 years old—the youngest of the managers interviewed. Furthermore, he started his first hedge fund at the earliest age—18—during his second year of college. As a freshman, he had traded options. This led to arbitrage trading, which led to convertible bond trading. In September 1987, as a sophomore, he launched his first hedge fund—Convertible Hedge Fund 1—with $265,000. The next month, during the crash of 1987, Griffin made money. He completed his Harvard degree in three years, and by the time he graduated he was managing $1 million.

The initial spark occurred at Harvard when he was about 17 years old. Griffin read an article in *Forbes* about the Home Shopping Network, that discussed how the stock was overpriced; Griffin bought a few put contracts. He profited as the stock declined and made a few thousand dollars. Griffin realized that the quality of the market maker's profit was greater than his own. This experience motivated him to learn more about options pricing theory.

During his college days, Griffin's role model was Carl Icahn, the leveraged buyout icon of the 1980s. Griffin's goal after graduation was to work at a firm like Kohlberg, Kravis & Roberts (KKR). He recalls meeting with a Harvard alumnus at a Boston bank. They talked about arbitrage and price relationships. The alumnus's firm focused on convertible bond arbitrage for its own proprietary money but did not recommend it to clients. This stayed in the mind of the 18-year-old Griffin as he formulated future plans.

In 1990, Griffin started the predecessor to Citadel Investment Group with approximately $4.6 million. The company focused initially on convertible bond arbitrage in the United States. Japan became an early focus as well. Most of his investors were entrepreneurs.

Ten years later, assets under management are about $5.0 billion in five funds. Two funds are for U.S. investors, and three are for non-U.S. investors.

There are over 250 investors. Griffin's clients are roughly 60 percent non-U.S. and 40 percent U.S. The global client base is represented strongly by Japan, Europe, and Southeast Asia. About 40 percent of the clients are institutions, while the remainder is split approximately evenly between family offices and fund of funds entities. According to the NACUBO annual survey, endowment clients include Oberlin College. Griffin and Citadel's other professionals combined are significant investors in the funds.

INVESTMENT BANK ORGANIZATION

Like most of the other managers, Griffin does not agree with the hedge fund label. He described his firm as a financial institution, one that trades proprietary capital but is capitalized with outside investors as well. "We manage risk and provide liquidity. We are not a hedge fund. . . . We use our capital base to provide liquidity to capital markets and to absorb the risk of risky assets." He likens his organization to an investment bank in the early to mid-1990s. "Our goal is to find underpriced and mispriced assets and hedge away the risk. . . . We mitigate the macro risks that global macro managers take. We are the inverse of macro fund managers."

Over time, Citadel has methodically and strategically developed into a multistrategy investment firm that uses a variety of relative value, event-driven, and fundamental-based investment strategies. Relative value strategies, since inception and through today, have been Citadel's primary focus. Relative value strategies include convertible bonds, statistical equity, and fixed-income arbitrage. Mathematical and statistical techniques are used to identify sets of long and short positions to capture mispricing between different components.

Event-driven strategies are also an important part of Citadel's portfolio. These include corporate life cycle investing in which one looks for opportunities created by mergers and acquisitions, spin-offs, and recapitalizations.

"At Citadel, we have a team of specialists. We have different businesses—statistical arbitrage, merger arbitrage, fixed-income arbitrage, convertible arbitrage, and long/short equity. We have specialists in each business." Citadel's funds account for about 1 percent of total daily volume traded on both the New York Stock Exchange and Tokyo Stock Exchange.

The firm is always changing to reflect investment opportunities. "If you're not aware of product evolution, you can't survive in the long term." For example, in the 1980s, index arbitrage represented a huge opportunity. Today, index arbitrage is a commodity product. Japanese equity warrants are another example. They were big in the early 1990s but are nearly nonexistent today; they largely disappeared in 1995 due to tax and accounting changes. Consequently, Griffin has moved people into new strategies.

The portfolio is equity dominated, but fixed income plays a growing role. One-third to one-half of the portfolio is outside the United States, and this has been the case for years. Europe and Japan play significant roles. The European office, based in London, employs about 30 people. Citadel's funds have had, from time to time, small emerging-market positions.

Citadel is active in the technology sector. Its geographic presence in San Francisco is helpful. The percentage of the portfolio invested in technology companies varies considerably, ranging from 5 to 50 percent. "We are significantly invested in the New Economy through mergers and acquisitions, convertibles and long/short equity positions. We always think about concentrated risk in telecom and the Internet. We invest in companies that we think will be survivors. There is an enormous revaluation taking place in technology and we are in the midst of it. Consumer gains do not equal profits."

Griffin allocated to another hedge fund manager once. He did so because he believed that the manager had an area of excellence and that allocating to him would diversify the portfolio and increase returns.

The firm engages in private equity investments, with allocations to the sector varying based upon opportunities available in the marketplace.

PROCESS-DRIVEN

When asked about a recent loss or one that stays in his mind, Griffin said that loss is a central part of their day-to-day experience. "We lose lots of money on hundreds of trades each day. We want to prevent losses that arise from making the same mistake twice." Griffin says that many of the things they trade are repeated—giving way to learning. "These are not one-off transactions like global macro traders with a Japanese yen–U.S. dollar trade. We are a process-driven firm from which we learn. The process is always changing, representing a learning experience." Lessons, negative and positive, are integrated into the learning process.

He feels some firms repeat the same mistakes because they are generalists without an edge. He also feels that some firms don't critically analyze what they're doing and how to do it better next time.

Since inception in 1990 through 1999, every year but one has been double digits to the upside for the longest-running fund. The exception was 1994, which was down 4.3 percent. Griffin says that 1994 was much like 1998 in that convertibles became extremely undervalued during the collapse of the bond market as competitors were forced to liquidate positions due to mounting losses. However, as these undervalued securities returned to more reasonable levels during 1995, Citadel earned significant gains in the portfolio. In 1995, the fund bounced back 36 percent.

LEVERAGE AND RISK MANAGEMENT

On the leverage front, Griffin says Citadel's leverage tends to be moderately higher than that of their peers, and this has been the case since inception. "However, we feel comfortable utilizing higher levels of leverage given what we think are superior risk management capabilities."

Citadel's goal is to try to eliminate beta (i.e., systematic risk). "We don't want performance dominated by beta. We try not to profit from market increases or decreases or interest rate increases or decreases." As a result, net exposure to the stock market is very low.

Citadel attempts to dilute risk by diversification. It forecasts and analyzes portfolio behavior based on historic and expected future volatility as well as extreme market conditions.

Citadel doesn't look for a specific return per trade but rather allows a certain risk per trade, and that varies by strategy. For example, the risk taken on a fixed-income arbitrage trade is often a fraction of that on a risk arbitrage trade.

For hedging, Griffin uses a full array of products—from shorting securities to shorting futures. "Each has a role in the portfolio depending on what you want to hedge. There is not always only one way to hedge."

Because Citadel attempts to mitigate macro risks, it feels comfortable using leverage. "Rewards can be small [with arbitrage], so we do utilize leverage. We really work to keep the portfolio hedged."

UNENCUMBERED BY BUREAUCRACY

Griffin says decision making is pushed down from the top. There are approximately 80 investment professionals who make decisions. "I want those nearest the information to be unencumbered by bureaucracy. They make the decisions."

The investment committee, consisting of a handful of senior portfolio managers, meets collectively, depending on the underlying volatility of the markets. Griffin says in 1998, they met several times a day. In 2000, they meet less frequently, perhaps once a week. The shifts in the underlying environment drive the frequency and duration of the meetings.

In describing the firm, Griffin provides an airplane analogy. The quantitative research group is responsible for building the engines. The technology team builds the plane's airframe, and the traders are the pilots in the cockpit.

Organizationally, there are five groups: (1) The Quantitative Research Group develops and enhances proprietary mathematical models to service Citadel. Numerous PhDs—mostly physicists—work on building models of the markets. They provide tools for portfolio management, stress testing of trades, and stress testing the portfolio under various market conditions. (2) The Investment and Trading Group identifies investment opportunities around the world using mathematical and statistical methods, proprietary valuation techniques, and fundamental analysis. (3) The Information Systems people provide the information technology that drives Citadel. They write and maintain code to keep systems current. They design the trading systems that support the analytics and trading efforts. (4) The Portfolio Finance Group is responsible for managing counter party and liquidity risk. (5) Operations, Legal and Accounting consists of approximately 80 people who monitor the transactions and positions. They are responsible for regulatory and financial compliance, and oversight of procedures. Every trade is reconciled every day.

For senior investment professionals, a significant portion of their compensation is based on overall performance of the firm.

Citadel has a comprehensive personal trading policy covering all employees which restricts employees transacting in securities included in Citadel account portfolios. All employee trades must be preapproved, says Griffin.

COORDINATOR, STRATEGIST ROLE

Griffin's role has changed over the years. In the early days, he did it all. Now, he is more of a coordinator and a strategist. He plays a role in developing new risk management techniques and capital allocation. "My technology and quantitative research people are better than I am. I coordinate. There are a lot of 'moving parts' at Citadel, and I spend a significant amount of my time making sure the firm is moving in the same direction."

One of Griffin's key focuses is how to manage the rate of growth correctly. "Alpha drives the capacity." His issue is where to get capacity in the future and how to get more capacity out of every strategy. The more alpha produced is spread over a larger asset base, and alpha is associated with more risk. Risk is also spread over a larger asset base. "How fast I can grow my business is a function of how fast I build alpha base and manage the risk that comes with an increase in alpha product."

Griffin is always working on new initiatives. The most recent addition was fixed income in 1999. The dislocation in fixed income in 1998 due to well-publicized problems in that sector resulting from the Long-Term Capital Management crisis helped free up a lot of talent, which made it possible to hire excellent people.

"I help build the team. We hired a very talented group of professionals from Salomon Brothers. I discuss the risks and transactions that appear attractive. I help them fit into the culture of our firm." Griffin describes the culture at Citadel as one where change is accepted. The firm is always assessing new strategies and implements those that are promising. But adding new strategies also adds new risks. "We can't rest on our laurels."

While Citadel may have a market leadership in several markets, its culture doesn't accept this thinking. "We go home every day and ask how we can do it better. . . . There is a huge emphasis on learning, sharing, and teamwork."

Griffin likes to hire people right out of college so he can teach them trading. "We are a very competitive organization. Most of the people are still in their thirties." He also feels that being in Chicago is an advantage—Citadel is one of the preeminent financial places to work in Chicago and there are few competitors. As a result, poaching is not common. Employees tend to be loyal, and a long-term outlook is part of Citadel's culture.

"I work with some of the brightest and most talented people in the world," Griffin says. All of us at Citadel are aware that we are building something very special. I love the challenges, the competition, the intellectual stimulation. That's what drives me."

While his business takes up most of his time, Griffin likes to play soccer and travel. He is on the permanent collection committee of Chicago's Museum of Contemporary Art.

THE INDUSTRY

Griffin feels that the 1990s have been a favorable backdrop for hedge funds. The one exception has been Japan, which has been difficult. The year 1998 was one of Citadel's best; the fallout of Long-Term Capital Management and other factors provided a great opportunity to acquire assets at distressed prices across the board.

He feels that a transition is taking place. In a bull market in equities, there is more money to go around. In a bear market, the markets are less easy, and consolidation will occur as the pie shrinks and the environment becomes more difficult.

He observes that the larger number of market participants has eroded some of the hedge fund managers' edge. Ten to 15 years ago, hedge fund managers could profit before institutional investors on the release of earnings reports and changes in Wall Street firms' opinions. But over the years, larger mutual funds and insurance companies have become more nimble in managing their portfolios. This situation, plus day trading, has taken away some of the hedge fund managers' advantages.

Griffin feels the future will be more challenging for global macro managers. In the 1980s and 1990s, macro traders had the advantages listed earlier as well as access to government officials and top economists. Now, with more broadly disseminated information, their edge has shrunk. The emergence of the euro and the emergence of a single euro yield curve have further exacerbated the situation. However, Griffin believes that global macro will persist as a strategy—though it will be much more challenging.

Net Performance (%) Longest Running Fund	
1991	43.00
1992	40.70
1993	23.50
1994	–4.30
1995	36.30
1996	23.00
1997	27.60
1998	30.50
1999	45.20
2000	52.00
Compound average annual return	30.80

Griffin also believes the hedge fund industry is immature in its response to institutional needs—from a transparency and business conduct point of view.

Griffin says the distinction between old and new generation is not clear-cut. However, a firm's comfort level with technology, quantitativeness, and information technology is telling and may be generational. Those managers who are under 40 years old seem more at ease in utilizing and integrating new technology into their businesses. Griffin observes that options pricing classes did not exist in colleges until the 1980s. The educational and technological environment has changed drastically since then. He also observes that it was the rapid adoption of technology that gave Salomon Brothers the edge in the 1980s and 1990s.

Succession planning? Griffin observes that most of the successful hedge fund management firms were built after a successful Wall Street career. How to capture an exit value or develop succession planning wasn't considered or even viewed as part of the process. Now these managers, late in their careers, are faced with issues they have spent little time contemplating. At Citadel, in contrast, a great deal of emphasis is placed on career development and grooming people for the next step.

KEN GRIFFIN
Citadel Investment Group

Organization

Inception	1990
Assets	
Current	$5.0 billion
Peak	$5.0 billion
Edge	Trading firm approach
Office and Affiliate Locations	Chicago, California, Connecticut, London, Tokyo
Number of People	Approximately 350
Type of Organization	Specialist teams
His Role	Coordinator, strategist, visionary
Investment Committee	Yes
Reward System	For senior investment professionals, significant portion of compensation is based on overall performance of the firm
Number of Investors	250+
Type of Investor	60 percent non-U.S. 40 percent institutional
GP/Principals' Ownership of Assets	Principals have substantial amount of their liquid net worth invested
Endowments (*Source:* 1999 NACUBO)	Oberlin College

Methodology/ Portfolio Composition

Style	Event-driven, relative value
Number of Positions in Portfolio	Varies
Trades Taken	Based on risk/reward dynamic for each trade
Role of United States	50 to 60 percent
Role of Technology	Varies

Role of Private Equity	Varies
Role of Macro	0 percent
Allocates to Other Managers	Once

Risk Management

Net Exposure	Net exposure to the market is low
Hedging Technique	Variety of ways
Maximum Leverage	Normal range in recent years is 3:1 to 7:1
Memorable Loss	Everyday experience
Risk Management	Hedging, diversification, and various quantitative and qualitative tools and analysis

Background Information

Initial Spark	College
Professional Background	Traded during college
Education	Harvard University
Motivation/Satisfaction	Competition
Age	32
Free Time	Soccer

JOHN HENRY
John W. Henry & Co.

Systematic, Disciplined Long-Term Trend Follower
Patient, Visionary, Analytical Whiz

John Henry is well-known in many areas. His company, John W. Henry & Co. (JWH), has long been the largest pure managed futures trader, measured by assets under management. Henry has been known as a visionary in the managed futures community. And, most recently, he purchased the Florida Marlins baseball team after owning a string of other baseball teams, including a 1 percent share of the New York Yankees.

I looked forward to my interview with John. I had first met him during my early days at Merrill Lynch in 1986. Merrill Lynch along with some of the other brokerage firms such as Dean Witter, Smith Barney, and Prudential Bache had long raised significant assets for the trader. During my career at Merrill Lynch, I went on road shows to the different Merrill Lynch offices describing the JWH's World Currency Fund or the Millburn/Henry Fund. I got to know John and his organization quite well. He had developed a strong following at the Merrill Lynch branch system in the United States and Europe during the 1980s, which continues through today.

PURE FUTURES TRADER

Henry, 51, has long held the distinction as the largest futures trader. Assets currently are at $1.2 billion compared with a peak of $2.4 billion in September 1997. As a percentage of the estimated $45 billion managed futures industry, a substrategy of the hedge fund world, JWH's assets alone have represented from 3 to 5 percent at various times. Henry trades worldwide financial and nonfinancial futures and forward markets, including currencies, interest rates, stock indexes, metals, energy, and agricultural contracts.

Henry views himself as a commodity trading adviser rather than a hedge fund but accepts the latter term as a matter of convenience. Unlike some of the other futures traders who evolved into global macro hedge fund managers, such as Louis Bacon or Paul Tudor Jones, Henry has remained a pure futures trader. Henry does trade a small amount of S&P futures and Nasdaq futures in a limited number of programs.

He says he trades stocks separately and not for clients. "I have thought about it for a long time but there are many who already do it well and there doesn't seem a need for us to provide that service. Clients already have their money invested in stocks and they don't need us to do that." He also observes that stocks are not the most liquid investments, especially when compared with futures.

In the managed futures subcategory, most of the traders tend to use computerized trading methodology rather than trade on a discretionary basis. They also historically charge higher fees, 4 percent management fee/25 percent incentive fee or 3 percent/20 percent, than the typical hedge fund manager's 1 percent management fee and 20 percent incentive fee. In September 2000, Henry changed his 4/15 percent fee structure to 2/20 percent. The fee reduction was a step to keep investors placated during choppy performances. The change also put more emphasis on the incentive component of compensation and less on the fixed management fee.

Low-key and unassuming, Henry has long carried considerable clout in the managed futures community. I have always known him to be a visionary. At an industry association conference in 1995, he delivered the keynote address where he talked about the need for managed futures traders to reduce fees and beef up risk management techniques to attract institutional investors. He felt that attracting institutional investors was the key to the long-term survival of the managed futures industry. Many of his peers were not happy to hear this, and even some in his own firm did not accept the thesis.[1] Yet in the long term, he will probably be proven correct.

Henry says JWH tries to follow a *kaizen* philosophy (i.e., continual improvement), which is similar to that used by Ned Johnson at Fidelity Investments.

JWH has often been the first to develop new products in the managed futures subcategory. Henry has made strides to develop efficient total-return swaps. While this product is not different than many of the swap products on traditional indexes, JWH has made significant advancements in the leveraging and deploying of capital in those swaps. JWH has also developed improved structures for notes that take much of the discretion out of the leveraging decisions. This should give greater comfort to buyers who want and need to know all of the rules for how a structured note will behave. Henry observes, "Being a disciplined, systematic manager applies not just to investing but to product development such as the structure of a note or swap."

JWH also has a number of proprietary trading accounts testing new ideas and methodologies. The firm is also doing preliminary work and trading in equity markets for defensive programs that can serve as an alternative to long-only investing. Currently, JWH does not allocate to other managers, but products along these lines are being developed.

LONG-TERM TREND FOLLOWER AND DIVERGENCE TRADER

If one theme summarizes Henry's philosophy, it is the knowledge that one cannot predict anything.

Henry is a long-term trend follower. His philosophy is based on the premise that market prices, rather than market fundamentals, are the key aggregation of information needed to make investment decisions. He says, "The markets are people's expectations," and these expectations manifest themselves as price trends. "We live in an uncertain world. One cannot predict the future of anything. In an uncertain world, identifying and following trends may be the only reasonable investment approach over the long term."

Henry feels that a mechanical approach has more value since no scientific approach or solid testing can be applied to discretionary trading.

Henry says that his edge is patience. He takes an extraordinarily long viewpoint and perspective. He expects to hold positions for months rather than days on an average trade. Holding a position for a year or more is not unheard of. Henry says that Wall Street executives tell him JWH is probably the most long-term of the futures traders they work with. He adds, "This [long-term] strategy tends to reduce costs and allows for faster growth."

Henry says that when he first researched the markets in the 1970s, he was looking for a methodology that would work through many market conditions. His research showed that long-term approaches work best over decades. "There is an overwhelming desire to act in the face of adverse market moves. Usually it is termed 'avoiding volatility' with the assumption that volatility is bad. However, I found avoiding volatility really inhibits the ability to stay with the long-term trend. The desire to have close stops to preserve open trade equity has tremendous costs over decades. Long-term systems do not avoid volatility, they patiently sit through it. This reduces the occurrence of being forced out of a position that is in the middle of a long-term major move."

He believes that patience during poor trading periods (such as the past three years for managed futures trading) is the most important weapon in one's arsenal. "I have never felt we have had a black box. We have a philosophy that follows trends as they change and emerge. We set our leverage to ensure we will be there after particularly poor trading periods. We don't seek to have large profits during those periods. We seek to remain in position to follow major trends that can last for years."

Leverage can be anywhere from three to six times capital. Leverage in the managed futures world is different than in the hedge fund world. It is the margin put up versus the value of the contract size, thus reflecting the dollar amount the manager controls.

Henry emphasizes how the markets are always changing. When he started, he observed the driver was money supply. Now there is no one driver of markets. Markets are constantly changing, and new variables and events become drivers. For example, now (September 2000), oil and currency movements are drivers. In the third quarter of 1998, it was the Asian crisis and risk contagion around the world. He says, "This understanding and accepting of change has been the hallmark of our philosophy. No one can predict the future. What drives a particular market in one period will not do so in a later period. That's the problem I have with convergence trading using historical models."

Henry feels that one of the biggest problems with investors is that they stay wedded to certain ideas or linkages. The failure of some traders is not that they do not see the importance of money supply or some other fundamental variable, but they continue to believe it is important long after markets have moved on to a new driver. Staying wedded to old experiences or out-of-date statistical linkages is more risky than accepting the inevitable tumultuous and changing dynamics of the markets.

Henry calls his type of trading "divergence investing" as much as trend following. "We generate returns when markets change and move to new equilibrium prices. When there are divergences from the status quo, there will be trends and these will be the times of greatest profitability. We do not predict times of change; we patiently trade a broad set of markets and remain posted to take advantage of trends when they appear." He emphasizes that this should not be confused with passive investing, because the programs are working 24 hours a day to identify these trend signals within the noise of the markets.

TIGHTENS RISK CONTROL

Henry has been known as having a volatile track record. Over the years, volatility has been reduced; 1992 was a watershed in this regard. For example, in 1991, the financial and metals program, the second longest-running and second largest program, was up 61.9 percent. In December alone, the program was up over 40 percent. But in 1992, the program lost 10.9 percent. It was this environment that caused him to tighten risk control. In 1993, the program bounced back 46.8 percent.

Henry says market moves that broad and strong leave long-term systems vulnerable to give-backs, and that is exactly what happened.

The volatility was too much for fiduciary investors to endure. While JWH made new highs before the year was out, he did cut the leverage.

He does not find his type of trading stressful. The major stress occurs for investors who don't understand what JWH does. "Every time we have extended bad periods, they wonder if our philosophy no longer works. I always get the question, 'Have the markets changed?' [and the complaint] 'There is too much money in trend following.' I always say they have changed and will continue to do so. That is why we are successful."

But true to his ideology, Henry views everything in the long term. "A methodology based on a valid philosophy will be successful value over the long run. There will be prolonged periods of poor performance, so leverage, if any, must be controlled accordingly."

Henry's philosophy has remained constant through the years—during up years and down years. His view is that the markets are constantly changing and are dynamic. "You must adhere to a philosophy that is based on change, and nothing adapts to change better than following trends in any industry or pursuit."

He says the essence of trend following is changing with the times.

Henry believes that all successful traders are trend followers—even if they say they're not. He feels the question really is "How do you define trends?" not "Are you a trend follower?" Some people define a trend as short-term while others are medium-term or long-term oriented.

MEMORABLE PERIODS

During stock market crashes, managed futures traders have historically shone. Often, they are the only investment category that does well in such periods. This occurred in October 1997 and again in August 1998. JWH is illustrative of this point.

In 1987, the financials and metals program was up 252.4 percent for the year. The fourth quarter was the best quarter JWH ever had. Recalling that period, Henry says he thought he was well-positioned for the crash. JWH was short equity indexes around the globe. Unfortunately, trends in interest rate instruments had them short in that sector. They did well the day of the crash, but on the following day's opening JWH suffered one of its worst days ever. Losses spilled over into currencies.

As with most disruptions, JWH was hurt in the beginning but ultimately had the best quarter of Henry's career. The dollar eventually declined precipitously, and financial and metals accounts open the entire year all made in excess of 200 percent net.

The Russian/LTCM crisis in 1998 caused large market disruptions leading to excellent profits. All of the JWH programs did well during this time frame. The financial and metals program made more than 30 percent in August and September while the stock market suffered losses. For 1998 as a whole, the financial and metals program was up 7.2 percent.

In 1999, JWH's financial and metals program was down 18.7 percent—its largest annual drop. Regarding the markets in 1999 and most of 2000, Henry says it is frustrating that the sectorwide moves that he is accustomed to seeing have not emerged. "Every time we have poor periods of performance you hear the cry, 'Trend following is dead. The markets have changed.' That's an oxymoron. I strongly believe that the markets are ever-changing and the time will come again for our basic philosophy to bring us to new and higher performance levels."

Henry kept to his methodology and strategy in a difficult 2000. After declining 25.9 percent through September, the financial and metals program rebounded sharply in the fourth quarter by 45.5 percent, giving the program a 12.9 percent gain for the year. JWH attributed the strong trading in the fourth quarter to strong trends in bonds and the dollar.

Identifying trends is key. Not that many people may be good at identifying trends, and in some periods they are more difficult to identify than in others. Examples are the past few years as well as the 1960s. During these difficult periods, you try to survive by keeping leverage low. This is where Henry's discipline becomes evident. His philosophy is "what is" is more important than "what should be," especially regarding price and direction.

DIVERSIFICATION

Henry says that he always perceived himself as a conservative investor, and that is one reason why he prefers his diversified programs. The aggressive financial and metals business, driven by client demand, overwhelmed the firm, however. At its peak, he estimates that 60 percent of their business was in financial and metals.

He is personally a conservative investor. In fact, reports indicate that when he bought the Florida Marlins he paid $150 million in Treasury bills. Principals' assets traded along with client assets range between $35 and $75 million. (The vast majority of the money is John's or JWH & Co.'s which is owned by John through a trust.)

Henry offers 12 programs in four categories—broadly diversified, financial, foreign exchange, and multiple style program. The programs have different combinations of style, timing, and market characteristics. Investment style differences are based on the number of directional phases that investment program uses for markets—long, short, or neutral—and how position sizes are determined. Timing refers to whether trends are recognized over a short-term to very long-term period. The programs can also be distinguished by the markets traded. Overall, JWH trades about 65 markets globally. On average, the firm holds about 50 positions.

The broadly diversified category programs include the original investment program, the global diversified program, and the JWH global analytics family of programs. Of this group, the original program is the largest, with assets under management totaling $226 million. The original program is a two-phase one, meaning that positions are held either long or short. The timing component is long-term trends. It is a diversified program that includes all major market sectors—interest rates, stock indexes, currencies, metals, energy, and agriculture.

Financial programs include financial and metals, the world financial perspective, global financial portfolio, international currency and bond portfolio, and worldwide bond program. In this category, the financial and metals program is the largest program with assets of $366 million. It began trading in October 1984. It seeks to identify and capitalize on intermediate-term price moves in currencies, interest rates, metals, and non-U.S. stock indexes. The financial and metals program won't invest in a market unless there is a clearly defined trend. It uses a three-phase investment style; in other words, the system can be long, short, or neutral. Henry observes that the financial and metals program does better during good markets and worse in bad markets.

In the foreign exchange category, the programs are the international foreign exchange program, G-7 currency portfolio, and dollar program. The largest program is international foreign exchange, with assets of $84.4 million. This program seeks to identify and capitalize on intermediate-term price moves in major and minor currencies, primarily trading on the interbank market. It can be long, short, or neutral.

The multiple style programs include the strategic allocation program. Begun in July 1996, it has recently become the largest program. At year-end 2000, assets totalled $519.3 million. In this program, JWH allocates to its different strategies. It is a discretionary approach to the selection of JWH programs and the allocation of assets among the programs. The decisions are made by the investment policy committee. Any or all of the 11 JWH programs may be included in the strategic allocation program. The allocation of assets among the different programs as well as the selection of programs to be used is dynamic, changing at the discretion of the investment policy committee. Generally, the maximum allocation to an individual program does not exceed 25 percent of the assets in the account.

CAPACITY

Henry observes that the markets of today are so much bigger than the markets of 1985. In 1985, he didn't trade globally. Initially, he thought the capacity for global diversified would be $100 million, but today it is about $400 million to $500 million.

JWH does slippage studies to examine the impact of position-taking on markets the firm is participating in. JWH has seen the problem decrease over the past four to five years. (Slippage is basically the difference between the first price on any give trade and the average price for the entire execution of the position taken.) But Henry observes that size can also work to a manager's advantage. If you have contracts to sell, someone will usually step up and pay your price.

But because of JWH's size, certain markets are not traded, such as orange juice, palladium, or oats. His focus is mostly on the more liquid financial and currency markets.

Henry says most of the clients today are U.S.-based funds consisting primarily of retail clients. JWH's clients are the largest pool operators such as Merrill Lynch, Dean Witter, and Prudential. Non-U.S. clients come via the U.S. brokerage firms. He observes that some non-U.S. investors perceive JWH as a black box because the firm follows certain rules. He disagrees. "Trading is a philosophy, not a black box. The markets are people's expectations."

Henry provides investors with a monthly report explaining what happened fundamentally in each of the major markets. Specific positions and details are not provided.

INSTITUTIONALIZATION OF THE FIRM

Henry has succeeded more than the other superstar hedge fund managers in institutionalizing his firm. Semiretired (i.e., not running day-to-day affairs) since 1986, he has a group of over 60 people working for him. Unlike most of the other hedge fund managers interviewed, he is not a fundamental trader. Perhaps it is his mechanical, long-term trend follower approach that allows him to be somewhat removed.

He admits never enjoying running a company, but he enjoys the vast majority of people who have been involved with the company.

The firm is structured by functional groups—trading, research, information technology, investment support, compliance, investor services and marketing, corporate finance, administration, and human resources.

For those activities that require cross-company expertise to enhance decision making, committees are used. The most important one is the investment policy committee, which Henry chairs. This senior-level advisory group is broadly responsible for evaluating and overseeing trading policies. Issues related to implementation of JWH's investment process and its application to markets, including research on new markets and strategies, liquidity, position size, capacity, and performance cycles. Besides Henry, Verne Sedlacek and Mark Rzepczynski are investment committee members. Sedlacek, who is president and chief operating officer, is also responsible for day-to-day management. He had been the executive vice president and chief financial officer at Harvard Management Corp. before he joined JWH in 1998. Rzepczynski is senior vice president of research and trading.

While all the factors relating to both individual and group performance are taken into account in determining the reward system, the primary driving factor is the performance of the firm.

Until 2000, there had been an office in Westport, Connecticut, where administration, compliance, and marketing were headquartered. The decision was made, partially because the Westport lease was up and also due to lackluster futures markets, to consolidate the office with the main Boca Raton, Florida, office. The Boca Raton office is where Henry is located and where trading and research are done.

Henry says he really does not have a typical day. And in his role, few things have to be done on a daily basis. "Watching the markets is a great waste of time in this business if you're not actually involved in a trade. My curiosity keeps me at quote screens much too often. There is always a story being told somewhere in the world in our markets, and there is a certain fascination in watching events unfold pricewise." Despite this, Henry does not go to bed until the Japanese markets close at 2 A.M. eastern standard time.

Henry spends his time researching. And more often than not, the research focuses on stocks. He focuses on correlation coefficients and ways to balance the portfolio. "You can't research the Holy Grail. You can't fine-tune. The more you do, the less efficient you will be in the future."

Henry says his role today is like a parent watching a child grow up. The rules and procedures are written down, and he observes that they are followed. He may call up the trader and ask, "Are we doing this?" rather than saying, "Do this."

Henry hadn't thought about completely retiring and the company carrying on without him. He has no interest in selling because that would give him cash and he already has plenty. But technically, because it is a mechanical system, the company could be sold.

DEFENSIVE APPROACH TOWARD STOCKS

Henry feels there has been too much money in too few hands and that the unravelling of some of the large global macro managers may be good for market participants in general and managed futures traders in particular. "The markets should be engaged in price discovery, not knee-jerk reactions."

In Henry's view, Americans have an irrational attitude toward stocks today. Their expectations are based solely on the past five years, and if one thing is certain, he says, what made them money in the past five years will not in the next five years.

These attitudes do not affect the futures market—just the stock market. A roaring stock market (at the time of the interview) does have a minimal effect on what he does regarding interest rates and currencies.

Henry has been researching stocks for many years, but stocks have a low priority since JWH has done so well in the futures niche. Henry says the firm will introduce equity trading as a separate endeavor and will be a different type of stock investor/manager.

The new endeavor will apply what they've learned in the financial markets over the past 20 years to specific equity portfolios. Henry explains, "We will certainly specialize in defensive methodologies that do not have a bias to either the long or short side. Our focus will be on using our basic philosophy that you cannot predict anything and therefore trend following is the most prudent way to invest. We will invest in particular groupings of equities and have a much larger number of stocks in a portfolio than most managers. We will not try to predict which particular stocks or sectors are going to do well. We would rather evaluate select stocks over the long term based on their trends and volatility."

Henry believes the long-term benefits of stock ownership are not in picking certain stocks that will outperform the market. He believes that if you choose a large enough number of stocks based on their characteristics rather than promise, you can make long-term profits long and short in much the same way insurance companies make money by insuring a very large number of individuals. This will enable them to make money in up and down markets, but the primary benefit of their large-diversification nonpredictive approach will be to mitigate the effects of being long only the S&P 500, for example.

ANALYTICAL WHIZ

Born in Quincy, Illinois, in 1949, Henry spent most of his childhood in Forrest City, Arkansas, where his father owned some farms. When John was 25, his father died and he took over his family's 2,000-acre farm and taught himself hedging techniques. He began speculating in corn, wheat, and soybeans. He eventually became a commodity trading adviser. He started his firm in 1981 with headquarters in Newport Beach, California. The headquarters then moved to Connecticut in 1989. That year, Henry moved to Boca Raton. The Connecticut office closed in 2000.

He has been quoted as saying he has average intelligence and a knack for numbers.[2] Philosophy has always fascinated him. As a child, crunching batting and earned-run averages in his head became a skill that came in handy for futures trading. He attended several community colleges and took several night courses but never received a college degree. While he was attending but was not registered for a UCLA class taught by Harvey Brody, the two of them published a gamblers' system for beating the odds at blackjack.

Henry says he has an ability to read between the lines. Discerning which sets of information have relevance to the future is very difficult and requires an ability to see beyond the pure numbers. He gives the example of raw diamonds going up in price for 25 consecutive years from 1955 to 1980. In New York City, everyone believed diamond prices could not go down. Diamond traders stopped doing business to some extent because they were making so much money just on their inventory appreciation.

Similarly at this time, he says, he owned farmland in the Midwest. Everyone believed prices of farmland could never go down, and many of the farmers he knew believed they had to purchase land at prices and interest rates that made it impossible to make money. "In 1980, I researched the history of markets and saw these as classic signs from the heartland of America to the streets of Manhattan that in certain hard-money sectors, individuals believed the world had fundamentally changed to a new landscape. That's how humans react to long-term divergences. They begin to believe that what is happening now will go on forever. The fact is new landscapes emerge and they last longer than anyone can foresee, wiping out convergence traders. But they do not last forever. Another landscape emerges. That's why I'm a trend follower. Twenty years later diamonds are still roughly 80 percent cheaper than they were at that time. Farmland in the Midwest still does not sell for what it did when I sold my land in 1980."

Henry believes that no one can predict the future, and the world is very uncertain. Therefore, one must have a certain aptitude for determining which, if any, data has significance for investing. "The current thinking is that stocks have outperformed everything else for 200 years. That may have little relevance for the next 25 years. But there is no one in the year 2000 that you can convince to jettison the belief that 200 years of performance will not cause stocks to grow to the sky. Right now people believe in data that supports the inevitable growth in prices of stocks within a new landscape or new economy. What will be new to them is an inevitable bear market."

BEING THE BEST

Henry loves competitiveness. He says he is motivated by being the best at what he does. Yet he acknowledges that no one can be the best all the time. "I know the markets will ultimately decide that, but to see your ideas tested in the real world is energizing over the long term."

He says he could have managed his own money as a speculator, but he wanted a business and he wanted it as a profession. He also wanted a simple organization where the goal was best returns, not necessarily being the largest.

BASEBALL PASSION

In addition to his futures trading business, Henry owns a recording studio and has one in his house as well. During college, he played in a band as the bassist.[3]

Henry is also a big supporter of the Democratic Party. In addition to making large contributions, he hosted a dinner for President Clinton at his home in 1997.

But baseball is his passion. In October 1998, Henry bought the Florida Marlins from Wayne Huizenga for $150 million. He had owned a 1 percent share of the New York Yankees since 1991. Having been involved with the Yankees for almost a decade, he says he has seen upwards of 150 games per year.

Net Performance (%) Financial and Metals Program	
1984	9.90*
1985	20.70
1986	61.50
1987	252.40†
1988	4.00
1989	34.60
1990	83.60
1991	61.90
1992	−10.90
1993	46.80
1994	−5.30
1995	38.50
1996	29.70
1997	15.20
1998	7.20
1999	−18.70
2000	12.90
Compound average annual return	**29.33**

*Trading started in October 1984.
†The timing of additions and withdrawals materially inflated 1987 rates of return. The three accounts that were open in 1987 achieved rates of returns of 138 percent, 163 percent, and 259 percent.

"When you are in touch with the intricacies of baseball and its strategies, it is incredibly interesting. When you get in a rhythm with a team, each night is like a new chapter in an epic novel."

In 1989, he bought the West Palm Beach Tropics, a now defunct senior professional baseball team. He then bought half of the Class AAA Tucson Toros baseball team. Over the years, he tried unsuccessfully to buy a National Hockey League (NHL) hockey franchise in 1990, the Miami Dolphins in 1994, and the Miami Heat in 1998.

Do similarities exist between baseball and trading? Henry says being patient and looking to hit home runs pays much better than looking for singles.

JOHN HENRY
John W. Henry & Co.

Organization

Inception	1981
Assets	
Current	$1.2 billion
Peak	$2.4 billion
Edge	Analytical whiz; patience
Office Location	Boca Raton, Florida
Number of People	Over 60
Type of Organization	Functional organization
His Role	Research; guidance
Investment Committee	Yes
Reward System	Primary driving force is firm performance
Number of Investors	Not disclosed
Type of Investor	Primarily U.S.-based funds with retail investors
GP/Principals' Ownership of Assets	$35 to $75 million
Endowments	Not disclosed

Methodology/ Portfolio Composition

Style	Futures; long-term trend follower
Number of Positions in Portfolio	50
Trades Taken	Not disclosed
Role of United States	Not disclosed
Role of Technology	N/A
Role of Private Equity	N/A
Role of Macro	N/A
Allocates to Other Managers	No

Risk Management

Net Exposure	N/A
Hedging Technique	N/A
Maximum Leverage	3:1 to 6:1
Memorable Loss	1992
Risk Management	Adjust leverage

Background Information

Initial Spark	Farming, hedging background
Professional Background	Farming, hedging background
Education	Varied
Motivation/Satisfaction	Competitive, being the best
Age	51
Free Time	Music, politics, baseball

MARK KINGDON
Kingdon Capital Management

Global Equity Long/Short,
Willing to Wait for Opportunities/Not Always Invested

Mark Kingdon's office is located in Carnegie Hall Tower, between the Russian Tea Room and Carnegie Hall. His office, on the 50th floor, offers a panoramic view of Manhattan.

With assets under management now over $4.4 billion, Kingdon Capital Management is virtually closed to new investors. Kingdon will take new capital only to offset withdrawals. While this has been the policy for years, investors were just formally notified of this in May 2000. "Being the largest hedge fund manager is not important to us," says Kingdon, 51. Kingdon employees and families are the biggest investors.

He says the principals have virtually their entire financial net worth invested in the funds.

He has three goals—to earn a significant risk-adjusted rate of return, to create an enjoyable work environment, and to build an organization with lasting value.

"What motivates me first is my love for the business," Kingdon says. "I enjoy the investment game—the intellectual and emotional challenge it represents. I like winning, and it's even more fun when you share the experience with teammates. I feel a sense of responsibility to our investors who have entrusted us with their capital and the employees who have put their capital and careers on the line to work here. At this stage in my career, money is just a way of keeping score, and asset size is a potential concern, not a goal."

Kingdon is a global equity long/short hedge fund. "One reason we have historically emphasized equity investing [as opposed] to macro trading is that it is possible to be more informed than other investors on the outlook of a given company, while macro is more of a judgment call."

From January 1995 through December 1999, global equities exposure peaked at about 90 percent in July 1997. By year-end 1999, global equities were less than 50 percent. Over that five-year time frame, equities averaged 56 percent. Of that amount, 41 percent were U.S. equities and 15 percent non-U.S. equities.

Macro trading (i.e., interest rates, metals, and currency exposure) has averaged 10 percent of Kingdon's assets under management during the same time period. Macro trading peaked at a bit over 40 percent in July 1998. By year-end 1999, it was less than 5 percent.

Cash makes up the difference between equities and macro trading. Cash reserves, futures, options, and short sales are used to hedge market exposure.

ALLOCATIONS BASED ON VALUATIONS, FUNDAMENTALS, AND CHARTS

Valuations, trends in fundamentals, and technicals (such as sentiment measures) make up the cornerstone of Kingdon's trading methodology. They are applied to the broad market and to individual stocks.

In order of importance, valuation (both asset- and earnings-based), earnings momentum, and relative price momentum are the three important criteria for selection of stocks. Management quality, balance sheet strength, and market liquidity are also important. Stocks are sold if they reach targeted prices or there is a significant deterioration in the selection criteria. Kingdon recognizes that some of the best opportunities are in underfollowed securities. When buying a stock, generally his goal is to look for at least a 30 percent gross return. There are about 200 positions in the portfolio.

Kingdon says they do not attempt to optimize the portfolio in any formal sense. "While we agree with the merits of portfolio diversification, our goal is to find stocks and industries with the best risk/reward ratio around the world, not mimic the S&P 500 or some other index."

Liquidity is also quite important. The majority of the firm's holdings represent less than one day's trading volume.

Kingdon observes that charts are often misleading. They are used to time positions. "Charts are used differently today. Today we use them more to determine support and resistance rather than as a reliable reflection of strength and weakness of the companies themselves. They are just another tool. We view them more skeptically today because of the noise in the market."

The high-growth sector, which includes technology, telecommunications, Internet companies, and health care, has ranged from 10 percent to 45 percent of the net assets over the past year.

Kingdon has invested in private equity for more than six years. "Although the category represents under 5 percent of assets, it provides an early window on developing technologies and sometimes offers outstanding returns."

Does Kingdon allocate to other managers? He says under 3 percent of the assets are allocated to a dozen other hedge fund managers. "We do not charge our clients a fee on top of those managers who charge us 20 percent, so the investments are primarily for relationship purposes. We have identified a number of specialty fund managers whose ideas and information we find helpful in our own stock selection process."

For Kingdon, his edge is doing solid fundamental research and having a strong trading discipline. The keys are a strong global research–driven organization (22 portfolio managers and analysts plus five traders), extensive contacts on the Street, and a strong trading discipline.

TRADING RULES

Kingdon maintains several trading rules. The first is to cut losses. The second rule is not to forget rule one.

The third rule is to find out what the Street considers the critical variables for the security and its industry. Kingdon says to use every legal means to monitor these on a timely basis. Other rules are: Don't try to turn a losing trade into an investment. If you buy a stock for a reason that is no longer valid, sell it. If you're brave (and dumb) enough to buy a stock in a bear market, trade and/or hedge it. If a stock is fully valued relative to its growth rate, comparable companies, or interest rates, it is a sale candidate. If the company misses the upper quartile of Street estimates, sell it. A technical breakdown or 15 percent decline from cost is a sufficient reason to reverse the trade. No matter how much time or money you have invested in the stock, it owes you nothing.

"We think about the consequences of being wrong before we invest," Kingdon says. "We are very concerned about liquidity."

QUIET, INTENSE CULTURE

Quiet and intense, Kingdon frequently uses sports analogies as he speaks. "You can't play the same game as everyone else and wonder if it's the eighth inning or the ninth inning. If you're wrong, it's like a game of musical chairs [and someone will be left without a chair]. It's not a game of baseball." Is the game worth playing? Yes, if sufficient potential return exists and downside risk is manageable.

Kingdon does not use a lot of leverage. In fact, there has been virtually no leverage for 13 years. "I haven't seen circumstances that would warrant lots of leverage." He avoids the use of leverage to try to turn mediocre returns into good returns. "A bad return is a bad return. Using leverage is only going to leverage you on the downside."

Being long value and short technology or vice versa isn't a hedged portfolio. It doubles your risk.

Resilience is an important word for Kingdon. Resilience reflects how a manager reacts to adversity or client withdrawals. "It is about believing in yourself and not confusing a bull market with brilliance and a bear market with stupidity. . . . Markets are markets. You can't take it personally."

Kingdon has a compound average annual return of about 23 percent since trading began in 1983. In the 18 years, only two have been negative. In 1984, the firm was down 18.4 percent.

The year 1994 was also a slightly down year for Kingdon, with the fund down 2.2 percent. He says that was a difficult year in almost all of the markets the firm trades. An example of a recent loss? The firm lost money on the General Motors/Hughes Electronics arbitrage because "we trusted someone's well-meaning but misinformed advice as to the amount of shares GM would accept in its tender offer. We should not have let his high confidence level outweigh our skepticism that perhaps he did not know what he didn't know—an old lesson we have learned before and will probably learn again several times before retirement."

Despite this loss, Kingdon feels that many factors came together in 1999 for him, resulting in great returns from both an absolute and a relative viewpoint.

For Kingdon, the typical day starts as he arrives in his office at 7:30 A.M. A daily half-hour meeting starts at 8 A.M. The macro traders give a two-page summary of overnight/market news. The European trader then gives a summary of what happened with overnight trading. The in-house technician discusses what is breaking out on a momentum model. Then the meeting is opened to everyone to discuss significant events. They talk about what is relevant and determine strategy for the day.

During the rest of the day, Kingdon often sees companies in the portfolio or a prospective investment. He talks to economists and to money managers. He works with internal managers on ideas in the portfolio. "I focus on what is going on in the real world, not just Wall Street."

Kingdon Capital consists of 15 profit centers (made up of teams and individuals). Of these, 12 are industry groups and three are regions. In the total organization there are 50 people.

An investment committee exists, but it is Kingdon's area to determine how invested the firm will be. The investment committee consists of Kingdon; Richard Rieger, director of domestic equity research; and Peter Cobos, the chief financial officer. "We take a top-down and bottom-up approach . . . bottom-up because the analysts and specialists (industry and geography) meet formally every morning as well as informally during the day. If a great idea emerges, capital is always available."

Rieger and Kingdon are the senior portfolio managers. Kingdon says, "We actively manage the entire portfolio. When we come up with an idea we like, we give the appropriate portfolio manager the option of taking it on his P&L [profit and loss statement] or leaving it with us. We work closely with our portfolio managers to determine their best ideas, set target and stop-loss levels, and determine appropriate position sizes."

A corporate culture has been established and is maintained as every portfolio manager can veto a prospective employee before he or she is hired. "We hire people who have a quiet intensity—not screamers; who compete with the markets, not with each other; and who take responsibility for their positions. The portfolio managers have their names assigned to a stock, thus giving them profit and loss responsibility." Authority is shared; all positions are discussed with either himself or Rieger.

The reward system is based on the performance of each portfolio manager's positions plus a bonus pool for the entire firm based on that year's performance.

Kingdon gets a great deal of satisfaction from seeing individuals within the firm develop. For example, Rieger joined the firm in December 1992 as an experienced analyst with no portfolio management or administrative experience. Kingdon says he has developed into a superb portfolio manager who has mentored several outstanding analysts in the firm and is his right-hand man today.

Four funds are traded: three for U.S. high-net-worth individuals and one for non-U.S. citizens. Kingdon Associates and Kingdon Partners are for U.S. investors. Their investment policy is nearly identical except that Kingdon Partners, the fund managed for investment professions, may not buy hot new issues. Kingdon Offshore NV is not subject to U.S. income taxes on capital gains. The fourth fund, Kingdon Family Partnership, began trading on July 1, 1993. There are over 300 investors in total.

Kingdon says that endowment allocations have become a bigger part of their business. The offshore fund (where endowments fall) is the largest segment. Investors in the offshore fund (including all endowments, pension funds, and non-U.S. investors) are not generally subject to U.S. taxes. As a result, Kingdon does not try to be tax efficient. According to the 1999 NABUCO study, public records indicate that those endowments that allocate to Kingdon include Bowdoin College, Colby

College, SUNY-Stony Brook, Yeshiva University, and the University of the South. Other significant parts of the investor base are high-net-worth individuals and fund of funds entities.

On the issue of transparency, Kingdon says the firm provides weekly performance data, quarterly data outlining performance by region and asset class, as well as month-end summaries of invested positions and quarterly SEC filings on long positions.

Kingdon tells investors that they must find a manager with a style that works for them. "If you like a roller-coaster ride, go to a highly leveraged fund. If you like low volatility, look for a more value-oriented, less leveraged fund."

DEFINING MOMENTS

Kingdon started his firm in 1983 with $2 million in assets. He recalls that during the first six years of being in business, his philosophy was to make as much money as possible any way you can. His returns averaged about 35 percent per year. Performance was strong but there was considerable volatility. After five years, his assets had increased from $2 million to only $8 million.

He realized that he could only justify charging investors an incentive fee for low-volatility, consistent performance, and avoiding big swings. He abandoned the risky path for consistent performance, providing above-average returns with below-average risk. The investment objective became one of maximizing risk-adjusted total return.

In 1988, he realized there was no need to be fully invested unless he was very bullish on the markets (which was rare). By 1989, he had achieved global diversification and had a different attitude; a Zen element appeared. "Happiness ensues when it is not pursued—investing is the same thing. Success occurs when you are willing to wait for opportunities." He quoted pro basketball player Al Houston of the New York Knicks—"'Let the game come to you.' There are always opportunities—long, short, or arbitrage."

The year 1990 was Kingdon's most painful one, after big up years in 1988 and 1989. In 1990, Kingdon was bearish; the Fed tightened the money supply, and the market looked expensive to Kingdon. He was mostly in cash, only 1 percent invested. He was sitting still, waiting. "Sitting still is the hardest thing to do. As Pascal wrote, 'The hardest thing for man to do is sit quietly in a room.'" By year-end, Kingdon was up 20 percent for the year; it caused people to notice. "It indicates the importance of doing what you think is right, if you have sound reasons. If it is a minority view, all the better."

MOTIVATIONS/INFLUENCES

Kingdon says his interest in trading developed when he received two shares of stock for his bar mitzvah. He found the stock market fascinating. As a competitive child, he liked to win. During the summer of 1965 when he was 16 years old, he worked at Hayden Stone.

He graduated from Columbia College Phi Beta Kappa and then received an MBA from Harvard Business School.

His first job was at AT&T, at the pension fund administration group. In 1975, he joined Century Capital Associates, a hedge fund, where he stayed for eight years. Here he worked for Jim Harpel as an analyst, a portfolio manager, and then as a general partner.

As a trader who is guided by fundamentals and an investor who uses trading techniques, Kingdon has been inspired/influenced by everyone from Benjamin Graham to Jesse Livermore, and a lot of people in between. "Jim Harpel was a major influence. During the eight years I worked for him, Jim taught me the importance of spending your time and capital where it can do the most good—by focusing on large potential return ideas and cutting losses."

Kingdon sees his New York location as a big plus. "Every IPO and secondary road show goes through here, and we are able to arrange one-on-one meetings with almost anyone we want to see. New York has more industry conferences, securities analysts, and money managers than anywhere else. The free flow of ideas outweighs the dangers of groupthink. The excitement and pace of the city, which has gotten cleaner and safer under Mayor Guiliani, is also a positive in attracting bright, energetic people to our company." In the future, Kingdon may consider adding small satellite offices in Silicon Valley, London, and Tokyo, but right now New York is the firm's only office.

Kingdon leads a balanced life. In his spare time, he studies tae kwan do (Korean karate); he is a third-degree black belt. He has been attending tae kwan do classes two or three times a week for the past 19 years.

He says this keeps him in shape mentally and physically, and it is fun. He also plays golf and travels with his family.

INDUSTRY OUTLOOK

Is there a new-generation versus old-generation hedge fund manager? Not really. Kingdon's view is that some things never change. "There were crazy hedge fund managers who blew up in the 1968–1974 bear market by using leverage and illiquid securities, and we'll see that again during the next bear market. The large hedge fund managers who recently retired did so after long, successful careers and should be admired for their achievements, not pilloried for their mistakes."

Net Performance [%] Kingdon Capital Management	
1983	44.70*
1984	−18.40
1985	101.60
1986	5.20
1987	0.00
1988	23.60
1989	50.10
1990	20.00
1991	41.40
1992	22.50
1993	38.30
1994	−2.20
1995	31.10
1996	15.40
1997	28.10
1998	7.00
1999	37.40
2000	11.60
Compound average annual return	**22.99**

*Trading started April 7, 1983.

Kingdon is concerned that many of the most successful mutual fund managers bought the "best" names regardless of price and have created a daisy chain that guarantees mediocre future returns.

Kingdon feels that over the past several years, day traders have moved the market as they jump on a move. He makes a distinction between day traders trading in parallel versus managers trading in series. Trading in parallel describes trading in the same direction as the market (i.e., buying strength and selling weakness.) Trading in series is the opposite—buying dips and selling rallies.

Day traders have caused managers to look more skeptically than ever at the message given by the market, observes Kingdon. "False, violent moves that are soon reversed occur more frequently and have created opportunities for us to be on the other side of the trade."

MARK KINGDON
Kingdon Capital Management

Organization

Inception	1983
Assets	
Current	$4.4 billion
Peak	$4.4 billion
Edge	Fundamental research; patience; sell discipline
Office Location	New York, New York
Number of People	50
Type of Organization	15 profit centers
His Role	Allocator, determining how much is invested, senior portfolio manager
Investment Committee	Yes
Reward System	Based on performance of each portfolio manager's positions plus bonus pool for entire firm based on that year's performance
Number of Investors	300
Type of Investor	Endowments are a growing part; high net worth and fund of funds are significant
GP/Principals' Ownership of Assets	Substantially all financial net worth
Endowments (Source: 1999 NACUBO)	University of the South Colby College State University of New York—Stony Brook Yeshiva University Bowdoin College

Methodology/ Portfolio Composition

Style	Global equity long/short; top-down, bottom-up

Number of Positions in Portfolio	Over 200
Trades Taken	Potential gross return of 30 percent
Role of United States	50 to 65 percent
Role of Technology	10 to 45 percent
Role of Private Equity	Less than 5 percent; provides window on diversifying returns and enhances returns
Role of Macro	Less than 5 percent
Allocates to Other Managers	Yes, under 3 percent of assets to 12 hedge fund managers

Risk Management

Net Exposure	58 percent
Hedging Technique	Cash, futures, options, shorting stock
Maximum Leverage	None used for past 13 years
Memorable Loss	General Motors/Hughes Electronics experience
Risk Management	Cut losses, don't try to turn a losing trade into an investment, sell if stop or target hit or fundamentals deteriorate; review positions if technicals break down

Background Information

Initial Spark	Bar Mitzvah
Professional Background	Pension plan; another hedge fund
Education	Columbia College, Harvard Business School
Motivation/Satisfaction	Intellectual/emotional challenge/see people grow
Age	51
Free Time	Family, golf, tae kwon do, yoga

10

BRUCE KOVNER
Caxton Corporation

Fundamental/Macro
Adapting to Survive and Creating Structures

Sitting in front of a wall-sized map of the world and surrounded by several computer screens in his New York City office, Bruce Kovner, 55, founder and chairman of Caxton Corporation, views himself as sitting in the cockpit of a plane, managing an enormous amount of information flowing in from around the globe. Kovner will trade anything that is liquid. Among the things he trades are currencies, fixed income, equities, indexes, commodities, and derivatives. "I trade world financial markets, all asset classes."

Kovner also has a photograph of one of his three oil tankers hanging on the wall. He first started purchasing tankers in 1987. They are not part of the funds but provide another source of information flow and intelligence.

Founded in April 1983 with assets of $7.6 million, Caxton Corporation now has assets of $4.5 billion. There are three hedge funds—Essex, GAMut, and Caxton Global—and a few small stock funds. Caxton Iseman Capital does private equity deals. (Caxton provides a home and capital for Fred Iseman.) A small percentage of assets of Caxton Global can be allocated to less liquid deals such as private equity.

Caxton Corporation consists of 160 to 170 people, of which about half are in the New York City office. Kovner sees New York City as a big plus. "You can see and talk to all kinds of people, government officials, scholars, economists. It is the world capital . . . I wouldn't want to be anywhere else." The Plainsboro, New Jersey, office serves as the back office and research center.

Kovner's goal is absolute return. With assets under management at $4.5 billion and assets at their peak, Kovner says, "I don't want to grow faster than capacity." He will allow money in if the firm is within liquidity limits of its capacity. Once liquidity limits are reached, he sends money back. For example, in June 1995 with assets at $1.8 billion, Kovner returned two-thirds to investors in order to improve performance. At the time, he said in a press release, "Under current market conditions, roughly $2 billion in trading capital is proving unwieldy. I think that a smaller capital base will help us return to our historically high profitability. . . . The lower liquidity in currency, fixed income, and commodity markets hurt our performance as our funds grew larger. In addition, I think Caxton has gotten too big and bureaucratic. This downsizing will help us respond in a more focused and agile manner." Kovner expects to pay out dividends from time to time so as not to grow faster than capacity.

Caxton principals' assets vary as a percentage of the total, and are currently under 30 percent of the assets.

DIVERSIFICATION WITH 27 TRADING CENTERS

Kovner describes Caxton's approach as top-down. "We make a judgment on what the world is like. Then we ask, given that the world is like this, where are the opportunities? Some periods are great for stocks; other periods are great for commodities." Kovner observes the environment and tries to develop a strategy to take advantage of that environment. He tries to identify the different styles, elements, and configurations of the economy—inflation/recession, low interest rates/high interest rates—and politics.

Kovner trades what is uncorrelated to the stock market. "The rule is to try hard to have uncorrelated strategies." He believes this is one of his edges since other managers may not do this carefully. Many analytics are used to measure noncorrelation of markets and trades under a number of varying conditions—even conditions that don't exist today.

For Kovner, diversification is more than just a platitude; it is a way of life. "The objective is to trade any political or economic environment well. One defining characteristic is that we want to seize opportunities in many markets. We try to keep the portfolios balanced so if we are wrong or if an exogenous event occurs, we don't pay such a high price." He doesn't risk more than 2 percent of the fund's equity on one idea.

Kovner does not want to be committed to any one approach. He doesn't want to be among those players who say, "The market is wrong or doing something it shouldn't be doing," or "I'm unsympathetic to the market/events." Rather, he wants a diverse, robust group of income streams that are uncorrelated to help control risk and correlation.

As a result, Kovner has 27 trading centers that provide this diversification. While the teams range in size from two to ten people, they are usually two to three people. Some represent regions; others represent trading strategies such as macro, equity, arbitrage, or quantitative techniques. Each trading center is strong on its own and not highly correlated to the others.

"With this structure, we are able to take advantage of different environments and we are not excessively at risk by relying on one style," Kovner explains. "The key is to constantly adapt and find the strategy that works."

He says, "It is wrong to assume [a specific] environment will continue forever." For example, he notes that value investing is not good now (May 2000) due to money flows. But at some time, value investing will again become good. He finds it useful to develop signposts that mark when an environment is ending. Examples of such signposts? While none are foolproof, one good example is a high degree of consensus, which tends to create opportunity in the other direction.

To those that predict the demise of global macro, Kovner disagrees and says such predictions usually occur at the end of popularity cycles. "You need to avoid crowd judgment." When business cycles swing (e.g., the Fed chomps down or central banks are active), big shifts are created. In periods of instability, global macro will make lots of money. Kovner says now that there is higher stability and regular currency movement, it is a great period for other styles. "Our structure allows us the opportunity to focus and choose the trading style that is most appropriate for the period. . . . Global macro will be back."

Currently, global macro accounts for 25 to 30 percent of the portfolio. Though this amount varies based on the period, it is a smaller percentage than it had previously been. The typical allocation is more in the range of 30 to 60 percent. "Over the past 24 to 30 months, rewards from global macro have been low. So risk attached to it is low."

Today, Kovner sees many opportunities. "The hard part is balancing those risks. Every asset class is in disequilibrium—currencies, fixed income, commodities, and stocks." Kovner says that many investors ask whether the European currency consolidation has eliminated currency trading opportunities. "There are so many more opportunities than before. Some currencies have been lost [with the advent of the euro], but more currencies can be traded now such as those in Eastern Europe. And as the financial markets develop, more tools exist. In the 1970s when I began trading, there were only T-bills and GNMAs; today there are over-the-counter structures. As the financial markets develop, there are so many more tools to express a view. There are hundreds of instruments now."

Kovner does not like to be publicly quoted on market direction because he doesn't want to be perceived as a market guru. He also needs the flexibility to change his mind—without encumbrances—in the event he has to.

In 2000, Caxton's Essex fund was up 33.4 percent. Kovner says, "Caxton's diversified portfolio worked about the way we had hoped. Macro was poor in the first half, excellent in the second; equities strong in the first half and okay in the second. Our absolute return and quant strategies worked well throughout the year."

Kovner spends most of his time developing strategy, risk control, and risk allocation. "Most people don't know that I am not the principal trader. I get other people to trade well and allocate resources to them. I develop structures that do it well. I pay attention to how you grow it [the business] and make structures that work." Kovner believes that by developing different strategies, a manager can grow the size of the fund. Each strategy can handle X amount; add them up and you can continue to grow until you hit a limit.

"My goal is to develop a company that works without me in 10 years, or doesn't have a lot of input from me," says Kovner.

INFORMATION TECHNOLOGY

Kovner says that his total long exposure to the stock market has always been low. Currently, it is about 17 percent, which is historically low. This reflects a moderate bearish view on the equity environment. Technology is only a very minor percentage of the total portfolio.

"Some managers get sucked into trading what they shouldn't. . . . They tend to be momentum traders. Some managers move to where the action is. They got into Nasdaq, a big roller coaster. For example, while it may be easy to get into technology, it may be difficult to get out. It is difficult to cope with the volatility."

Nevertheless, technology is important to Kovner. Technology is needed to gather information globally. "It is hard to handle [all the information flow] without information technology," he says. This may be one of the defining success factors between the old generation and the new generation of hedge fund managers.

He suggests that some of the older hedge fund managers may not have wanted to learn new technologies—which may lead to their demise or put obstacles in their way of surviving. "The survivors will be those who are able to adapt to new markets, adapt to information technology, and instill rigorous risk control."

INTELLECTUAL HONESTY

Kovner says that Ed Banfield, his academic mentor at Harvard University, has been the biggest influence on his life. "He was an intellectual leader of the New York conservative movement; really he was a complete iconoclast. . . . I learned intellectual honesty from him. There are lots of things you don't know. You've got to be aware of that. Be honest about what you don't know. . . . I never thought I could do as well as he [Banfield], so I moved [out of academia to this area]."

In applying this philosophy to trading, Kovner says it is not so much about being right all the time but rather being able to adapt and find a strategy that works. "I am wrong a lot. While the analogy may be pushing it, you can think of a painter painting many brush strokes. He can be wrong a lot; no one stroke is right or wrong. We are constantly painting a picture."

Kovner says they have losses all the time because they are testing ideas in the marketplace. The implications are minor; a loss tells you that something isn't right now. But if the losses are larger than predicted or expected, those losses have to be examined. Why? What happened? What was wrong with the analysis? Kovner is most concerned when risk levels are exceeded. The teams are given maximum risk levels and they can trade within acceptable risk levels.

RISK CONTROL, RISK CONTROL, RISK CONTROL

When asked what his edge as a manager is, Kovner acknowledged that it is a "complex game we are in and the edges are subtle . . . . In real estate, the key is location, location, location. With money management, the key is risk control, risk control, risk control." He spends considerable time and resources on understanding and managing risk. Kovner says that unlike other hedge fund managers, he usually takes smaller positions. "We don't like to see big volatility in the fund. We have seen volatility steadily lessen in the last five years as we understand risk better. It is probably half what it was five years ago."

While Kovner uses leverage, it is used cautiously. If leverage is a feature of hedge funds, leverage magnifies the mistakes as well as the benefits. There are plenty of ways to get returns but there are plenty of ways to lose it, too, says Kovner.

Kovner notes it is difficult to measure how much leverage he uses. He acknowledges that the term "leverage" creates lots of confusion. "We measure risk precisely every day. We do lots of analysis on risk. The term 'leverage' doesn't specify risk."

Caxton has a department that focuses on risk management, and risk is measured in many different ways. Considerable stress testing is done on the portfolio every day. That is, what happens if there is a big shift in stocks? What if interest rates change or a political crisis occurs? While Value-at-Risk (VaR) is measured every day and the numbers are very low because the portfolio is balanced with short and longs, Kovner feels VaR isn't good at capturing basis risk. "We've developed techniques to understand risk outside VaR."

Kovner acknowledges that market volatility can be both a friend and an enemy. Day traders have had an impact on market volatility as well. But generally Kovner finds market volatility is an opportunity. "We've learned how to take advantage of volatility—not let it hurt us." Kovner feels this is another edge—something that other managers may not have been able to solve as well as Caxton has.

Kovner feels that many of the long stock traders that call themselves hedge fund managers will eventually go through a shakeout in the inevitable bear stock market because they don't have adequate risk control.

PERSONAL SATISFACTION

Kovner did considerable economic analysis in his undergraduate and graduate days at Harvard University and a good amount of political work. From 1968 until 1970, he was a teaching fellow at Harvard. He had articles published in *Commentary*, *The Public Interest*, and *New York* magazine.

From 1970 until he joined Commodities Corp. in 1978, Kovner did consulting work on public policy questions for the likes of the U.S. Congress, the National Science Foundation, the University of Pennsylvania, Harvard University, and the State of New York. Eventually he gave up academic life. Sitting in a room writing articles was not for him. It bothered him that he didn't know if he was right or wrong—there was no feedback.

Kovner feels his career has been a natural progression. "I love what I do. I'm in the cockpit managing information, coming in from all over the world. . . . I can hire people who help me understand it. I have friends and associates all over the world in every major financial capital. How many people are willing to take calls at 3 A.M.?" Creating a community of people who are smart and whom he can talk to gives him a great deal of personal satisfaction.

Kovner also gets satisfaction in developing new strategies. The process motivates him and he finds the intellectual work interesting. "It is fun to figure things out. The markets are like puzzles. If you're right, the market tells you and you are rewarded financially. I get a sense of accomplishment when I get it right. This is interesting and satisfying."

MOST MEMORABLE TRADING PERIODS

Kovner borrowed $3,000 on his MasterCard in early 1977 and began trading on his own. He made $1,000 on his first two trades—copper and interest rate futures.[1]

Kovner says his earlier trading experiences were the most memorable. The first time he lost control of the trading process was in the soybean market. "It is seared into my memory."[2] A shortage developed in soybeans, running his $4,000 position up to $45,000 in six weeks. "In a moment of insanity, I discarded a hedge limiting losses if prices turned down, which they did." In a panic, he liquidated his position, escaping with a loss of $23,000. Yet he still had $22,000, five times what he started with.[3] "I had a huge gain but lost half before getting out. . . . I lost half the profit in an hour. I closed out the trade and was physically sick for a week. In retrospect that was a very good thing," says Kovner. "It helped me understand risk and create structures to control risk."

Other memorable periods? During the 1987 crash, Kovner recalls how the markets were disoriented in unison for 72 hours. He remembers watching each market after another cascade all around the world; they were limit-down and there were no bids in sight.

The year 1987 turned out to be one of his best, with a net return of almost 100 percent. The gain was mostly in currencies. "I made lots of profits in currencies and fixed income . . . I made profits on light short stocks. The volatility was horrendous . . . I made millions on small short stock positions but made hundreds of millions of dollars in currencies and fixed income."

INSTITUTIONAL INTEREST

Kovner sits on many endowment committees. He observes how the role of bonds is now being questioned by endowments and other institutions. Because bonds have generated very low returns and many institutions allocated about 30 percent of their portfolios to them, the institutions are getting something like a 3 to 4 percent rate of return. After inflation, fixed income return is very low. As a result, some of the institutions are lowering their fixed income allocation. Where are they putting it? Equities have peaked, so the search is on for diversification. Therefore there is demand for top-quality alternatives.

Kovner feels that institutions now have a higher sophistication level on portfolio theory and alternative investments. "There is an increasing perception of absolute return investments (i.e., those investments that are not correlated to the S&P)—that these are a good thing to have . . . Over the next 10 years, their perception will grow that it is good to have investments uncorrelated to the S&P that can also do well when the S&P does well or does not do well—inverse correlation." These investments will provide relatively stable returns with a high Sharpe ratio and low standard deviation. Kovner expects that those investment vehicles with low correlation to the S&P and a high-quality rate of return will see demand grow over the next 10 years and see cash flow into them from institutions.

MUSIC, EDUCATION, AND RARE BOOK COLLECTING

Kovner is quite enthusiastic about his activities outside work as well. He is very much into music. Even though he says he is a bad piano player, he plays every day. He is active with the Juilliard School—to play music as well as to listen.

Education reform is a second passion. In 1996, he set up a foundation with $6 million for school reform. The School Choice Scholarship Foundation gives scholarships to poverty-level students in New York City, in first through sixth grade, to go to private school. Vouchers are offered to 1,300 children, paying up to $1,400

Net Performance (%) Essex Limited	
1985	17.33*
1986	56.16
1987	92.76
1988	−0.85
1989	54.53
1990	39.43
1991	23.28
1992	22.89
1993	40.41
1994	−2.19
1995	16.24
1996	21.30
1997	36.99
1998	17.16
1999	24.43
2000	33.40
Compound average annual return	**29.02**

*Trading started September 1, 1985.

per year for three years. Vouchers give parents the financial where-withal to opt out of designated public schools and put their kids in private schools of their choosing.[4]

Rare book collecting is also a passion. Caxton—the name of his firm—was taken from William Caxton, the first printer in England. In fact, at the end of our interview, Kovner proudly showed me a new Bible that has been illustrated by Barry Moser—a designer, printmaker, illustrator, and engraver. Released in October 1999, it is the only Bible illustrated by a single artist in the twentieth century. It has 250 illustrations and took Moser four years to complete. The Pennyroyal Caxton Press edition of the Holy Bible is a two-volume rendering of the King James Version of the Bible. There are only 400 copies of the limited letterpress edition printed, and each costs $10,000. (There is also a Viking Studio trade edition priced at $65.) True to form, Kovner said, "I put the structure together for it." He underwrote the $2 million cost of producing the Bible.[5]

BRUCE KOVNER
Caxton Corporation

Organization

Inception	1983
Assets	
Current	$4.5 billion
Peak	$4.5 billion
Edge	Trades what is uncorrelated to stock market; risk management
Office Location	New York, New York; Plainsboro, New Jersey
Number of People	160 to 170
Type of Organization	27 trading centers
His Role	Overseer
Investment Committee	No
Reward System	Individual performance is heavily weighted but group performance is also given some weight
Number of Investors	500 to 600
GP/Principals' Ownership of Assets	Under 30 percent
Endowments	Not disclosed

Methodology/ Portfolio Composition

Style	Top-down; macro
Number of Positions in Portfolio	Thousands
Trades Taken	Diverse
Role of United States	Variable
Role of Technology	Variable but usually modest
Role of Private Equity	Minor
Role of Macro	30 to 60 percent (typical range)
Allocates to Other Managers	Minor on a limited basis

Risk Management

Net Exposure	10 to 25 percent (typical)
Hedging Technique	Diversified portfolio, noncorrelated
Maximum Leverage	Varies
Memorable Loss	Everyday experience
Risk Management	Maximum 2 percent risked per idea; takes small positions; uses leverage cautiously; stress tests portfolio

Background Information

Initial Spark	Postgraduate school; sees opportunities in futures markets
Professional Background	Academic, politics
Education	Harvard University
Motivation/Satisfaction	Challenge/community of smart people
Age	55
Free Time	Books, music, educational reform

11

DANIEL OCH
Och-Ziff Capital Management

Merger Arbitrage/Event-Driven Investing
Low Volatility with Consistent Positive Performance

After working at Goldman Sachs for 11 years in the risk arbitrage department and heading proprietary trading and the U.S. equities department, Dan Och left in February 1994 to found Och-Ziff Capital Management in partnership with Ziff Brothers Investments. He had an arrangement with Ziff Brothers in which Ziff would commit capital for a multiyear period and in exchange Och committed not to run money for others. This arrangement allowed Och to build the business slowly and steadily. As planned, this arrangement ended on December 31, 1997, but the Ziff family remains a significant investor. There are now about 170 investors with total assets of $3 billion. Assets are at their highest level.

Undoubtedly Goldman Sachs has had an influence on Och's business structure and style. Och said among the many things he learned at Goldman was how to invest, how to hire, how to build a business, and how to think.

Och listed Robert Rubin, his first boss, as a significant influence. He declined to name others because he might leave someone out. It was obvious that he was a big admirer of Teddy Roosevelt. An Andy Warhol silkscreen of Roosevelt hangs prominently in his office. Och's modification of "Speak softly and carry a big stick" is "Do what you think is right for the long term rather than what is popular thinking."

FOUR DISCIPLINES

The investment methodology is event-driven investing. There are four major disciplines: merger arbitrage, convertible arbitrage, event-driven restructuring; and distressed credits. The distressed credits strategy was added in August 1999; the other three disciplines are original strategies of the firm. Och said the decision was made to build the distressed credit business unit in October 1998. It was a great time since Wall Street was cutting back in the area. Over the ensuing period, he has hired six professionals. "We have built the unit well in advance of the opportunity."

Generally 40 to 50 percent of the portfolio is in merger arbitrage; this equates to 50 to 60 positions. Merger arbitrage deals—mergers, tender offers, proxy contests, rights offerings, exchange offers, and leveraged buyouts—include only those that have been publicly announced. Examples of positions in this area include MediaOne Group, which was acquired by AT&T, and Mannesman, which merged with Vodaphone.

Another 20 to 30 percent is in convertible arbitrage (about 50 positions). The convertible arbitrage part of the business takes a mathematical approach combining hedging of warrants and other derivatives with market experience. Fixed income and currency exposures are fully hedged.

The remainder of the portfolio is made up of equity restructurings and distressed credits—about 20 restructuring positions and 20 credit positions.

The equity restructuring unit, which had been downplayed for the past two years, is now growing due to fundamentals creating new opportunities. Many instances exist where publicly traded subsidiaries have become more valuable than their parents. One can buy the parent for less than the value of its holding in the subsidiary. Boards are therefore taking corporate action. Examples include General Motors spinning off GM Hughes and Bell Canada spinning off Nortel.

The distressed credit unit is different from the other disciplines regarding liquidity, duration of investment, and potential mark-to-market loss. The special situations part of the business includes spin-offs, split-offs, liquidations, recapitalizations, reorganizations, divestitures, and share class discrepancies. Market exposure here is fully hedged.

"It is a very diversified portfolio," says Och. Opportunities determine portfolio composition; there is no predetermined commitment to a given investment discipline.

EUROPEAN COMPONENT

Currently, about 25 percent of the overall portfolio focuses on Europe. Four years ago, when the firm didn't have an office in London, that percentage was quite small. Now that 25 percent is fairly constant. The London office, which opened in August 1999, has been critical in the diversification of the portfolio. Having an office in Europe has been essential to Och-Ziff's ability to analyze and invest in European deals.

Of the merger arbitrage portfolio, about 35 percent is invested in European arbitrage and 65 percent in the United States. The U.S. team has seven analysts and the European team has four.

In convertible arbitrage, new opportunities are being found globally. The majority of the convertible portfolio is comprised of Western European and Japanese bonds.

BOTTOM-UP DECISION MAKING

The firm is research-driven with bottom-up decision making. Qualitative and quantitative analysis are used. Och emphasizes that while sophisticated analytics and tools are used, all decision making is done by people. Quantitative aspects are used to hedge equity currency and interest rate exposure. The firm focuses on specific assignment of responsibility for all positions and exposures; portfolio diversification; monitoring of industry exposure; and risk analysis, including embedded optionality.

Qualitative aspects include the focus on permanent loss of capital and the experience in managing risk.

In deciding which positions to take, risk-adjusted returns are key. "We focus on the risk component," says Och. "We avoid positions which have an explicit or implicit correlation to the market."

FOCUSED MANDATE

Och is very clear on what the investment mandate of the firm is: to provide consistent positive absolute returns in the mid-teens. These returns will be neither correlated with nor dependent on the stock market, and will have low volatility. Another goal is not to lose money. Och makes the distinction between quantitative low risk and qualitative low risk, and he feels his firm has both. This means that in addition to very low risk as measured statistically, such as low correlation, low volatility, and high Sharpe ratio, the firm must also have low risk of permanent loss of capital.

Och says Och-Ziff's edge is that the disciplines are designed to fit the mandate, and he believes they have the best team in the world. "The individual business units are among the best at what they do. The team is stronger than the components." Och discusses the interaction that occurs between the business units such as cross-border mergers or debt for equity swaps on distressed convertible bonds. The introduction of the London office has helped reinforce this strength.

Och notes that in six years the firm has lost only one professional person. People are key to the organization's success. "The story at this firm is not about me. We have a strong and deep team which has been together for many years. All of our professionals are integrated into the decision-making process. This is not a one-man show."

The firm is able to focus on more unusual and complex securities where its hedging and analytical capabilities create a competitive advantage. As the world becomes more integrated and more complex, the combination of Och-Ziff's diversified business units with its team approach becomes even more powerful.

NOT CORRELATED TO EQUITIES

Och says the firm has produced consistent returns in this area with little market correlation because non-event–related risks are hedged and the portfolio is diversified. Furthermore, the firm has expertise in legal, regulatory, and accounting analysis.

Och has learned that investing in noncorrelated strategies requires more than a statistical analysis. One example he gives is cash tender offers for companies. Historical statistics indicate noncorrelation. However, with the 1987 crash, a noncorrelation relationship to the stock market went to a multiple correlation when stocks fell 50 to 70 percent. As a result of that experience, Och limits the percentage of the portfolio that is in cash deals. He also limits the risk from any one position in the portfolio to 1 percent of the equity. Except in convertible arbitrage where leverage is 3:1, which is low relative to his peers, Och does not use leverage.

Och says the firm is also good at reducing allocations quickly if a situation becomes unattractive. This may occur when spreads get tight. In contrast, other firms may use such a situation to leverage. This is what caused the bloodbath in 1998, he says. Because Och wants the ability to change his mind if a situation changes, liquidity of positions is always taken into account.

Net exposure to the stock market is usually less than 10 percent.

LEADER OF THE BUSINESS UNITS

There are about 50 people in the firm, located in both London and New York. The New York City headquarters overlooks Central Park from the 39th floor of a building on 57th Street.

The firm has 17 analysts and seven traders. There are six people in information management whose job it is to monitor 85 news services, contact companies with which the firm is involved, as well as monitor the Internet.

Information technology—information flow and information management—is critical at Och-Ziff. Four in-house people focus on information technology on a full-time basis. On the front end, information technology is used for the traders, analysts, and portfolio managers. In the back office, technology is harnessed for position and portfolio monitoring, and tracking exposure on a real-time basis.

In addition to the four business units, there is a financial controls group business unit that develops systems; monitors positions and exposure; maintains relationships with prime brokers, banks, accountants, and legal specialists; monitors counter party risk; provides internal checks and balances; provides external controls (written confirmation on all corporate reorganization activity, next-day confirmations on all international trades); and conducts exposure analysis with prime brokers and daily reconciliations of positions, market value, and cash balances. This unit has 18 members, including the chief financial officer.

As managing member, Och is responsible for everything yet he knows how to delegate. He is very involved in portfolio decisions and is focused on the investment process. He leads the arbitrage/restructuring unit and is part of their daily meeting as well as that of the European group. While he is not part of the daily meetings of the convertible/distressed group, he is part of the process before any positions of size are put on.

Och's typical day starts on the way to the office when he speaks to the London office. At 8:15 A.M., the morning meeting begins and lasts until about 9:30. During the day, he is in constant touch with London, the analysts, and the traders.

Och focuses on the capacity issue as well. He looks at the firm's capabilities, its business units, depth of these business units, and the ability to get the team to work together. He plans for maximum capability and capacity. A recent example was the adding of the distressed credit unit.

As the business grows and becomes more complex and global, Och sees a bifurcation taking place. The available universe for Och-Ziff is different from that of other companies. "They can't compete with us. Take, for example, cross-border situations and distressed convertibles. As the business becomes more complex, a bifurcation is taking place."

Going forward, is there an area the firm may focus on more? So far, Och has not invested much in Asia because trades are usually directional or involve a credit bet or sovereign credit. Within the next five years, he feels true event-driven arbitrage and restructuring opportunities will become more available in Asia.

Technology positions in the portfolio are not a large percentage. There is no intentional underweighting or overweighting.

Och does not invest in private equity. He also does not allocate to other hedge fund managers.

There are seven partners in the firm including Ziff Brothers Investments. All of the business heads as well as the chief financial officer are partners. Och says about 80 percent of his net worth is in the firm and for the others it is also a substantial part.

The culture is one of teamwork where the whole is bigger than the component parts. While individuality exists—the people are excellent at what they do and may have strong personalities—they are part of the team culture. This culture carries through to the back office and control groups as well. The reward system is based on the profits of the overall firm, not on each of the four individual units. By giving people unlimited growth, it helps keep them and helps develop the next line of talent, says Och.

1994 AND 1998

The best environment for Och-Ziff is when there are many events such as mergers.

What is unusual about Och's track record is that in the seven years traded, there have been no down years and only four down months. The largest of those was a 3.2 percent decline in August 1998. Unlike most other hedge fund managers, Och generated positive returns in 1994 and 1998 of over 28 percent and 11 percent respectively. The firm has a negative correlation with declines in the S&P 500.

There is very little volatility in the track record. Downside risk is controlled by having a diversified portfolio, being truly hedged, and being noncorrelated to the stock market.

Using an arbitrage strategy has permitted consistent performance. Och believes that institutions want a clearly delineated investment strategy and business plan executed with consistency.

Despite this low volatility and consistent performance, Och says there have been many defining moments. For example, 1994 was a tough year. In the summer of 1996, there was a small-cap meltdown. In 1997, there was the blowup of the Office Depot–Staples and MCI British Telecommunications merger. "One of our most important goals is to preserve capital and not lose money during these difficult environments."

INVESTOR BASE

Investors in Och-Ziff make a two-year commitment. This has helped create a stable investor base and also ensures high-quality, committed investors.

Och observes that investors in hedge funds have changed over the years from the individual who wants returns to the institution that uses asset allocation for its decision making and wants excellence. Och-Ziff's investor base has always been institutional. This has solidified the firm's disciplined focus on its business mandate. According to the NACUBO 1999 annual survey, endowment clients include Amherst College, Carnegie Mellon University, Colgate University, Middlebury College, University of Michigan, and Yeshiva University. Fund of funds entities are not a large part of the investor base.

Following 1998, a bad year for hedge funds in general, Och observes that investors are not asking for any different information. "Because we delivered what was expected and have always been clear about what we do and don't do, investors are not so concerned about transparency."

Och provides his investors with a quarterly letter that lists the top positive contributors and negative contributors to performance as well as the basis points they added or took away. He also provides information on portfolio allocation and sizable positions. He is always available to meet with investors.

There are three funds. Each has a U.S. limited partnership and an offshore corporation. The OZ Master Fund is the multistrategy global fund. In addition, the firm offers two dedicated funds, OZ Europe, which focuses exclusively on European arbitrage, and O&F Credit Opportunities Fund, which focuses on distressed credits. All funds charge 1.5 percent management fees and 20 percent incentive fees. The minimum investments range from $5 million to $10 million. There is a two-year lock-up of capital.

MOTIVATION

Och originally had been a chemistry major at the University of Pennsylvania. But after his freshman year, he transferred to Wharton where his interest in finance was encouraged.

His first full-time job was at Goldman Sachs in the risk arbitrage department; he was there 11 years. Och left Goldman Sachs so he could build his own firm. As people go up the corporate ladder at Goldman, he says, they are moved from investing toward management. He wanted to focus on investing.

His motivation is to have the best firm in the world. He expects that the firm will outlast his involvement there. He points out that in five years, there will be eight senior people who've been with him for 10 years. "This is a by-product of how we run the business rather than an end goal."

Och emphasizes that he leads a very balanced life. He enjoys skiing, golfing, and other outdoor activities. He is also involved in a few charities. He is chairman of the Wall Street division of United Jewish Appeal (UJA) and is on the board of City Harvest. Facing History in Ourselves is another project he spends time on.

Net Performance (%) Och-Ziff Capital Management	
1994	28.49*
1995	23.53
1996	27.36
1997	26.65
1998	11.15
1999	18.80
2000	20.50
Compound average annual return	**22.02**

*Trading started in April 1994.

INDUSTRY

The new-generation manager runs a different type of business than the earlier hedge fund managers ran. A business exists, and there is more than one decision maker.

DANIEL OCH
Och-Ziff Capital Management

Organization

Inception	1994
Assets	
Current	$3.5 billion
Peak	$3.5 billion
Edge	Focus on mandate, focus on unusual and complex securities, team
Office Location	New York, New York; London, England
Number of People	50
Type of Organization	Business units
His Role	Leads the four business units; managing member
Investment Committee	Yes
Reward System	Profits of the overall firm
Number of Investors	170
Type of Investor	Institutions, endowments; mostly U.S.
GP/Principals' Ownership of Assets	80 percent of his net worth
Endowments (*Source:* 1999 NACUBO)	Amherst College Carnegie Mellon University Colgate University Middlebury College University of Michigan Yeshiva University

Methodology/ Portfolio Composition

Style	Research-driven, bottom-up
Number of Positions in Portfolio	140
Trades Taken	Risk-adjusted returns; avoids implicit/explicit correlation to stock market
Role of United States	75 percent

Role of Technology	Minor
Role of Private Equity	None
Role of Macro	None
Allocates to Other Managers	No

Risk Management

Net Exposure	Less than 10 percent
Hedging Technique	The strategies allow for hedging of individual positions and the overall portfolio
Maximum Leverage	Uses leverage only in convertible arbitrage, 3:1
Memorable Loss	Not disclosed
Risk Management	Reduces allocations quickly, limits percentage of cash tender offers, maximum risk of any one position is 1 percent of portfolio

Background Information

Initial Spark	College
Professional Background	Goldman Sachs, trader
Education	Wharton School of Finance and Commerce
Motivation/Satisfaction	Build the best team
Age	39
Free Time	Skiing, golf, philanthropy, children

12

RAJ RAJARATNAM
Galleon Group

Technology Sector
Bottom-Up Research

Raj Rajaratnam differs from most of the other superstar managers in that he focuses specifically on the technology sector and does not use leverage at all.

Assets under management have grown rapidly in the past several years. Assets now stand at $5 billion versus $1 billion in 1998. Galleon Group closed to new investors on April 1, 2000, and to existing investors on June 30, 2000. The funds, however, are open to strategic investors (i.e., executives of technology companies and health care companies).

STRONG WORK ETHIC

Rajaratnam, unlike most of the other superstar managers, is not U.S. born. He was born in Sri Lanka and educated in England, and came to the United States to attend the Wharton School of Finance and Commerce. He came as a student and stayed. He feels this background has had an influence on him. Because he didn't have a support system in the United States, he has never been complacent and has a strong work ethic. Nothing is taken for granted and he doesn't think life owes him anything.

Rajaratnam compares this business to getting a report card every day. "I am very focused and disciplined. You need a toughness. You need to take it personally, yet if you take it too personally, it could wear you down. It requires a lot of stamina. You could have the right analysis but be wrong on the market."

NEEDHAM CONNECTION

After graduating from Wharton, Rajaratnam worked at Needham & Company. In December 1991, at the age of 34, Rajaratnam became president of Needham. After a few months, he realized the job was not for him; he didn't want to manage people, and he needed other challenges. So with the company's permission, he started a hedge fund, Needham Emerging Growth Partnership, in March 1992 with $15 million. Most of the money was from technology company executives he knew. He ran the hedge fund and continued his duties as president of Needham.

By mid to late 1996, he knew he wanted to focus all his time on the hedge fund. By then, the hedge fund assets had grown to $250 million. He bought the fund from the company and renamed it Galleon. Galleon refers to the boats in the Spanish Armada that carried the gold while navigating rough waters. On January 2, 1997, when Galleon officially started, assets stood at $350 million. Throughout the office, a visitor will see ship models and ship prints of galleons.

Gary Rosenbach, Krishen Sud, and Ari Arjavalingam went with Rajaratnam.

COMBINES TRADING AND RESEARCH

Galleon has a strong trading department and a strong research department—neither dominates. Of the seven partners, three are in technology analysis, two in health-care analysis, and two in trading. This dual strength is something not usually seen at a hedge fund, where traders tend to have short-term horizons and those in research have long-term time horizons.

This dual focus has to do with the seven partners coming from the brokerage side. Rajaratnam, Rosenbach (who coheads trading and risk management), Sud (portfolio manager of the Galleon Healthcare funds), and Arjavalingam (comanager of the Galleon Technology funds) came from Needham Investments. Jeff Bernstein (who comanages the Galleon New Media Funds) as well as Prem Lachman (who comanages the Galleon Healthcare Funds) came from Goldman Sachs. David Slaine (who coheads trading and risk management) came from Morgan Stanley.

Galleon trades actively around its core positions. One example of this is if Galleon owns 500,000 shares of, say, Intel, and the stock falls by 7 percent for no apparent reason, the traders may buy another 100,000 shares. They can buy and sell 25 percent to trade around the core position. By doing this, Galleon generates incremental returns while minimizing market exposure. Therefore trading velocity is high. It also means senior traders are in these positions, and the traders own about one-third of the company.

The traders are not rewarded by how much they make. "They are the defensive line; they don't score points. They are there to limit losses. I don't want them to try to hit home runs," Rajaratnam says.

Bottom-up research prevails. Over 300 companies are visited per month. Galleon views Wall Street analysts as its competition, and its goal is to arbitrage research and consensus thinking with its positions. So if a brokerage firm analyst feels that the personal computer industry will grow at 10 percent and Galleon's research indicates it will grow at 15 percent or 3 percent, Galleon will arbitrage the difference in the two perspectives.

Rajaratnam observes that typical sell-side analysts spend one-third of their time chasing initial public offerings, secondary offerings, banking business, and mergers and arbitrage; another one-third of their time making institutional visits; and only one-third of their time doing research. He feels this gives his analysts an edge since they spend 100 percent of their time on research. They are not encouraged to write 30 to 40 pages of pretty reports, but rather one page that lists the issues.

Eight of the 10 Galleon analysts are engineers by training, have worked in the technology industry, and therefore understand the trends and know the right questions to ask. "They don't get blindsided by the marketing hype," says Rajaratnam.

The analysts are encouraged to travel as much as they want and to visit as many companies as they can. They are not limited by a travel budget. The one rule, however, is that at the end of each day, they must e-mail or fax an explanation of what they learned that day that they didn't know before. If they do not do this, they don't get travel expenses reimbursed.

Unlike many of the other hedge fund managers, the analysts are neither penalized for losing money nor rewarded for making money in their sector. No one points fingers at each other. Rather, they are rewarded for increasing their expertise or edge. Every analyst follows 35 companies. At the start of the year, Rajaratnam asks each analyst how many he or she has an edge on. This includes contacts in senior management, suppliers, customers, and competitors. It is that number, at the end of the year, that determines the analyst's reward. The goal is to have it increase significantly. For example, if it increases from five to ten, that is good. If it increases from five to six, that is not so good. Rajaratnam points out that the main factor that could hinder the firm's growth is the ability to hire excellent people.

Integrity is also key at Galleon. No personal trading accounts are permitted. Employees are asked to sign a statement attesting to this. In one instance it was violated, and the person was terminated.

Rajaratnam says many of the staff have known each other for 10 to 15 years and have close ties. They are personal friends as well as business acquaintances. As a result, there is no tension from within the firm. Most are in their early forties. This atmosphere helps reinforce the team approach culture.

AGE OF SPECIALIZATION

While Galleon is very narrow, it is also very deep. There are 35 people within the firm—ten technology analysts, five health-care analysts, six traders, and various back office and support staff including accounting and investor relations people and a chief financial officer. Besides the office in New York where most of the traders are located, there is an office in Santa Clara, California, where the semiconductor, data networking, hardware equipment, and software exposure analysts are located. By being in Silicon Valley, they can develop good contacts with the companies they follow.

The analysts in New York follow wireless, telecommunications, Internet, software, and health-care industries. Communication between the two offices is seamless, making them feel like one group.

Rajaratnam covers companies as well. He is the managing general partner and portfolio manager of the Galleon Technology and New Media funds. He describes himself as the quarterback of the team. He is involved with everything in the firm and often accompanies the analysts to their company meetings. Rajaratnam meets with two to three companies a day. One week out of every month, he visits about 25 companies in California.

His typical day starts with a walk to work. From 7:30 to 8:45 A.M., he listens to the brokers' calls to hear what the Wall Street analysts have to say. At 8:45 A.M., Galleon has its own meeting, which lasts for about an hour. Every issue is discussed regarding the companies being followed. Because the companies are all interrelated, it is educational for all to have an idea on each other's areas. Conference calls are held with the California office. By 10 A.M., the day's game plan has been formulated.

Everyone sits in a bull pen to facilitate the communication between the portfolio managers and the analysts. There are five portfolio managers in the various funds. These include Rajaratnam, Arjavalingam, Bernstein, Sud, and Lachman (coportfolio managers of Galleon Health-care Partners).

Unlike most other hedge fund managers, Galleon does not have an investment committee; they work as a team. Galleon is a thematic investor rather than optimizing the portfolio by sector. Five to six powerful themes are identified and trades are placed based on those themes. One example of a theme is the growth of the Internet. Rajaratnam says they are an agnostic when it comes to market capitalizations of a stock. Liquidity is not a concern.

Rajaratnam makes it a point to meet with investors. He meets with investors any time after 4 P.M., when the markets have closed, until late in the evening. He feels this is critical and something he will always do. Once a year, the partners go to Europe where they meet with investors. "Investor relations are something we take very seriously," Rajaratnam says.

There are about 550 investors in total. In the United States, there are about 200 investors, of whom about 125 are strategic investors (i.e., executives of technology companies). Outside the United States, most of the investors are institutions. How transparent is Galleon? A monthly letter is sent out that details the long and short positions as well as the top five positions. Galleon does not fax the portfolio details out to investors.

Tax efficiency is not a major priority, though it is considered in the October through December time period.

Galleon has a board of advisers consisting of Stanley Druckenmiller, Don Maron of PaineWebber, and two offshore advisers. The group discusses growth strategies for Galleon. While they have discussed the role of private equity, no plans are in place at this time.

FOUR FUNDS

Assets total $5 billion in four funds. All assets are in equities. The specialties are technology, health care, Internet, and communications. Rajaratnam points out that these sectors comprise about 45 percent of the S&P—technology, Internet, and communications make up about 32 percent of the S&P while health care is about 10 percent. "These are the growth sectors of the economy."

The original fund, Galleon Technology Partners I, a $3 billion fund, focuses on technology. For the past year, on the stock side, the theme has been strong demand for communication bandwith, the cyclical recovery in both the semiconductor and semiconductor equipment industry, and continued growth of the Internet.

About 70 percent of the profits came from the long side and 30 percent from the short side. On the short side, the bulk of returns recently came from the wireless and Internet sectors. Money was made on shorts in the business-to-consumer sector of the Internet. The net exposure in 1999 was 30 to 40 percent.

Galleon Healthcare Partners focuses on pharmaceuticals, medical devices, biotechnology, health-care services, and health-care information technology. The health-care fund, started in October 1994, has grown to $1.2 billion.

In biotechnology, Galleon is focusing on companies with products experiencing accelerating growth and companies with products in late-stage clinical trials that are underappreciated. In genomics, the firm focuses on infrastructure companies that will benefit from the focus on gene validation and do not have associated patent issues. In health-care services, the view is that health-care providers will do well with premiums up over 10 percent. Galleon also believes the margins for drug distributors are poised to expand. The firm is selective with brand-name pharmaceuticals. In medical devices/hospital supplies, it is neutral toward cardiology companies since the U.S. stent market is maturing. And in health-care information technology, it is net short traditional companies and those disintermediated by Internet-based solutions.

The Galleon New Media Fund, formed in June 1999 to invest exclusively in the Internet sector, is now at $500 million. Given the early stage of market development, most Internet stocks are volatile. As a result, this fund has a higher risk/return profile than the flagship technology fund. The core belief that shapes the investment strategy is that in the Internet sector, there will be a few large winners and many losers. The strategy is to identify those few large winners, build investment positions in them over time, and trade around these core positions to decrease the volatility as well as enhance returns. Galleon shorts companies whose business models are fundamentally flawed or where the demand drivers are moderating.

The firm segments the Internet sector into five subsectors: Internet infrastructure, Internet software, business-to-consumer, business-to-business, and Internet consulting services. Galleon believes the Internet infrastructure, Internet software, and business-to-business are the areas with attractive return. The driving trends are rapid deployment of information technology budgets away from Y2K-related exposure to e-business strategies among the Fortune 2000 companies. The shorts are in the business-to-consumer and Internet consulting services sectors. Worries over dot-com companies being able to obtain adequate funding and the softening demand for Internet-related advertising caused the fall in stock.

The newest fund, the communications fund begun in July 2000, is already at $125 million. The Galleon Communications Fund focuses exclusively on investing in companies in the communications sector. This includes electronic communications, voice communications, and data communications.

Rajaratnam says Galleon has grown by word of mouth and hasn't focused on marketing. One organization has developed a fund for Galleon, but that is only about $50 million out of the total.

The partners and employees of Galleon have over $300 million invested in the various Galleon funds. Any employee can participate in Galleon ownership.

MANAGE VOLATILITY AND DOWNSIDE RISK

Rajaratnam believes that investors invest in hedge funds because the downside risk is managed. They are willing to give up some on the upside to manage the downside. He points to the Goldman Sachs Internet Index, which was down 45 percent for the first half of 2000. In contrast, the Galleon Internet Fund was up 30 percent. "We were able to manage volatility on the downside," he explains.

There are about 100 positions in the portfolio. One situation cannot have more than 5 percent of the portfolio, although a position can grow to 7 percent before it is trimmed. About five have a 5 percent allocation, and about 20 to 30 of the positions each make up 1 to 2 percent of the portfolio.

Most of the trades are U.S.-based or American depositary receipts of non-U.S. companies such as Nokia or Ericsson. He likes companies with ADRs because they report according to U.S. GAAP (generally accepted accounting principles) standards, he can attend investor meetings, and he has access to management. He wants to stick to local expertise in order to avoid any expensive lessons.

Leverage is not used. For hedging purposes, Galleon prefers shorting stocks. While options are used, they tend to be expensive. As an interim measure, he may use Nasdaq options on Morgan Stanley High Technology Index. Shorting is very important to the firm. Often, says Rajaratnam, the long and short exposure is less than 100 percent. For example, in 1999, when returns were 100 percent, 70 percent of that was from the long side and 30 percent from the short side. Rajaratnam points out that because technology is the greatest wealth creator as well as wealth dissipator, there are many opportunities for short positions.

Furthermore, because of the short product cycles in technology, there are additional opportunities for short positions. Rajaratnam observes this is similar to the old-fashioned (A. W. Jones) model because shorts are as important as long positions.

Moving to cash is another alternative sometimes taken. Given the turbulent second quarter of 2000, Galleon reduced its risk profile of the New Media Fund by raising a significant amount of cash.

LOSSES AND OTHER POTENTIAL PROBLEMS

Galleon's objective is to provide investors with a 20 to 25 percent average annual return over an 18-month period. In actuality, the results from inception in 1992 to today are about 36.0 percent. Rajaratnam observes, "If we go through a tough 18-month period, it could indicate that size is a problem. If that did happen, Galleon would return money to investors."

Have they gone through such a period? Rajaratnam says Galleon has had three-month rough periods, but not six-month periods, and has not had any down years. When there have been losses, Rajaratnam says they had read the chief executive officer or other senior management the wrong way. "We didn't understand their motivations and got caught in the marketing hype."

One memorable rough period was the fourth quarter of 1997 during the Asian crisis. Part of the problem was Galleon's lack of a good macro view of the world, and the firm got caught long technology stocks, losing 10 to 12 percent for the month of October 1997.

The lesson learned was to spend more time on macro issues. And if the fund is down 4 to 5 percent a month, the manager now reduces exposure.

PRIDE AND COMPETITIVENESS

Rajaratnam describes himself as a competitive person. "It is pride and I want to win. After awhile, money is not the motivation. I want to win every time. Taking calculated risks gets my adrenaline pumping."

Rajaratnam wanted a level playing field on which to compete. While he was at Needham, he felt that in investment banking a level playing field did not exist. Some of the non-U.S. banks that were getting involved had enormous resources. In hedge funds, however, he felt a level playing field did exist, and that was attractive.

He gets personal satisfaction from seeing the team work together and from the knowledge that they have built a culture with little bureaucracy. "It is the consistent cooperation and focus on one goal. People enjoy working here."

Rajaratnam likes to travel with his family. Every year, they visit two countries they have never been to. "It's like an adventure." He is also intrigued by international politics, particularly with Sri Lanka, his homeland, which is undergoing civil war. On the sports side, he likes to play tennis and squash and to swim.

Net Performance (%) *Galleon Technology Fund*	
1992	33.20
1993	21.10
1994	29.30
1995	56.10
1996	34.80
1997	6.60
1998	30.50
1999	96.30
2000	16.00
Compound average annual return	**33.98**

"I find that playing sports fuels my competitive bent and desire to win, while time with my family provides a balanced perspective on life, reminding me that there is more to life than portfolio returns."

INDUSTRY OUTLOOK

Rajaratnam is not certain that there is a new- or old-generation distinction between hedge fund managers, but he does see the hedge fund industry increasingly move toward specialization. "Each hedge fund manager has to understand his edge."

Rajaratnam feels institutional investors will assert themselves. More transparency will develop because of investor demand. Investors want more accessibility to the organization.

He also expects a shakeout will occur since there are too many hedge funds, many of which are run by long-only managers using considerable leverage. "It is almost too easy now. And there are so many excesses."

RAJ RAJARATNAM
Galleon Group

Organization

Inception	1993
Assets	
Current	$5 billion
Peak	$5 billion
Edge	Hard work; culture; trading and research; specialization
Office Location	New York, New York; Santa Clara, California
Number of People	35
Type of Organization	Team combining analysts and traders
His Role	Portfolio manager
Investment Committee	No
Reward System	Overall profitability and increasing expertise and knowledge
Number of Investors	550
Type of Investor	U.S.—primarily strategic investor; non-U.S.—institution
GP/Principals' Ownership of Assets	$300 million
Endowments	Not disclosed

Methodology/ Portfolio Composition

Style	Bottom-up; sector focuses: technology, health care
Number of Positions in Portfolio	100
Trades Taken	Arbitrage Wall Street analysts' research
Role of United States	100 percent
Role of Technology	100 percent
Role of Private Equity	0 percent

Role of Macro	0 percent
Allocates to Other Managers	No

Risk Management

Net Exposure	30 to 40 percent
Hedging Technique	Short stocks; cash
Maximum Leverage	None
Memorable Loss	Asia 1997
Risk Management	No leverage; move to cash; 5 percent maximum per trade

Background Information

Initial Spark	Needham Investments
Professional Background	Brokerage
Education	Wharton School of Finance and Commerce
Motivation/Satisfaction	Pride, competitiveness
Age	43
Free Time	Travel

13

PAUL SINGER
Elliott Associates

Arbitrage/Distressed
Process-Driven Activities

After graduating from Harvard Law School in 1969, Paul Singer practiced law at two top New York City law firms, but he became interested in investing as a hobby. "I was passionate about investing. It was an obsessive hobby. I found it fun to study the relationships. It was interesting, like a game or a puzzle." Elliott Associates—taken after his middle name—was formed in 1977; initial assets were from friends and family. His goal was not to lose money.

In talking with Singer, one distinctly gets the impression of a tenacious individual who is highly principled. He is articulate and to the point. He is organized in thinking and speaking as well as hardworking.

As we sit in his conference room overlooking Central Park in New York City, Singer, 56, discusses his diversified, opportunistic approach. "The world has a rapidly shifting set of opportunities. You have to be there and you can't stay in too long. It's like the Welcome Wagon in front of your house for 10 minutes. You don't want to be too late and miss the cookies." He also emphasizes that being eclectic is different from being whimsical and a dilettante.

His objective is to achieve a rate of return as high as is consistent with his goal of capital preservation. Distressed securities and arbitrage are two big parts of his business. At the moment, due to where the opportunities are, arbitrage strategies like investment trust arbitrage and related securities arbitrage represent the largest deployment of capital. Long-term equity-linked positions, largely derived from his distressed and convertible investing, represent another significant area of capital deployment. Distressed investing, which had been the largest area in the past, is now shrinking.

Early on, a good percentage of his business was in convertible arbitrage. But after the crash of 1987, Singer found the paper was too crosscorrelated, too correlated to the stock market, and too difficult to hedge. "It is an overstatement—but not too much of an overstatement—to call them bull market instruments." For example, convertibles have not had an easy time in test periods such as the 1973–1974 market weakness, 1987, 1994, 1998, and April/May 2000. He feels that in a sustained bear market, convertibles may not trade well. Interest rate hikes and bear markets are just a few factors that make convertibles vulnerable. Since then, convertibles have diminished to a smaller percentage of what he trades. Convertible hedging in Japan, which was active from 1988 to 1993, has also since diminished. Today, he approaches convertibles on an opportunistic basis.

There are typically about 200 positions in the portfolio. Regarding portfolio optimization, Singer says that he uses both quantitative and qualitative measures but does not provide further details. This situation is reassessed continuously. Liquidity of markets traded ranges from low to high.

EFFORT-LADEN MANUAL ACTIVITIES

He focuses on process-driven activities where he can add value. For example, with distressed securities, he is a hands-on activist trader who gets involved in negotiations and committee work; he is close to the companies. An example is where the value of the business may not be the main uncertainty but perhaps a legal decision is key to the rate of return or return on profit. The hands-on activity also is evident in arbitrage strategies. For example, with investment trust arbitrage, he observes, "We don't trade just relationships; we try to make things happen."

Singer likens what the firm does to what private equity managers do but with smaller positions. Whereas a private equity manager may have 10 positions, private equity-like investments could represent 1 percent of Elliott's diversified portfolio.

The characteristic that makes Elliott Associates different from many other managers in similar businesses is that they apply more resources to the task—they work harder. There is a higher unit of effort to money invested, and more complexity per unit of risk. He focuses on those areas that are effort-laden—where manual effort is required. Unlike some other managers, Elliott is usually not just buying cheap stock in bankruptcy. It takes a one-on-one approach to one-off situations.

Singer adds that they have quant cleverness skills but are not a quant shop. Many of their trades have arbitrage, quantitative, and derivative elements but those are just part of the equation. "We also know the company, are close to the companies, have done the work, and know the numbers." In other words, their approach combines qualitative and quantitative skills; both are critical elements.

Singer doesn't like to use the term "edge" since he is not competing against anyone. He is trying to get it right. "Compared with stock pickers and value players, destiny is in our own hands. It is based on the quality of work and the quality of decisions—it is about getting it right."

THE TEAM

There are about 60 people in the New York and London offices. Senior portfolio managers are responsible for the different sectors, industries, and types of situations. Analysts support the senior portfolio managers. Then there are traders. While most of the portfolio focuses on the United States, the London office is a good base for global trading. There is no investment committee. The bonus reward system is based on Singer's discretion.

As general partner of Elliott Associates, Singer is responsible for all positions. He is the senior risk manager and has input on position size. His goal is to delegate responsibility to people and let them make decisions. He is the mentor and makes creative additions. He approves and validates what the person has done—to make sure that person has done the thinking correctly.

During the typical day, Singer first looks at the world through the newspapers, computers, and news events. After he assesses the price movement, he then talks to the portfolio managers, analysts, and traders as well as his contacts on the Street. He tries to move positions along and put out fires. He has input on positions that can be built up. He looks at different segments of the portfolio to see what needs to be adjusted. Is the timing right? Is the size right? "I try to add value and subtract pain." He does not spend much time talking to clients.

Singer achieves satisfaction on many fronts—making money for the fund, doing something clever, and helping someone to learn.

Singer, his family, and the principals are the largest investors in the fund. A no-trading policy exists which means no employee can have a personal trading account. All employee trading money is invested in the Elliott funds.

RISK MANAGEMENT

A manager cannot rest on his laurels; he is only as good as his previous quarter's performance, says Singer.

For the period since Elliott's track record began in 1977, the average annual return is about 15 percent. The year 1994 was a flat year for Elliott while most other hedge fund managers were down. Singer attributes 1994 to a credit squeeze and unusual cross-correlation. The first down year occurred in 1998.

He is of the view that the markets have been benign and that tougher markets lie ahead. He feels the stock market is in the process of changing. It is a challenging, whipsaw environment. He feels a humble approach needs to be taken. Limiting leverage is the most important risk management tool at the moment. Elliott Associates uses a very low amount of leverage except in fixed-income arbitrage positions. Leverage, ranging from 1.3:1 to 1.5:1 in all businesses, is low relative to his peers. In fixed-income arbitrage, leverage is 20:1, which is in line with his peers, says Singer. This strategy has not changed over the years.

Singer has long emphasized risk management and recently spoke about this topic at a conference in New York. In recalling the crash of October 1987, he questioned whether it really was a 10 sigma event—like an asteroid hitting earth. Was it a once-in-a-lifetime event or a sign of things to come? Since 1987, he observed, we have experienced crashes also in 1994 and 1998.[1]

Singer sees three major risks—model risk, herding risk, and equity market risk. "Those who trust the models do so at their own peril. They will be hurt, as the models are wrong. The world may be different than those used in the models' history." Further exacerbating the change are developments in technology, easy access to leverage, instant communication, and herding—the piling on of momentum trades.

To lessen the impact of herding, Singer suggests finding out who else owns the spreads that you own and determining their motivation. If there are too many players, the position can be a trap. They can also impact the exits as well. People getting into trouble can also have a herding effect. Two examples of these were the Quest–US West merger as well as General Motors–Hughes Electronics. In both cases, the amount of arbitrage activity was significant and turned out to have painful implications for Wall Street. Another example was Bell Canada, which owned and spun off a big stake in Nortel. The arbitrageurs expected higher valuations than actually resulted when the stub started trading. "Now the arbitrageurs are sitting and choking on this. It will take a long time."

One of Singer's goals is to attempt to do as much as possible that is uncorrelated to the stock market (i.e., stay away from stock market exposure), because it is becoming so difficult to hedge.

He observes that the term "stock market" is increasingly not a single concept. More variation is occurring in the sectors of the market.

If the stock market should turn downward, Singer is well protected.

The types of distressed securities that he favors are uncorrelated to the stock and bond markets. His arbitrage positions, in the aggregate, he believes are largely insulated from a bear stock market. His long-term equity-linked positions are subject to their own execution but are also subject to stock market forces. Elliott attempts to hedge those exposures. Hedging is done by shorts in stocks, indexes, options, volatility positions, volatility swaps, and use of derivatives.

NOT STRESSFUL

Singer doesn't feel he will be faced with capacity constraints in the near term. Assets in his two funds—Elliott Associates for U.S. investors and Westgate International for non-U.S. investors and U.S. tax-free investors—currently total about $1.9 billion, their historic peak. "The financial markets have grown as we have grown. There are many opportunities. For example, during the Drexel years, the amount of paper in the high-yield issuance market was $150 billion total. In the 1990s, it has been $650 billion."

Singer doesn't find his work stressful. "Stress is not caused by managing over $1 billion; it is caused by people, relationships, mistakes, and losses." Singer has used that philosophy to run an investment style that attempts to minimize stress. His goal is to continue his path of delegating to smart, talented, risk-conscious individuals so that he can be creative in managing risk.

Balance is important to his life and work. "I'm an incremental guy, not a burnout guy." He can do what he is doing for the long haul. "I don't believe in retirement."

Outside of work, he runs a family foundation, is active on different boards, and is involved in social policy groups. He is a firm believer in the power of the individual to make a difference.

INVESTOR BASE

Singer estimates there are 300 investors, including individuals, fund of funds entities, and endowments. According to the 1999 NACUBO survey, one of those endowments is Vassar College.

On the transparency front, Singer provides investors with quarterly reports and annual audits but no information on exact position size. Tax efficiency is considered in the U.S. fund. He says excellent tax optimization is achieved with the goal being long-term gains.

INDUSTRY VIEW

Singer finds it simplistic to delineate a dichotomy between the old-generation and the new-generation hedge fund manager. "Each has its own approach. Managers fit their own personal skills, styles, and personality quirks in varying degrees into an organization. It depends on each of their own experiences and the kind of adversity they have faced."

Singer feels some of the new managers may not be fully aware of the extent their success in their pre–hedge fund life and their initial success in their hedge fund life has to do with the unusual markets that have existed for 5, 18, or 26 years—depending on how you measure trends. Essentially, the bull market has been roaring since October 4, 1974, through early 2000.

He describes the market up through early 2000 as extraordinary with a high degree of public speculation. "Uninformed performance chasing and momentum chasing. It is a mob, a crowd." He recalls a book he read many years ago "which basically said 'the power of the public on a stampede is incalculable.' There is no connection to value in many sectors of today's market." Day traders (i.e., Internet traders) and technology have made the stock market incredibly dangerous for professional investors. Staggering moves occur in the stock market that have nothing to do with rationality or anything fundamental. "It makes the markets more volatile and less efficient. It is harder to sell short."

Singer also observes how quickly an environment can change. "Ideas, tones, markets can go in one direction for so long supported by one concept—and on a given moment's notice, and unpredictably, it may be over and replaced by a whole other feeling and last another 20 years." He recalls the 1968 to 1982 period, which was a grueling environment and devastating for many managers.

Singer also sees the institutional investor community as deteriorating in its professionalism. There is more performance chasing, more momentum chasing, and more throwing money at the latest stars. Furthermore, many of the institutions don't know when to get off the stock market train or are afraid to get off. Singer believes that more institutional allocations are coming into the hedge fund community since the stock market will not be able to return 15 percent per year over the long term on a low-volatility basis. He feels the indexes are over-owned and overpriced.

As a manager for over 23 years, he respects the select number of managers who can consistently make money for the long term in different environments—periods of inflation or no inflation, low interest rates or high interest rates, trade deficit, dollar collapse. In contrast, some of the new-generation managers (in 1999 and early 2000) were engaged in bull market stock-trading strategies. Gradually the investor community will realize they are not getting their money's worth. The ability to chase stocks in a bull market may be less attractive as time goes on. "In each whipsaw environment, a few managers will be lost. Few managers can create businesses with finesse and risk control combined." Singer also

Net Performance (%) Elliott Associates	
1977	6.70*
1978	9.90
1979	16.60
1980	22.60
1981	23.40
1982	17.60
1983	22.10
1984	16.40
1985	22.50
1986	10.70
1987	6.60
1988	13.40
1989	23.80
1990	13.40
1991	12.40
1992	15.10
1993	21.60
1994	0.00
1995	18.30
1996	19.00
1997	12.10
1998	−7.00
1999	18.10
2000	24.00
Compound average annual return	**14.71**

*Trading started February 1, 1977.

acknowledges the importance of investing as well as business decision making. Both are needed. It is an art, not a science.

PAUL SINGER
Elliott Associates

Organization

Inception	1977
Assets	
Current	$1.9 billion
Peak	$1.9 billion
Edge	Does not like the term "edge," works hard, process-driven activities
Office Location	New York, New York; London, England
Number of People	60
Type of Organization	Portfolio managers, analysts, traders
His Role	Risk manager, input on size
Investment Committee	No
Reward System	Discretionary
Number of Investors	300
Type of Investor	Individuals, fund of funds investors
GP/Principals' Ownership of Assets	Singer, his family, and principals are largest investors
Endowments (*Source:* 1999 NACUBO)	Vassar College

Methodology/ Portfolio Composition

Style	Opportunistic, distressed arbitrage
Number of Positions in Portfolio	200
Trades Taken	No special criteria
Role of United States	Majority
Role of Technology	Small
Role of Private Equity	Similar, but smaller positions
Role of Macro	None
Allocates to Other Managers	No

Risk Management

Net Exposure	Attempt at zero net equity market exposure
Hedging Technique	Stocks, indexes, option volatility swaps, derivatives
Maximum Leverage	Low leverage except fixed-income arbitrage
Memorable Loss	Northampton/Ponderosa de-inked paper mill bonds
Risk Management	Find out who else owns spreads and their motivation, uncorrelated

Background Information

Initial Spark	Hobby
Professional Background	Lawyer
Education	Harvard Law School
Motivation/Satisfaction	Challenge, fun, puzzle; help someone grow
Age	56
Free Time	Public issues, foundation

14

BRIAN STARK
Stark Investments

Arbitrage Focus with Convertible Arbitrage Core
Finding Inefficiencies Outside the U.S.

In the suburbs of Milwaukee, one can find Stark Investments—an 85-person firm managing about $1.7 billion. Stark Investments, which focuses on convertible arbitrage, risk arbitrage, private placements, and capital structure arbitrage (in that order), has a track record going back to 1987. The firm started as Stark Partners.

Interestingly, the firm has it roots in New York City and then Greenwich, Connecticut, but Stark eventually moved it to Mequon, Wisconsin, in August 1993. Whitefish Bay, a suburb of Mequon, is where Brian Stark grew up. Mike Roth, who met Stark at Harvard Law School and who became his partner in 1992 when they formed Stark Investments, also comes from Wisconsin.

The two main funds are multistrategy. In October 1994, Stark Investment LP was formed, and in July 1995, Shepherd Investments International began trading. About 60 percent of the firm's assets are in the former fund and 40 percent in the latter fund. There are a few specialty funds—a Japanese convertible arbitrage fund and another focusing on European convertible arbitrage. There is also a private placement arbitrage fund.

Trading from Milwaukee, Stark Investments has perhaps a more global focus than many of the superstar managers who are located in New York City. Since its inception, the firm has been active internationally. "The inefficiencies are greater internationally. In 1987, when I started, there were not many arbitrageurs. And those that were arbitrageurs were mostly U.S.-focused. The locals in those markets were less cognizant of arbitrage opportunities."

Much of that focus has been on Japan, which, along with the United States, is the biggest convertible bond market. Stark says that the European focus has historically been small because of lack of product and rich valuations. But in the past year that has changed. There are more issuances at attractive valuations.

Stark moves capital to where the most attractive opportunities exist. As a result, the percentage of focus that is U.S. to non-U.S. swings greatly. Historically the percentage is 65 percent non-U.S. to 35 percent U.S. Now the mix is about 70 percent non-U.S. and 30 percent U.S. The highest percentage the U.S. has ever been was about 65 percent, while twice non-U.S. was as high as 90 percent.

The first of those periods began around July 1987 and lasted until mid-year 1990. Stark had pretty much exited the U.S. markets at that time because of inability to find good value in the U.S. convertible market, the much greater inefficiencies in the non-U.S. markets at that time, his concern about U.S. equity valuations, and the degree of speculation occurring in the U.S. markets. Again, beginning in late 1993, Stark began significantly to reduce U.S. exposure. By the end of the first quarter of 1994, the firm was less than 10 percent exposed to the U.S. market. "Pricing in the U.S. convertible market had become quite rich by historical standards, and accordingly we did not believe U.S. convertibles would hold up to an adverse environment."

Stark came back to the U.S. markets in a significant way at the beginning of the fourth quarter of 1994, with the U.S. exposure reaching as much as 65 percent of the portfolio at various points between then and 1998.

In addition to its location and heavy global focus, other factors make Stark Investments different from the typical superstar managers. Stark and Roth are both Harvard-trained lawyers. Stark says that background helps them in their risk arbitrage work where evaluating regulatory risks and analyzing documentation are very important. Regulatory obstacles and litigation can often become elements affecting the outcome of a risk arbitrage transaction. "A legal education helps us in the analytical process. It instills a discipline."

Talking with Stark, one sees the implications of his legal background—he is very prepared and thorough, and is a meticulously analytical thinker.

BOOKS READ AND WRITTEN

Stark worked for his father, an accountant and active investor, one summer while he was in high school. While he didn't enjoy the accounting work, he turned his focus to investing at the suggestion of his father, who gave him Edward O. Thorpe's *Beat the Market: A Scientific Stock Market System* to read. This book focused on warrant arbitrage. If the strategy were applied scientifically from 1946 to 1966 (the book was published in 1967), an investor would have made money every year. This got Stark and his father investing in warrant and risk arbitrage.

Stark worked on his own book beginning in his senior year at Brown University and then while at Harvard Law School. Published in 1983 by Dow Jones-Irwin, *Special Situation Investing: Hedging, Arbitrage and Liquidation* was about special situations and why persistent opportunities exist in what appears to be an efficient market.

The book caught the attention of a couple of important investors, including two of the other superstar managers—Paul Singer of Elliott Associates and Donald Sussman of Paloma Partners. Stark and Sussman eventually became co–general partners of Stark Partners; that fund operated until early 1992.

ARBITRAGE FOCUS WITH CONVERTIBLE ARBITRAGE CORE

Stark Investments' objectives are absolute returns, low volatility of returns, preservation of capital, low correlation with equity and bond markets, and specialization by focusing on arbitrage.

Stark emphasizes the importance of being multistrategy. Arbitrage is the firm's specialty; convertible arbitrage is its core, and the other strategies are built around it as additional incremental strategies. Assets are shifted to where the best risk-adjusted opportunities exist.

Five years ago, Stark Investments did only convertible arbitrage and risk arbitrage internationally. Private placements were started only three and a half years ago with a small percentage of the assets but have since provided important performance. Currently, the firm is incubating three other arbitrage strategies, including high-yield arbitrage. A large percentage of high-yield arbitrage is capital structure arbitrage (i.e., long a more senior piece of paper and short a more junior security). At this point, the firm is testing the strategies with small amounts of money, building systems, and paper trading. "We are building up experience before putting in real capital."

Convertible arbitrage and risk arbitrage have been consistent performers throughout the years, yet risk arbitrage is at least theoretically prone to somewhat more volatile performance. In private placements, the results are lumpier. Nothing happens for a while; then the market gets volatile and opportunities appear to both profitability close earlier investments and establish new positions, observes Stark.

Portfolio optimization is not done by a computer program but rather is an amalgam of qualitative and quantitative analyses. Stark Investments screens strategies on a worldwide basis for risk and expected return. In convertible arbitrage, they will look at theoretical mispricings—mispriced by quantitative options analysis. If there is a mispricing, they will then look at creditworthiness of the convertible and at the fundamentals of the underlying equity. In addition, overall portfolio analysis is applied. "We want diversification by strategy and geography as well. We want the portfolio to do well in all environments. Accordingly, we look at both the risks in the general macro environment as well as the riskiness of the individual position and how it fits into the balance of the overall portfolio." A similar process is used in risk arbitrage.

Stark says the trading strategies make money in three ways. First is cash flow from the interest or dividends from the convertibles and rebates on the short sale proceeds. Second is making money from volatility. Typically, to maintain market neutrality, they must short more stock when stocks rise and buy back some of the shorts when stocks fall. Thus, they capture trading profits from volatility while maintaining market neutrality. In addition, when the markets are volatile, more inefficiencies occur. Third is mispricing (i.e., buying below theoretical value and selling either when the convertible or risk arbitrage spread reaches fair value or the risk arbitrage deal closes).

NET EXPOSURE

Net exposure varies considerably, but on average shorts are 70 to 90 percent as big as the longs. Stark feels that it is not a good indicator of their true exposure since you could be quite short with the short side being only 70 percent of the longs. Convertibles move down more slowly than do equities. Furthermore, cash tender offers have no short side.

Stark thinks of exposure in terms of how the hedge ratios compare to what quantitative models say their theoretical deltas (i.e., hedge ratios) are. On a portfolio basis, they are theoretically heavy 5 to 10 percent and sometimes more. They do this because there tends to be a skew in arbitrage positions. They tend to do better than theory predicts when stocks are rising strongly and worse than predicted when stocks are falling significantly.

LEVERAGE AS A TOOL

"Leverage is a tool that needs to be used carefully and the right way. It varies based on the macro environment and the degree of undervaluation of the portfolio." Stark's range is between 1.5:1 and 7:1. "We adjust the leverage downward when the macro environment becomes more of a concern or the degree of arbitrage mispricing diminishes, and tend to increase leverage when the macro environment becomes friendly or the degree of arbitrage mispricing increases."

Stark says the usual thinking of investors is that greater leverage means greater risk. But in arbitrage that correlation breaks down. Stark says that situations can exist where leverage is very high but risk is quite limited. For example, a convertible arbitrage position involving a bond with almost no premium and hedged 100 percent requires almost no capital to set up. The position can generate very high static returns and be quite profitable if the underlying common stock drops significantly. While the leverage is nearly infinite, the credit and equity risks of such a position are *de minimus*. "We believe that reasonably leveraged and well-hedged arbitrage portfolios are considerably less risky than unhedged, outright equity portfolios."

The amount of leverage used is determined qualitatively and quantitatively. Stark explains, "The higher credit quality of the portfolio means that more leverage can be taken. If a significant portion of the convertible portfolio is asset swapped or otherwise default protected, then there is limited credit risk. We can create quality positions without the credit risk of companies going bankrupt."

Stark discusses how they build in macro considerations. For example, when arbitrage spreads tighten, they are more cautious. If the equity markets are speculative and frothy, such as in 1987 and first quarter of 2000, pricing can be wild. In those situations, positions will be heavily hedged and generally carry lower leverage since the risk of a significant market correction is higher. Often in such corrections, arbitrage spreads widen, causing mark-to-market pain if not compensated through higher hedge ratios and lower leverage.

Stark says they try to hedge most risks in the portfolio and do so more than the typical equity hedge fund. "We are typically overhedged on a theoretical basis. Generally, when the equity markets are rising, we will do better than theory predicts we should because the outright community, in an effort to keep up with their benchmarks, will buy convertibles at expensive premiums. Conversely, when the equity markets are falling, convertibles will do worse than they should because the outright community, which has no downside protection, is selling convertibles cheaper than theory says they should. We offset this skew by overhedging."

The firm's currency exposure is fully hedged but the degree to which interest rate exposure is hedged is variable. This is because the correlation between convertible pricing and interest rates often is much less than theory predicts. Moreover, the costs of running a continuous full-interest hedge can be quite high and over time is likely to be a losing proposition. Thus, in the United States, the firm is typically only partially hedged. On the other hand, when conditions warrant, they will fully hedge interest rates. For example, in Japan, interest rates are very low. They don't want to be on the wrong side when the market turns. Therefore, they are fully hedged.

Where it is possible to asset swap the credit or buy default protection at reasonable levels, they will do so. They may also short high-yield bonds, short other convertibles, short credit derivatives, or buy credit derivatives. But to fully hedge all credit risk on a continuous basis would be very expensive so they take an opportunistic approach.

Some trades are on for days while others are four to five years old. Stark Investments will hold a trade until the mispricing corrects itself.

Why do these arbitrage strategies remain attractive? Why do these inefficiencies persist? Stark says arbitrage securities tend to be very complex, technology skills vary, financing arrangements differ, and people analyze instruments from different perspectives. All of the major arbitrageurs have different competitive advantages. Stark also observes that the markets are heavily moved by greed, panic, and fear. Sometimes these emotions dominate and create inefficiencies.

How large a role does technology play in the portfolio? Technology companies have been some of the primary issuers of convertible products in the United States and Japan. Thus, a convertible arbitrage fund will typically have a fair amount of exposure to technology names. Stark says, "We are no different, though we are probably underweight technology relative to the convertible indexes because we tend to be skeptical of the creditworthiness of many new-economy companies."

Where on the continuum of convertible arbitrage does Stark Investments fit? If at the left end of the spectrum is the pure black box and at the right end is the manager who invests and hedges based on a fundamental view, Stark would fit between center and the pure black box end. "Models tell us where to be but we qualitatively adjust at the margin. We are quantitatively driven but not purely," says Stark. Human input is used to adjust hedges as well as do fundamental and credit analysis that provide input into the models.

OVERLAP IN THE ORGANIZATION

Unlike other specialist organizations, Stark Investments has overlap.

Stark heads up the convertible arbitrage area while Roth heads up risk arbitrage. Underneath them, there is a layer of portfolio managers who are experienced and talented and who have significant input into and influence on portfolio construction. Stark refers to this as senior redundancy. Thus there are at least two sets of experienced eyes monitoring each of the strategies and geographic areas within a strategy. In addition, most of the traders are experienced at and trade both risk arbitrage and convertible arbitrage positions. They believe Stark Investments differs in this respect from many of the major arbitrage firms.

Stark says they prefer this overlap because risk arbitrage can quickly become convertible arbitrage and vice versa. For example, in risk arbitrage deals today, there are often caps and collars that create embedded optionality in the positions. Trading optionality is the essence of convertible arbitrage. Therefore the Stark traders are active in both, knowing how to trade and price each.

Stark Investments has just gone through a growth spurt. A year and a half ago, the firm was half its current size. At 85 people, the firm has outgrown its space and is looking perhaps to construct a building somewhere nearby.

Stark emphasizes the team approach. Senior people include chief operating office, chief financial officer, and a technology officer. There are nine research analysts, two quantitative analysts, and about 20 information technology people, plus two consulting groups that are helping with technology products. A weekly portfolio meeting is held where trading staff members discuss the best and worst trades and make comparisons.

Both Stark and Roth are responsible for the overall allocation of assets. They also are sounding boards for the portfolio managers. Stark and Roth sit on the trading desk—this is their office. For about 80 to 85 percent of Stark's time and somewhat less of Roth's, they are investment managers; they keep on top of market developments and talk about individual trades as well as take care of capital allocation.

After trading hours and whenever required during the day, they run the business side.

Stark and Roth are the principal equity owners, and three senior managers have an equity stake. Stark expects that number to grow over time because they want people for the long term and want them to have a stake. The predominant source of compensation is based on the overall performance of the firm. Some years, a certain part of the portfolio will do better than others, yet compensation is very much the same if all traders are doing a great job. "You can do a great job in a tough market and still lose money. You should not be penalized because you faced a tough market environment in your niche and another trader dealt in a sector where everything was being bid up."

Located in Wisconsin, Stark feels they are less influenced by herd mentality because less interaction exists with their peers or brokers. In hiring staff, he is looking for a certain person who wants a certain quality of life. Many have Midwestern ties. "They are loyal and stable. We are looking to hire for the long term. We have low turnover."

Stark likes to hire people from MBA programs and develop people in-house. The firm recruits from the University of Chicago, Northwestern University, the University of Wisconsin, and the University of Indiana; but they typically do not hire people from banks or brokerage firms. When they are looking for more experienced candidates, they hire from other buy-side firms such as insurance companies, mutual funds, or hedge funds.

Stark describes the culture as a cautious one. "We are slow to bring on new strategies. In risk arbitrage, we do not invest in rumor deals; we wait until the deal has been announced. We are always hedging. You could describe our personality as risk-averse."

NO FIXED LEVEL OF CAPACITY

Stark answered the capacity concern question a bit differently than some of the other superstar managers. He observed that capacity changes with the markets and the environment. "There is not a fixed level of capacity. . . . At points when there is not sufficient opportunity or there are significant macro risks, taking capital is not the right thing to do. At other times, capacity can be beyond the capital of even the largest arbitrage fund."

Now, Stark says, in convertibles the amount of issuance has been increasing and the size of the deals has been getting bigger. In Europe recently, one company issued 2.5 billion euros of a convertible. Ten years ago, $200 million was a decent size for a new issue. In risk arbitrage, there is tremendous opportunity now as deal after deal comes out.

Discussing the advantages of being a large fund, Stark says advantages to size include obtaining better financing rates. Size is important to borrowing rates, rebates, and obtaining stock lending. Size impacts which funds get to keep their shorts on, are allocated new issues, receive the first call on secondary blocks, and can afford to maintain presence and key relationships in markets that are currently unattractive but may become opportune at a moment's notice sometime down the road. Large teams of analysts are needed to evaluate the creditworthiness of companies. Technology is another area where size is important.

EVOLUTION

Stark says the firm's philosophy, strategy, and goals have remained unchanged since inception. "Our goal is to make money independent of the direction of the market. We are risk-averse. We want to protect our principal but earn 20 percent-plus. We always do this through arbitrage."

The tactics and instruments, however, have changed through the years. Some types of convertibles no longer exist. There are more convertible investors. The techniques are more sophisticated, and more emphasis is placed on technology information. The degree to which hedging is done is more sophisticated.

Stark recalls that 10 to 15 years ago there were few arbitrageurs and the markets were smaller. At that time, you could rely on a spreadsheet. Today, the number and complexity of instruments is very high. Instruments need to be screened on a worldwide basis, and potential trades need to be monitored. Stark says that one position could be intertwined with 10 to 15 trades. Today, technology is required to bring it all together. Equities, options, and convertibles are all involved, and they each have different hedge ratios. This requires powerful risk management tools, powerful screening tools, and a large staff to maintain it all. Technology is very important to Stark Investments in terms of screening opportunities, keeping track of risk exposure, execution of trades, and the like.

PERFORMANCE

The year of the crash, 1987, was the first full year that Stark was professionally managing money. He did quite well that year, perhaps because he was concentrated on the non-U.S. markets and totally out of the U.S. markets.

The year 1990 was characterized by a junk bond scare. Many arbitrageurs didn't do well that year. Stark did; he was up 6.4 percent, while the S&P 500 was down 3 percent.

For hedge funds in general 1994 was a tough year. Interest rates turned, and people got caught. Stark was up 10.36 percent in 1994.

In each of these tumultuous times, Stark Investments has deleveraged, hedged well, and exited the U.S. markets before things turned sour.

The year 1998 was different. Arbitrage spreads widened dramatically with the collapse of Russia, Asian currency fears, and liquidity pressure brought on by the near collapse of Long-Term Capital Management. It was the first down year for Stark Investments; the main fund was down 7.9 percent. Stark says they recognized the Asian situation early on. By September, they had reduced their U.S. exposure and deleveraged. However, this time, they didn't sell out of their U.S. exposure entirely. Convertible product had so cheapened that they decided to hold onto a good part of the U.S. portfolio. They felt the United States would be seen as a haven from worldwide turmoil. They were highly hedged and positioned to be a substantial buyer in an anticipated fourth-quarter equity sell-off. Then the Long-Term Capital Management crisis happened. Some people had to sell. "It was incorrect, at least in the short term, to think the United States would be a safe haven. Liquidity was the driver, and a liquidity crisis occurred. Fortunately, we were in the position to be able to hold onto our portfolio."

Stark Investments benefited from that decision in 1999 and 2000 when annual net returns to the investor of, respectively, 25.9 percent and 28.8 percent were generated.

Are there lessons from 1998? Stark says 1998 reinforced the vital importance of being able to maintain arbitrage positions through market maelstroms; even if you are correct about the long-term fundamentals, short-term liquidity constraints will dominate arbitrage pricing. Accordingly, they have further increased the diversification of what has always been a very diversified portfolio—diversification in terms of both strategies and geography. At any one time, they typically hold 400 to 600 positions spread through the G-7 countries. In addition, they now place even more emphasis on the component of the portfolio that is derived from credit. More investment-grade product is used in all kinds of environments, even if it is not as cheap as lesser-grade products. Stark Investments has also significantly increased the extent to which asset swapping and default protection are used.

An asset swap is the process by which the manager sells out the bond component of the convertible bond, leaving only the equity option of the convertible (plus an option to call back the bond component from the asset swap buyer). The asset swap buyer is interested in buying the asset swap for yield, and is buying the straight bond without any call on the equity. Stark likes to asset swap because it eliminates any credit risk associated with owning the convertible.

Based on 1998's experience, Stark Investments narrowed position limits even more. Formerly the firm would generally risk 4 percent in any one position. Today, those limits are 3 percent for convertible arbitrage and 2 percent for risk arbitrage holdings.

MEMORABLE TRADES/MOTIVATION

When discussing memorable trades, Stark has a long list going back to 1987. He talks about intermarket trading of Nikkei puts back in the late 1980s as an example. This was a period in which the Japanese equity market was in the process of crashing with violent day-to-day swings in the Nikkei index (the Japanese equivalent of the Dow Jones Industrial Average). North American investors were clamoring for ways to profit from the debacle. A variety of U.S. and Canadian underwriters met this demand by issuing Nikkei puts. Each put was a security whose value was determined by the price of the Nikkei; the lower the Nikkei went the greater the value of the put. The price of each security was determined by some form of trailing average of a series of closing prices for the Nikkei.

Complexity was added by the fact that these puts traded when the Nikkei was closed, had a variety of strike prices, involved up to three different currencies and cross-currency rates, and differed in key respects regarding the manner of converting the securities into cash. Through mathematical formulas, as well as real-time pricing and currency feeds, one could equalize the securities. Huge disparities in prices simultaneously occurred between different classes of these securities within a market and between markets. This was because trading was dominated by speculators emotionally betting on the next day's move in the Nikkei and because these investors were not cognizant of the existence of all of the other puts available or lacked the means or understanding to quickly equalize them or to borrow the securities for shorting. Significant low-risk profits could be made by simultaneously buying one type of put and shorting another type. In addition, investors would commonly overreact to news occurring in North American hours, ignoring or underestimating how much less the determinant moving average would change than the next day's move in the Nikkei. This made possible purchases or sales of the puts that created trades with an extremely high probability of profit unless the Nikkei moved by some phenomenal amount.

It is trades like this that motivate Stark. "I get a kick out of it. I like to find something that the market misses. The markets should be rational and efficient, making it intellectually satisfying when you find a substantial mispricing. It is like solving a perplexing riddle or finding a great bargain at a flea market—it is fun."

He continued, "Moreover, the market is a performance-oriented business. It is a real-life puzzle since you and your investors' money are on the line. A risk element exists that is missing in many other intellectual endeavors." Stark also alluded to the market as a good outlet for his competitive spirit.

INVESTORS FROM 22 COUNTRIES

Early on, the investor base was primarily high-net-worth investors. But now there is a growing percentage of institutional investors. "Institutions have the longest time horizon and are more stable. They have an understanding of the business. You need to see things through in arbitrage; you need to stay the course. Institutions do this."

Investors are located in 22 countries. The number of Japanese investors is also on the rise. Arbitrage has seen increased interest from Japanese investors due to regulatory changes; Japanese institutions are now able to invest outside of Japan much more readily. In addition, the Japanese are becoming more knowledgeable about arbitrage and how well it meshes with their search for stable, consistent returns. Due to demand from a Japanese investor, Stark created a product solely focusing on Japanese arbitrage strategy.

Stark also has a fund of funds investor component. In fact, some of their oldest investors are funds of funds. "While you must be cautious about which funds of funds to include in your investor base, those which are truly committed to market neutrality, rather than chasing the fund with the hottest hand, can be extremely stable. Such funds are dependent on managers like ourselves to provide consistency. Thus these funds tend to make us a core part of their portfolios."

Stark disclosed that he is selective with his client base and is not hesitant to turn potential investors away. He wants investors who have stable, long-term capital and who understand arbitrage. "The greatest risk in arbitrage is if capital leaves at the wrong time. You are attempting to exploit temporary mispricings between one security and another. Much of your success comes when the correct relationship between those securities is restored. When the relationship is out of whack and your capital leaves is when you get hurt."

About 95 percent of his and Roth's net worth are in the funds. The general partners and staff members' investment in the funds are about 8.3 percent of the total assets.

On the issue of transparency, Stark says that with arbitrage a manager can be harmed if people know about individual trades. Stark provides information on leverage and the geographic distribution of positions. Beyond that, if investors want specific information about particular positions, Stark requires that a confidentiality agreement be signed. He also will permit on-site reviews of the portfolio.

Stark and Roth are always available to talk with investors. While they have three people in marketing and client services, the two principals will always take investor calls.

WORK AND HOBBY CLOSELY INTERCONNECTED

Stark admits that he no longer comes to the office of weekends. Whatever free time he has is devoted to his wife, their two children, charitable board work,

Net Performance (%) Stark Investments	
1987	22.44
1988	26.78
1989	15.41
1990	6.40
1991	20.22
1992	21.63*
1993	39.75
1994	10.36
1995	42.89
1996	27.30
1997	19.35
1998	–7.88
1999	25.89
2000	28.80
Compound average annual return	**20.71**

*Trading did not occur in March and April.

and exercise. He views his work as fun and reminds me that it started out as a hobby while he practiced law. He says the days fly by and that the concept of work and hobby are closely interconnected.

How long does Stark plan to work at Stark Investments? He points to his father, now at age 83, who has an office in the firm and comes in every day to work on his personal portfolio. Stark plans to work for at least 10 more years, and he sees no reason why the organization couldn't function without him. "I have great confidence in the people here. I would want my capital to still be managed here, even if I were to retire from money management."

BRIAN STARK
Stark Investments

Organization

Inception	1986
Assets	
Current	$1.7 billion
Peak	$1.7 billion
Edge	Global focus, team experience and orientation, brokerage and investment banking relationship
Office Location	Mequon, Wisconsin
Number of People	85
Type of Organization	Arbitrage specialists with redundant oversight
His Role	Heads up convertible arbitrage area; responsible for overall allocation of positions
Investment Committee	Yes
Reward System	Predominantly based on what firm does overall
Number of Investors	215
Type of Investor	Fund of funds, institutions, family offices, high-net-worth investors; investors from 22 countries
GP/Principals' Ownership of Assets	95 percent of his net worth; general partner and staff comprise about 8.3 percent of total assets
Endowments	Not disclosed

Methodology/ Portfolio Composition

Style	Convertible arbitrage, risk arbitrage, private placement, capital structure arbitrage
Number of Positions in Portfolio	400 to 600

Trades Taken	Risk-adjusted returns with portfolio considerations
Role of United States	Varies, but typically about 35 percent
Role of Technology	Fair amount of exposure; technology companies are prime issuer of convertible products in United States and Japan
Role of Private Equity	Limited amount of late-stage private equity in Baystar, private placement fund
Role of Macro	None
Allocates to Other Managers	No

Risk Management

Net Exposure	Shorts are 70 to 90 percent as big as the longs
Hedge Ratio	5 to 10 percent
Hedging Technique	Arbitrage
Maximum Leverage	1.5:1 to 7:1
Memorable Loss	1998
Risk Management	Diversify by strategy and geography; use investment grade product when necessary; Maximum risk per position is 2 percent for risk arbitrage and 3 percent for convertible arbitrage

Background Information

Initial Spark	High school
Professional Background	Lawyer
Education	Brown University; Harvard Law School
Motivation/Satisfaction	Solving a puzzle; finding something the market misses
Age	45
Free Time	Children, sports

15

S. DONALD SUSSMAN
Paloma Partners

Market Neutral Focus
Opportunistic Internal Multistrategy Investment Pool

S. Donald Sussman, founder of Paloma Partners in 1981, calls himself the "chief opportunistic officer." Focusing solely on market neutral strategies, his role is figuring out where the opportunities are. Once those opportunities are identified, he will then find the people who can execute the appropriate strategy.

Sussman, 54, has been farming out allocations to managers since 1981. These are usually exclusive relationships where Paloma is the sole backer of the manager. Sussman says he does not own a piece of these managers and doesn't receive the incentive allocations (the managers do). Currently, he allocates to 22 managers and another three are in the pipeline. The number of managers and strategies provides diversification. The trading groups function as distinct business units. Historically, since Paloma's inception, there has been virtually no market correlation (0.05) to the stock market. Assets currently total approximately $1.6 billion. Peak assets were about $2 billion in 1998.

DIFFERENT STRUCTURE

Because of this structure, it is unclear to some what Paloma is. Is it a fund of funds or a manager? Sussman says that in some respects similarities exist with a fund of funds: Diversification is provided; multiple managers are used, as are multiple strategies.

But many important differences exist as well. First, Paloma typically has exclusive relationships with its managers or maintains separate accounts. In contrast, a fund of funds has pooled accounts with its managers. Second, on the risk control front, Paloma has complete transparency on each transaction done by its managers. It knows in aggregate the concentration by sectors and positions. It also adds a portfolio overlay based on options volatility which uses a small percentage of capital but pays off geometrically. It identifies undervalued options and protects the portfolio when there are large moves. In contrast, most funds of funds receive only monthly returns and don't have the daily knowledge on concentration risk or the ability to manage risk.

In allocating capital, Paloma takes a bottom-up perspective. Capital allocation changes are made daily. "We are opportunistic. We take advantage of the ebb and flow of the markets. Opportunities disappear and reappear." A fund of funds, however, tends to take a top-down, macro approach, and usually a termination of capital will end the relationship between the manager and the fund of funds. In contrast, it is not uncommon that Paloma will reject a manager's trade or idea in the short term and let positions unwind but still maintain a relationship for when future opportunities appear.

All of Paloma's central back office, credit, legal, and stock loan activities are done in-house; about 175 people are housed at Paloma's headquarters and another 50 are located around the world. With a fund of funds, most managers maintain their own administration and financing, so there is no economy of scale achieved through centralized operations as there is at Paloma. So the conclusion is that Paloma is an internal multistrategy investment pool that is managed by the investors' representative, Sussman, not the manager.

Quantitative and qualitative factors are used. Paloma does credit analysis on securities and counter parties but is quantitatively driven for actual selection.

Are there maximum limits a manager can be allocated? There are no formal written rules, but generally Paloma does not allocate more than 5 percent of its capital to a manager.

A substantial majority of Sussman's liquid net worth is in his funds. Over 10 percent of the overall Paloma portfolio assets are insider capital.

GROWING EMPHASIS ON STATISTICAL ARBITRAGE

When Sussman started Paloma, the business was a fund of funds and allocated 100 percent to convertible arbitrage. Allocations were made to two managers—Paul Singer's Elliott Associates and Princeton/ Newport Partners. The focus of both was convertible arbitrage. At that time, Elliott was a relatively conservative convertible bond arbitrageur and Princeton/Newport Partners was more leveraged, using more aggressive instruments. By late 1985, Paloma was allocating to about 16 managers. Sussman started to prune them and bring management in-house.

Over the years, Sussman added other market neutral strategies based on where he saw the opportunities. In the mid-1980s, merger arbitrage became a large percentage of the portfolio. By 1987, the profits in merger arbitrage strategies were dwindling and Sussman closed out this exposure by the end of September 1987. Two weeks later, the crash occurred.

Today, Paloma's three largest strategies are convertible arbitrage (42 percent) in the United States, Canada, Europe, and Asia; merger/event arbitrage (28 percent); and statistical arbitrage (24 percent). The remainder is made up of volatility arbitrage (2 percent), securities lending (2 percent), G-10 fixed income (1 percent), and miscellaneous (1 percent).

Diversification is critical. More than one manager is trading each of these strategies. For example, there are 13 managers in statistical arbitrage and five in Japanese convertibles. Sussman makes it a point that each manager uses a different strategy—thus providing diversification. Whereas other firms will have morning meetings, Sussman doesn't want the managers communicating or sharing information. He wants to keep them separate. Managers have the choice of being located in the Greenwich headquarters or wherever else they want. As a result, about six are in Greenwich. One division is in Melbourne, Australia, and another is in Seattle. "Risk management is here [in Greenwich]; trading centers are everywhere. It is only relevant that the trader be based where he or she can be most productive," says Sussman.

Sussman acknowledges that at some point diversification has limits (i.e., overlaps may exist in portfolios between the managers). If overhead isn't high, the additional manager is worth it. If overhead is high, the additional manager is not worth the expense.

Today, Sussman is very interested in statistical arbitrage and feels this is the area where growth will occur. Statistical arbitrage uses high-level mathematics to trade large baskets of related securities. The three new allocations will be to statistical arbitrage managers. He feels that if these strategies work, it will expand overall capacity of the firm by several hundred million dollars.

Sussman says the statistical arbitrageurs can reap some of the profit made by the market makers and specialists. "They have 10,000 orders in the system and monitor them all and can be the bid-ask spread in any one of them. If they don't like how it's going, the manager can pull out." By replicating the role of the specialist, these arbitrageurs can earn extraordinarily good profits, with little leverage and volatility.

Among Sussman's successes has been his relationship with David Shaw of D. E. Shaw Investments. Back in the late 1980s, when Shaw had just a dream but no track record, Sussman was the first to give him the research and development funds to create a business and was his primary backer. Sussman benefited for many years. In 1998, however, when Paloma was down about 20 percent for the year, much of that loss was a result of the investment with Shaw. Sussman still maintains an account with Shaw, but Shaw has refocused out of fixed-income arbitrage and into convertible arbitrage and statistical arbitrage. Andrew Lo from M.I.T. (where he heads the Laboratory for Financial Engineering), who joined Paloma in 2000, is now trading a statistical arbitrage strategy. Sussman believes this may be the next big advance in computerized trading techniques.

Interestingly, Sussman has been the first investor of a number of the other superstar managers interviewed in the book. In addition to allocating to Singer back in 1981, Sussman was one of the first investors for Bruce Kovner and Brian Stark.

RISK MANAGERS ARE IN CHARGE

Sussman makes the point that his team—not the manager—makes the allocation decision at Paloma. In most funds, says Sussman, the manager-founder makes the allocation decision. Undoubtedly the manager's ego may make him myopic about his trades. Sussman feels this can lead to bad results or at least greater risks.

At Paloma, the risk manager makes these decisions, and the risk manager is independent of the manager. The process is a mix of qualitative and quantitative factors. The percentage allocation is driven by opportunity. The computers spit out expected return and expected risk of each investment owned. Opportunities are analyzed and simulations done. From a subjective viewpoint, Sussman looks at rates of return earned in various businesses, simulations of what could be done, correlations to other strategies, and what the risk-adjusted return's impact is to the portfolio.

Overlay of judgment is important to Sussman. He feels that the main problem that Long-Term Capital Management, as well as David Shaw, had in 1998 was that they had ultimate faith in statistics; no overlay of judgment was used.

CHANGES AFTER 1998

Since its inception in 1981, Paloma has enjoyed double-digit returns in all full years of trading except two: it incurred a 5.4 percent loss in 1994 and a 20.9 percent loss in 1998. Its average annual return since inception is 14.3 percent.

What about 1998? Sussman says they could see problems developing in May and June in fixed-income arbitrage and they started liquidating their positions. By the time the Long-Term Capital Management debacle occurred, they were completely sold out of their fixed-income positions. But they still had the investment with David Shaw.

The bulk of the losses were in bond arbitrage as interest rates on the safest government bonds fell while rates on most other debt shot up. As world bond markets collapsed, illiquidity occurred. As a result of LTCM, spreads went to historically wide levels. Yet, Japanese asset swap spreads (reflecting the credit distinction between Japanese government and bank credit obligations) actually went to zero. Sussman says this was an anomalous result because it meant that Japanese government bonds (the better credit) were trading at yields equal to Japanese bank bonds (the lesser credit) of the same maturity. Historically when flights to quality occurred (such as in 1994 with the Mexican bank crisis) these spreads widened dramatically, as one would expect they should. Paloma expected this spread would widen during a liquidity meltdown, and this trade was on the books in large size as insurance for other types of fixed-income arbitrage trades in the portfolio. Why, then, didn't it work in 1998?

It turned out that one of the few liquid instruments in LTCM's portfolio was Japanese government bonds, and LTCM needed to sell these to support less liquid parts of its book. Thus, spreads went backward to flat; bank paper had the same yield as government paper. The fixed-income markets were so illiquid that LTCM was unable to move even some medium-sized positions in short-term government bonds. Sussman decided to bail out of his whole-fixed income book when he saw the spreads go backward; he could tell something was happening that he didn't know about at the moment. "The risk system at Paloma worked—we were able to get out."

In 1998, there were three investment managers whose balance sheets were greater than $1 billion—Long-Term Capital Management, Paloma, and D. E. Shaw. Unfortunately, Sussman says, we were two out of the three places. "Competitors weren't big enough to be in the business. That turned out to be an advantage for them."

As a result of 1998, among other things, Sussman learned never to put capital where he is not in control of what's going on, such as in the Shaw situation back then. Based on the multiyear exclusive agreement Paloma had going back to 1993 with Shaw, they mutually locked each other up. Shaw didn't have to listen to Sussman—and he didn't. Yet Sussman couldn't pull his money. Today, the exclusive relationship with Shaw continues, but Paloma has much greater liquidity with him and Shaw has limited the scope of his trading authority.

The current Paloma portfolio has leverage of 3.5:1, which is down about 100 points from earlier in 2000 and much lower than in 1998 when leverage was about 8:1 across the entire book. As a result of Sussman's decision to get out of fixed-income arbitrage at the end of 1998 and focus more on convertible arbitrage and statistical arbitrage, leverage has declined a great deal.

Today, Sussman feels high leverage is no longer needed. "1999 was Paloma's best year, up 30 percent following our worst year . . . . High leverage wasn't needed." Sussman describes how the LTCM situation resulted in most of the proprietary trading desks, except Goldman Sachs's, closing down. This lessened competition and provided more opportunities for those still trading. He sees this as a generational issue since banks and insurance companies are unlikely to go back into proprietary arbitrage business anytime soon. Recent mergers between Credit Suisse First Boston and Donaldson, Lufkin & Jenrette as well as J. P. Morgan and Chase take out further players.

Today, Sussman prefers highly liquid securities and convertible bond trades that produce high cash flows. He avoids Reg D convertibles (i.e., an event-driven strategy that invests in micro- and small-capitalization public companies that are raising money in private capital markets), which he feels could be like a game of musical chairs if the stock market turns bearish. Until now, he says, the bull market has bailed out these securities. These companies, using very expensive financing, are usually in financial distress or at least weak.

In 2000, Paloma Partners had another strong year, up 27 percent, closely following its record year in 1999. Sussman commented, "We are positioned to take advantage of the opportunity occurring in part because of lack of capital in the arbitrage world. This is a result of mergers of many banks who had previously been competitors and the withdrawal of capital because of 1998."

OTHER BUSINESS

Sussman is also the chairman of the New China Management Corporation, an investment manager for the Cathay Investment Fund, which was established for the purpose of undertaking direct investment in China. Within Cathay, there are six publicly listed companies (on the New York Stock Exchange, as well as the China, Hong Kong, and Singapore exchanges). There are also seven private unlisted companies in Cathay, including an infrastructure project, food production company, and Internet companies. So, it is part private equity. Paloma's other investment category includes a small investment in the Cathay Fund (less than 1 percent of aggregate capital).

In 1990, Sussman founded London Global Securities, an independent securities lending firm, to service the internal convertible bond managers and to assist in trade financing, while generating revenue for the fund through third-party fee income from securities lending. In 1997, LGS was sold to Donaldson, Lufkin & Jenrette, although Paloma remains in the securities lending business primarily for its internal traders.

FEES

While Paloma has been criticized for its fee structure in a 1999 business publication,[1] Sussman maintains that the fees are considerably lower than those of a fund of funds. Paloma charges a management fee of 1.5 percent of assets as long as the fund is profitable on a rolling 12-month basis. The underlying managers typically are paid 20 percent of net profits, subject to a hurdle and loss carryforward. Sussman does not share in the incentive compensation.

TRANSPARENCY

Paloma provides taxable clients and non-U.S. clients with monthly reports. U.S. tax-exempt clients receive quarterly reports. Sussman actively discusses the portfolio with clients, including percentage capital allocation to strategies, balance sheet leverage on the overall portfolio and by strategy, number of trading positions overall and by strategy, average static returns and hedge ratios on the convertible book (broken out by the United States, Canada, Japan, and Europe), and year-to-date profitability attribution by strategy.

Sussman is willing to sit down in Greenwich with any client and review the specifics of trading, the allocation process, and strategies.

PAST AND FUTURE

Sussman was a convertible bond trader at a brokerage firm in the late 1960s. He understood the return/risk characteristics that were appropriate for wealthy individuals. Whereas most wealthy investors used municipal bonds, Sussman felt that convertible arbitrage was superior.

On an after-tax basis, people could make twice as much without taking interest rate risk or market risk. He later became chief financial officer for a privately held multinational trading company and, after that, managed money for partners at a New York law firm.

He started Paloma Partners in 1981. The firm is named after Paloma Picasso, the Tiffany & Company jewelry designer. Sussman's career has been driven by intellectual stimulation, pride in a job well done, as well as professional respect.

Sussman describes the culture as entrepreneurial as well as where a premium is placed on intellect. A large number of the professionals have advanced degrees with significant experience. Sussman also describes the culture as a big family atmosphere—easygoing in dress and demeanor. "We encourage people to seek an environment that makes them most productive."

Today, four funds are offered to U.S. investors and three to offshore investors. There are over 300 clients; most are U.S.-based. Insurance companies, family offices, and institutions are the core investors. Paloma Partners is the oldest and largest. Paloma Partners Institutional Investors, Capital Preservation Partners, and European Merger Fund also are offered to U.S. investors. Paloma International Fund, Capital Preservation Partners Limited, and European Merger Fund Limited are available to offshore persons.

Where does Sussman see Paloma going? His goal is to build the firm into an institutional entity, yet retain his role as the person identifying opportunities and allocating capital.

Sussman sees the hedge fund industry growing in the years ahead. His main concern is that empire building will lead to some problems as some managers grow uncontrollably. "Investors need to know who is trading the money and how much they are getting paid to trade it." In some cases, says Sussman, the main manager hires lesser-known managers, who are paid considerably less, to handle subportfolios. Another issue is that when asset size is too large, a manager may have difficulty getting out of wrong ideas.

PASSION FOR THE ENVIRONMENT

In addition to sailing, Sussman has a passion for the environment. He says this interest was sparked by his two children, who have been vegetarians since an early age. He supports sustainable forestry. In Maine, he has been fighting the paper industry, which would like to cut down more trees and has been a big polluter. He has donated considerable money and resources, and has a full-time lobby person in Maine where he has a vacation home.

Sussman, a liberal Democrat, has supported President Clinton in the past and Al Gore in 2000. Throughout the years, he has supported Senators Chris Dodd and Joe Lieberman.

Sussman also finances and supports pure science research at the Weizmann Institute in Israel. He has chaired the American fund-raising arm and is a deputy chairman of the international board of governors. In 1996, he established the Sussman Family Building for Environmental Sciences on the Weizmann campus. He is also a trustee of Carnegie Hall and is cochair of the board of trustees for the Ethical Culture Fieldston School in New York.

Net Performance (%) Paloma Partners	
1981	7.80*
1982	17.41
1983	18.77
1984	13.46
1985	25.09
1986	16.51
1987	25.75
1988	16.69
1989	20.73
1990	11.32
1991	19.31
1992	11.01
1993	15.45
1994	−5.41
1995	11.66
1996	19.87
1997	17.33
1998	−20.95
1999	30.45
2000	27.00
Compound average annual return	**14.34**

*Trading started in December 1981.

S. DONALD SUSSMAN
Paloma Partners

Organization

Inception	1981
Assets	
Current	$1.6 billion
Peak	$2.0 billion
Edge	Exclusive manager relationships; daily position transparency; sophisticated risk management systems
Office Location	Greenwich, Connecticut— headquarters
	Various trading centers in New York metropolitan area, Seattle, Toronto, London, Tokyo, and Melbourne
Number of People	200+
Type of Organization	Exclusive managers
His Role	Chairman and director of asset allocation and risk management
Investment Committee	No
Reward System	Typical group earns incentive over a hurdle
Number of Investors	300+
Type of Investor	Insurance companies, family offices and high-net-worth individuals, pensions, foundations, offshore persons, and entities
GP/Principals' Ownership of Assets	Exceeds 10 percent of total capital
Endowments	Not disclosed

Methodology/ Portfolio Composition

Style	Market neutral
Number of Positions in Portfolio	2,500+

Trades Taken	Opportunistic within market neutral universe
Role of United States	Historically varies from one-third to two-thirds of portfolio
Role of Technology	Immaterial
Role of Private Equity	Immaterial
Role of Macro	Immaterial
Allocates to Other Managers	Yes

Risk Management

Net Exposure	Longs typically matched with shorts
Hedging Technique	Each individual position is hedged; in addition, entire portfolio has volatility options overlay; able to move to cash daily
Maximum Leverage	Not predetermined, but unlikely to exceed 5:1
Memorable Loss	1998
Risk Management	Diversification by strategy and number of managers; proprietary internal risk management system

Background Information

Initial Spark	Summer job at brokerage firm
Professional Background	Convertible bond trader
Education	New York University, undergraduate and MBA
Motivation/Satisfaction	Professional respect; intellectual stimulation; pride in a job well done
Age	54
Free Time	Children, philanthropy, environmental causes, sailing, modern art

16

DAVID TEPPER
Appaloosa Management

Opportunistic Event-Driven
Getting Back to Basics

Located in Chatham, New Jersey, a 45-minute drive from New York City, Appaloosa Management has a suburban mood and setting. During my visit, David Tepper, 43, spoke openly and candidly about his business. He had recently made the decision to shrink the business and go back to its original core. At $1.6 billion, he felt the portfolio was too big. By returning money to investors, he believed the firm could become more focused and be more profitable. He estimated the optimal size to be about $1 billion.

Tepper wants to bring more discipline to the firm. "I want to get rid of the more fluffy positions and only have great positions on rather than those that I think can be great." Tepper also wants to reduce the number of positions so the firm can focus more on what it has. Generally, Appaloosa has 50 to 70 different types of positions on. At the moment (September 2000), it has 30. He likes the more concentrated approach. Tepper derides the theory of diversification. "You can't make money with a diversified approach." Typically, about one-third of the portfolio has exposure to the stock market.

In taking a position, he is opportunistic, usually looking for double the return on small caps and perhaps a 50 percent return on larger caps. Tepper says size of the position determines how much a manager can lose. When getting into a position, he also needs to know how they're going to exit.

Tepper, the ultimate trader, is casual and down-to-earth. Gut feeling is important to him. At the moment, Tepper is holding a lot of cash because he doesn't like the markets. He feels the market is not going anywhere and has underlying risk. He believes a high probability exists of a bad outcome. "I don't have the guts now because the probabilities are not there." While he feels the near term is not great, he sees great potential for 2001.

In the quest to be more focused, Tepper sees high-yield bonds, also known as junk bonds, as being the focal point, but the firm won't just invest in junk companies. He sees them as the window to look at and find other opportunities.

VALUE-ORIENTED OPPORTUNISTIC

The core of Appaloosa's business is and has always been high-yield bonds and distressed securities. At the moment, junk bonds and distressed comprise about one-third of the portfolio, but Tepper sees that percentage going higher. He described the approach as value-oriented opportunistic. They take a credit orientation; they analyze the capital structure of a company.

Appaloosa is opportunistic and will be in and out of various instruments and markets. But it will always have U.S. capital structure on the books.

One example was its buying of McDermott bonds. McDermott is an oil driller. One of its subsidiaries, Babcock & Wilcox, went bankrupt due to the asbestos scare. Tepper says everyone was tossing the bonds, but he found it opportunistic to buy them at such a low price.

Tepper and I talked in the conference room where there were mementos of recent deals Appaloosa had participated in. These included Kmart, Kroll, Intermedia Partners IV, Goodman, United Industries Corp., and Parker Drilling Corp. The variety of sizes, and types of deals underscored Appaloosa's opportunistic approach.

Tepper describes the methodology as 95 to 100 percent fundamental. The goal is to provide returns higher than those of corporate bonds.

EMERGING MARKETS/RUSSIA AND KOREA

Tepper gave several examples of his micro opportunistic approach. Tepper has gone into emerging markets where others fear to tread. He openly says that what makes him different from many other traders in sovereign and emerging debt is that he is willing to take bigger positions and be more aggressive. "We often catch the bottoms. We'll be there at the turning points."

After the Russian default on government bonds in 1998 in which many hedge firms got hurt—Appaloosa was down 29 percent that year—Appaloosa was in there heavily buying Russian bonds in November. Tepper said he felt comfortable doing this because it all boils down to probabilities—one of his favorite themes. The bonds were selling at 15-cent coupons and trading as if the worst case had already happened. Probabilities that the bonds could go lower were not great but the upside potential had a great probability. Worse-off emerging market disaster cases such as Congo bonds or Vietnam bonds were trading at 10 cents. Wall Street desks were no longer allowed to buy the bonds. It was this aggressive action that generated a 60 percent gain in 1999 for Appaloosa.

Did the 29 percent loss in 1998 lead to any changes? Not really. "We fell asleep with a sense of false liquidity. We thought liquidity was there but it wasn't. Things happened so fast in Russia and we couldn't get out."

Again by being opportunistic, Appaloosa was also the first Western firm to buy Korean Treasury bills in November 1997. None of the major U.S. investment banks were willing to be in Korea. Credit-rating agencies were beginning to downgrade the country from investment grade, which pushed the debt price down so far that it yields as much as 8 percent over U.S. Treasuries, or 13 to 20 percent.

In September 2000, only 4 percent of the portfolio was in non-U.S. instruments.

Tepper acknowledges a major vulnerability to his approach. "You can't stay too long in such situations. You are fighting on a micro level and it's not your battlefield." He then brings the conversation back to junk bonds and distressed securities—which are his battlefield and what he knows best.

Tepper admits that it is hard to hedge distressed securities, junk bonds, and emerging markets. They tend to use S&P futures and Treasuries. "It is an art, not a science, and the percentage moves around. We may not have a hedge on if we are really bullish."

The Appaloosa portfolio has not used leverage in two years. The high had been 3:1. One example of high leverage was its buying Columbia Gas investment-grade bonds where the yield was 600 basis points over Treasury bills and relatively little risk. If it is a safe, lower-volatility asset such as Columbia Gas or McDermott bonds, Appaloosa feels comfortable adding more leverage. The typical leverage, however, is about 1.5:1 to 2:1. In Thoroughbred Fund, a secured bank debt fund, leverage of 4:1 to 7:1 is used.

THREE-YEAR LOCK-UP

At the end of 1998, Tepper says investor withdrawals were normal. This is partly because many of the investors are long-term in nature and had been with him for a while, and performance had been excellent. He also requires a three-year lock-up of assets.

Because of the three-year lock-up, he does not have many fund of funds investors or European investors. Clients tend to be endowments, family offices, and high-net-worth investors. According to the 1999 NACUBO study, Davidson College and Middlebury College are two endowments that allocate to him. Overall, there are about 150 investors.

Regarding transparency, he gives investors the investments by category on a quarterly basis. He lists the percentage in U.S. stocks, the emerging markets by country, as well as stock investments by country. But he does not provide individual names.

All the funds are named after horses. Appaloosa Investment LP I is for U.S. investors; Palomino Fund Ltd., which invests in parallel to Appaloosa, is for non-U.S.; and Thoroughbred LP I is a secured bank fund. The minimum investment for each is $5 million with a 1 percent management and 20 percent incentive fee charged.

ORGANIZATION

Appaloosa consists of 25 people, seven of whom are partners. Tepper, the sole stockholder, owns 100 percent of the voting rights. He is the decision maker when positions require size. He is very involved in the portfolio and focuses on different areas ranging from bankruptcies to emerging markets to equities. The general partner and its principals own more than 10 percent of the partnership's total assets.

There are six industry analysts who do credit analysis. There is also an in-house lawyer for the bankruptcy work.

A relatively loose organization exists. There are no investment committee meetings, and discussion is casual as everyone sits in a bull pen close together. Once a month, he and partner Jim Bolin, along with Ron Goldstein, the chief financial officer, review the portfolios over lunch at a nearby Mexican restaurant.

Appaloosa does not allocate to other managers. Allocations to private equity occur just in special situations.

Appaloosa had been indirectly linked to Michael Smirlock. In 1994, Tepper hired Smirlock to trade mortgage securities and raise a new fund—Mustang Investments. Smirlock was a principal. By 1997, Smirlock ran three hedge funds—Mustang, Shetland, and Trakehner. In August 1997, Smirlock created Laser Advisers, a new registered investment adviser, to manage the hedge fund and real estate investment trust. At this point, Laser was not an Appaloosa entity. Smirlock, as chairman, owned 80 percent of the entity of Laser Advisers, and Tepper owned the rest.[1] After Smirlock mispriced securities, he eventually resigned as chief executive officer of Laser Advisers, the management company advising the hedge fund and the REIT, and was ousted as chief executive officer of Laser Mortgage.

BACKGROUND

Tepper says he initially became interested in investing as an 11-year-old watching his father trade stocks. In college, he developed an options scheme where he'd buy at $\frac{1}{16}$ and sell at $\frac{1}{8}$.

Upon graduating from the University of Pittsburgh, he became a securities analyst at Equi Bank in Pittsburgh. Then he attended graduate school at Carnegie Mellon Business School. After graduation, he worked at Republic Steel in Ohio and then Keystone Mutual Funds in Boston. Then he went to Goldman Sachs in New York in 1985 when the high-yield group was initially formed.

Tepper had been at Goldman Sachs for about eight years as head trader on the high-yield desk. His primary focus was bankruptcies and special situations. He left in 1993 to start Appaloosa with Jack Walton, who was formerly senior portfolio manager for Goldman Sachs Asset Management. Walton was in the office the day of the interview, but is no longer active in the firm.

Why are the funds named after horses? When they started the company they originally wanted the name Pegasus but the name had already been taken. Since Pegasus was a horse, they looked into other horse possibilities. Appaloosa was the first name in the horse book. Also being the first letter in the alphabet, it had the additional plus of getting information first if faxed or called.

Tepper says he is motivated by the game. When he's not trading, he enjoys golfing and swimming. He also coaches baseball, softball, and soccer teams of his three children.

Net Performance (%) *Appaloosa Management*	
1993	57.62*
1994	19.03
1995	42.06
1996	78.46
1997	29.54
1998	−29.19
1999	60.89
2000	0.03
Compound average annual return	**27.59**

*Fund started in June 1993.

DAVID TEPPER
Appaloosa Management

Organization

Inception	1993
Assets	
Current	$1.2 billion
Peak	$1.6 billion
Edge	Experience, opportunistic
Office Location	Chatham, New Jersey
Number of People	25
Type of Organization	Trading
His Role	Actively involved in all areas
Investment Committee	Yes
Reward System	Performance of overall firm and specialty
Number of Investors	150
Type of Investor	Heavily U.S.; family offices, endowments; no fund of funds
GP/Principals' Ownership of Assets	10 to 15 percent
Endowments (*Source:* 1999 NACUBO)	Middlebury College, Davidson College

Methodology/ Portfolio Composition

Style	Opportunistic, event-driven
Number of Positions in Portfolio	
Average	50 to 70
Current	30
Trades Taken	Opportunistically
Role of United States	Varies
Role of Technology	Varies
Role of Private Equity	Selectively, rare

Role of Macro	Varies
Allocates to Other Managers	No
Risk Management	
Net Exposure	One-third of portfolio
Hedging Technique	S&P futures, Treasuries, cash
Maximum Leverage	3:1 in low volatility, safe situations; very little in last few years
Memorable Loss	Russia 1998
Risk Management	Little leverage; moves to cash; 5 percent maximum per trade
Background Information	
Initial Spark	Watching father trade stocks
Professional Background	Head trader at Goldman Sachs
Education	University of Pittsburgh; Carnegie Mellon Business School
Motivation/Satisfaction	The game
Age	43
Free Time	Coaches children's sports teams, golfs, swims

17

BRUCE WILCOX
Cumberland Associates

Enfranchisement—Three Generations
Long-Term Value Investor

Cumberland Associates is the only hedge fund that has managed to succeed beyond its first generation. In fact, it is on its third generation and has a 30-year track record. It was founded in 1970 by Don Cecil and Walter Mintz, two veterans of Shearson, Hammill & Co. In 1982, Cecil and Mintz turned management of Cumberland Associates over to Richard Reiss and K. Tucker Andersen. In 1996, when Reiss and Andersen stepped down, the next generation was in place. It converted from a general partnership in 1997 to a limited liability company.

    The Cumberland interview was conducted with Bruce Wilcox, current chairman of the management committee and one of the six partners, as a representative of the firm and proxy for the other partners. "It is our organization, not my organization," he emphasized.

Fittingly, the firm does not carry the name of any individuals but rather that of the hotel in London at which the founders struck their agreement to enter the venture.

CUMULATIVE WISDOM

Wilcox says their edge is the cumulative wisdom of the organization and its experience over 30 years and the ability to keep its current and retired principals nearby. Insight and context are also key.

Wilcox says Cumberland is truly different from most other hedge funds because it operates as a true partnership. The senior portfolio managers have discretion over the capital, and they have significant equity in the enterprise.

The partners include five portfolio managers and the chief financial officer. The funds are managed on a decentralized basis with each of the portfolio managers directly running, for example, 20 percent of the firm's capital. This means that all of the portfolio managers have about 80 percent of their own capital run by the other partners. This situation makes them interdependent on each other. It also means they care very much how the overall portfolio is run. The portfolio managers argue passionately about their differences yet they depend on each other. The result is a lot of give-and-take, challenge, debate, and compromise, says Wilcox. Thus the culture can be described as a true partnership with enfranchisement.

The management committee consists of Wilcox, Andrew Wallach, and Gary Tynes, the chief financial officer. The committee has broad authority to control the extent to which the overall portfolios are invested and sets specific guidelines on how capital is used by each manager. These are not sector allocations; they are risk limits. The job of the committee is to formulate a consensus and make a final determination.

The management committee allocates to each portfolio manager at the start of each year and adjusts if needed during the year. The allocations are based on several factors including the immediate opportunity for any given portfolio manager and his individual style as well as the demands from the other portfolio managers. The process is consultative and debated. Cumberland takes a bottom-up approach: The portfolio is built one position at a time. There is no top-down sector allocation.

Wilcox focuses on oil and gas, the financial industry, and financial-related technology. Wallach's expertise includes communications, media and entertainment, technology, capital goods, pollution control, and distressed securities. Oscar Schafer, who has been at Cumberland since 1982 after nine years as a portfolio manager and then a general partner at Steinhardt Partners, focuses on health care, chemicals, conglomerates, cosmetics, paper and forest products, railroads, textiles and apparel, and trucking. (Schafer retired at the end of 2000.) Glenn Krevlin specializes in beverages, foods, household products, lodging, restaurants, retailing, and consumer services. Dipak Patel specializes in the Internet, electronic commerce, technology, and entertainment.

The portfolio is heavily U.S.-biased because this is where disclosure is outstanding and the partners have a strong understanding of how company managements work. About 5 percent of the portfolio is outside the United States.

A snapshot look at the portfolio at the end of August 2000 indicates that consumer cyclicals comprise 23 percent of the long exposure and 6 percent of the short exposure. Technology makes up about 17 percent of the long exposure and 3 percent of the short exposure. Financials, health care, and energy come in next, each with about an 8 to 9 percent long exposure.

Two meetings are held each week. On Monday morning, the portfolio managers review the calendar, discuss what markets are moving, examine significant purchases and sales, and assess the general atmosphere. On Friday morning, they review the portfolios and positions in depth. Ad hoc interaction takes place throughout the week.

Each quarter, each portfolio manager does a formal review of his portfolio. Managers are required to write an internal memo for each security position initiated.

Wilcox says information alone is not an edge; information is now a commodity. It is insight that is a competitive edge, and they are able to maintain it through the cumulative wisdom of the organization. They keep the retired people overtly in the fold or close to it. Cumberland still has three of the original seven limited partners involved. Cecil and Mintz still have offices at Cumberland. Cumberland has an economic interest in Reiss's Georgica Partners, a hedge fund that focuses on media stocks. Andersen, who has an office at Cumberland, acts as an informal consultant.

Of the assets under management, about 10 percent are the current partners' and retired principals' assets.

With this structure, turnover is low. In hiring people into the firm, they do not necessarily look for Wall Street people. They look for people with experience in appraising companies. Patel was from McKinsey, and Larry Rifkin was from an investment bank. "We pay a lot of attention to personality. We want people for the long haul. We want an equity owner. We don't want hotshots or hired guns," says Wilcox.

Money is not the primary motivator. Self-realization and fulfillment are key.

LONG-TERM VALUE ORIENTATION

Throughout the 30-year track record, there has been very little variation in the approach and structure of the firm. There have generally been four to six portfolio managers.

While each of the five portfolio managers has his own individual approach and style, they all adhere to long-term value investing. Generally, they look at discounted cash flow adjusted for large opportunity or risk parameters.

On the black box–fundamental continuum, Cumberland is definitely at the fundamental end. They seek out securities that are significantly mispriced on an earnings per share, cash flow, and/or private market value basis.

Wilcox says they see growth and value investing as reconcilable. They seek to quantify the reasonable current value of businesses based on future net cash flows, discounted at an appropriate cost of capital. "This eclectic definition of value enables us to adapt to different market and business cycles and to a wide range of industries and capitalization sizes. Generally, we seek out situations on both the long and short side which have not only a large differential between market price and value but also some form of catalyst to optimization of market price and therefore shareholder value."

As value investors, they ask primary questions such as, "What is the company worth? What is the value accretion rate? What can we buy it at?" They look at the value per share in contrast to the trading price per share. Price and value are not necessarily the same. They think about the likely future trading range per share relative to their notion of value. On the long side, the ideal situation is if they can buy $100 worth of value at $60 and that the notional $100 of value is increasing over time.

In the past two years, as the volatility in the stock market has increased, share prices have fluctuated widely while the value per share has changed more slowly. "It is more likely that $100 worth of value may trade between $10 and $175 than the narrow ranges of the past. There is more overvaluation and more undervaluation," says Wilcox. "We need to think widely. The environment is now more challenging but it is better suited to our skill set."

The best environment for Cumberland's trading approach is a flat to slightly up environment with considerable volatility, such as 2000. A volatile market presents a challenge for their long-term orientation since they are less likely to take a buy-and-hold strategy. The worst environment for Cumberland is an indiscriminately rising market such as the late 1990s.

"We're running a marathon," says Wilcox. "It is an investment organization, not a trading organization. It is not unusual to hold an investment for many years."

Cumberland focuses most heavily on companies with equity capitalizations of between $500 million and $10 billion. The weighted market capitalization is about $6 billion. The firm runs a diversified portfolio of over 100 positions.

Since inception, the compound average annual return of Cumberland Partners has been about 19 percent. There have been six down years, including 1973, which was down 2.2 percent; 1987, which was down 3.5 percent; 1990, which was down 18.8 percent; 1994, down 6.4 percent; 1998, down 3 percent; and 2000, down 0.5 percent.

The year 1990 was a memorable one in which Cumberland learned a significant lesson. Their analysis of the companies was excellent but the distressed high-yield markets in which they were heavily invested became illiquid. At year-end, they had redemptions that had to be funded despite the illiquid market. That situation taught them to pay greater attention to portfolio liquidity.

Usually a tough year is followed by a very good year, says Wilcox. The down years (since 1987) were always followed by large gains.

RISK MANAGEMENT

The portfolio managers' own assets are aligned with those of investors, and are invested in highly diversified and liquid vehicles. The portfolio managers are subject to ongoing systematic review. Leverage is rarely used and is viewed as a double-edged sword.

Wilcox emphasizes that gross exposure to the stock market is as important as net exposure because it is sometimes possible to lose money on the long side and short side. Gross exposure is the sum of the long and short exposures, while net exposure is the short exposure taken from the long exposure.

Shorting stock is done to make a profit rather than to hedge. The managers will also hold cash. Occasionally they use paired-securities tactics to create stub values. They may use index and company-specific options to effect short strategies.

DURABLE BASE OF INVESTORS

In addition to managed accounts, there are six funds. Cumberland Partners, which began in 1970, is the flagship fund. The first of the four LongView Partnerships began in 1987. They feature a preferred return to investors of 8 percent annually. Net profits in excess of 8 percent are allocated 80 percent to the investors and 20 percent to the general partner. Cumber International began in 1984. Cumberland Benchmarked Partners began operations in January 2000. The profit allocation is 25 percent of the excess over the market benchmark provided that the partnership is in a positive gain position and ahead of a high-water mark.

In 1999, Cumberland adopted its formal benchmark consisting of the average of the S&P 500 and the Russell 2000. This blended benchmark reflects the characteristics of its portfolio companies. Exceeding this benchmark is part of the goal set for all the funds and an explicit part of the incentive fee for Benchmarked Partners.

In addition to the 10 percent of assets that belongs to current and retired partners, 25 percent of the investors are U.S. nontaxables including endowments and foundations. The offshore component is small. The remainder is high-net-worth investors as well as executives of companies they've researched who have been impressed by them and decided to invest with them.

Wilcox feels Cumberland is one of the most transparent hedge funds. Each month, it shows investors its top 30 long positions in dollar terms and as percentage of equity, and the respective gain/loss. Also shown is the portfolio composition with regard to gross long and gross short positions as well as long call options and short call options. Portfolio concentration by industry on both the long and short side are shown. In addition, there is often a fairly detailed write-up of one or more portfolio positions.

SURFING AND MUSIC

Wilcox enjoys what he does and finds that it fulfills his eclectic tastes and interests. He joined the firm in 1986. What had attracted him to Cumberland was not that it was a hedge fund per se but rather its investment philosophy and that he aspired to own equity.

He had previously been an analyst–portfolio manager at Central National–Gottesman after working as a lending officer at Continental Illinois National Bank. He became a member of the management committee in 1997 and the chairman in 1998. He spends about 60 percent of his time interacting with the management of companies, an-

Net Performance (%) Cumberland Partners	
1970	34.70*
1971	26.00
1972	10.70
1973	−2.20
1974	4.10
1975	45.20
1976	38.40
1977	13.90
1978	20.20
1979	38.40
1980	40.70
1981	11.70
1982	34.50
1983	29.70
1984	7.30
1985	41.70
1986	18.40
1987	−3.50
1988	21.00
1989	26.40
1990	−18.80
1991	37.50
1992	24.10
1993	31.10
1994	−6.40
1995	21.40
1996	17.90
1997	32.00
1998	−3.00
1999	35.00
2000	−0.50
Compound average annual return	**19.04**
*Trading started on June 1, 1970.	

alysts, and other industry participants and another 20 percent on management.

He gives considerable attention to the health of the organization. "I don't spend a lot of time staring at my screen."

His passion for surfing is evidenced by a photograph of him riding the big wave at Sunset Beach in Hawaii. He also loves music and plays rock guitar in the No Dancing band. He is the chairman of the board of the Piatigorsky Foundation, which brings live classical music to places where it may not otherwise be found such as rural districts of North Carolina or a boys' correctional facility in Texas.

THE FUTURE OF THE INDUSTRY

Wilcox believes the hedge fund industry has rapidly expanded and may soon go through a consolidation phase. "Some managers haven't earned their 1 percent management fee/20 percent incentive fee," says Wilcox. "As a result, you could see some differentiating in pricing." One such example could be the increasing use of the hurdle benchmark such as Cumberland instituted with Benchmarked Partners. He expects to see more performance-based fees as the 1 percent/20 percent structure comes under pressure.

BRUCE WILCOX
Cumberland Associates

Organization

Inception	1970
Assets	
Current	$750 million
Peak	$1.2 billion
Edge	Insight, context, cumulative wisdom of the organization, keeping retired people close
Office Location	New York, New York
Number of People	22
Type of Organization	Team; five portfolio managers
His Role	Portfolio manager, chairman of the management committee
Investment Committee	No
Reward System	Based on fund as a whole
Number of Investors	150
Type of Investor	25 percent U.S. nontaxable; executives of companies they've researched; high net worth
GP/Principals' Ownership of Assets	10 percent
Endowments	Not disclosed

**Methodology/
Portfolio Composition**

Style	Value investing
Number of Positions in Portfolio	100
Trades Taken	Opportunistically
Role of United States	95 percent
Role of Technology	17 percent
Role of Private Equity	Less than 5 percent, special situations

Role of Macro	0 percent
Allocates to Other Managers	No

Risk Management

Net Exposure	65 percent
Hedging Technique	Shorting stock, hold cash, paired securities, options, move to cash
Maximum Leverage	Generally not used
Memorable Loss	1990
Risk Management	Low leverage; diversification; liquidity

Background Information

Initial Spark	Cumberland philosophy
Professional Background	Banking
Education	University of California, American Graduate School of International Management
Motivation/Satisfaction	Eclectic interests
Age	46
Free Time	Surfing, music

PART THREE

The Reverse Side
of the Coin—What
Investors Have to Say

18

INSTITUTIONAL INTEREST

Family offices, high-net-worth investors, institutions, banks, and funds of funds are the main investor categories. Around the globe, the percentage sizes of the institutional and fund of funds categories are relatively constant at 25 percent and 14 percent respectively.

Distinct differences exist between family offices/high-net-worth investors and banks in the United States versus those outside the United States. Outside the United States, on a percentage basis, banks are a bigger allocator than in the United States. Individual investors are more active in the United States than abroad. Endowments and pensions are also more active in the United States than elsewhere. (See Table 18.1.)

Each investor category has its own particular needs and objectives regarding hedge funds. Geographic location also has implications.

FAMILY OFFICES/HIGH-NET-WORTH INVESTORS

Family offices are a growing phenomenon as very wealthy families set up offices to run their investment portfolios. In some cases it may be run by a family member, while in others it is run by outside professionals. Or it can be a combination of the two. The number of professionals varies widely. For example, the Rockefeller family office in New York has over 140 in staff, including managers, analysts, trust officers,

Table 18.1   Estimated Breakdown of Investors in the Hedge Fund World

	U.S. Investors	Non-U.S. Investors
High net worth/family offices	55.1%	34.8%
Institutions		
Endowments	8.8	2.2
Pensions	8.5	3.5
Corporations	3.8	7.3
Foundations	2.1	2.6
Insurance companies	0.3	6.7
Trusts	4.1	4.3
Banks	3.2	23.2
Fund of Funds	13.5	15.4
Other	0.6	0

Source: Joseph Nicholas, *Market Neutral Investing: Long/Short Hedge Fund Strategies*, September 2000, pages 22–23.

lawyers, and back office. It has been in existence since 1882, and manages over $5.5 billion for 178 family members in the third, fourth, and fifth generations as well as nonfamily members. Non-Rockefeller wealth accounts for about half the assets.[1] In sharp contrast are other family offices that are run as one-person offices.

In some cases, the family office may eventually broaden out and accept other families' and friends' money. For example, the Rockefeller family office started doing this in 1980, and introduced its first fund of funds in January 1999.

Multiple family offices are becoming more popular. Variations include family offices that have been developed for sports athletes or family offices for investors from a certain country or region. By bonding together, either formally or informally, the individuals in the group gain more clout.

As a group, individuals and families are concerned about after-tax returns. They often request to see performance numbers after taxes have been taken out. Fees are another area of concern. Family offices are often interested in a hurdle rate structure where the manager gets paid if he or she reaches a certain benchmark first, which could be Treasury bills, S&P, LIBOR (London Interbank Offer Rates), or other point of reference.

Up until 1997, there could only be 99 accredited investors in a hedge fund if the hedge fund were not registered as a registered investment adviser with the Securities and Exchange Commission (SEC). In the United States, an accredited investor is one who has a net worth of at least $1 million or an annual income of at least $200,000 for two consecutive years ($300,000 for a married couple). Under Section 3(c)(7) of the Investment Company Act of 1940 a hedge fund can now take up to 500 qualified eligible participants. Section 3(c)(7) came about with the passage of the National Securities Market Improvement Act in October 1996 and went into effect in June 1997. Qualified eligible investors must have $5 million in securities/investments, and institutional investors must have at least $25 million.

INSTITUTIONAL INVESTORS

I interviewed three large institutions from the United States, Switzerland, and Japan to get their feedback and experiences with hedge funds. While one would expect major differences due to geographic and cultural differences, some main themes existed.

Fund of Funds Approach/Diversification

The fund of funds approach is a common and comfortable way for institutions to start. Due to time zone differences, language hurdles, and complex strategies, these companies feel a fund of funds approach is a wise way to go.

Following the Long-Term Capital Management crisis, diversification of managers and strategies is seen as a way to reduce risk. In addition to taking the fund of funds approach, the Japanese institution allocates to 30 managers, while the Swiss insurance company allocates to 90.

Private Equity and Hedge Funds Viewed in the Same Light

The institutions view hedge funds and private equity closely and expect similar characteristics from each. For example, Swiss Life Insurance Company made a 5 percent allocation to hedge funds—the same amount it made to private equity. The California Public Employees Retirement System (CalPERS) is interested in crossover or hybrid funds that contain a component of private equity and equity long/short. Many of these crossover funds came from the private equity sector. The Japanese institution received a good amount of transparency in venture capital and expects the same with hedge funds. Institutions would also like to know who the other investors are and details of the portfolio.

Transparency

Transparency is something that the institutions would like more of because hedge fund strategies are very different from long-only investments to which they are accustomed. Furthermore, the risks of different strategies are hard to map together. Transparency would help resolve this concern.

Managed accounts also enable more transparency and help manage risk. With managed accounts, investors can more quickly spot a problem and react if the manager is not performing as expected.

Happy with Returns

Though the programs have been in existence for differing time periods, the institutions feel their objectives have been met. CalPERS is using hedge funds to fill in gaps in its portfolio; the Japanese company has a smoothed portfolio and noncorrelation to Japanese stock market exposure.

Distribute to Others

Interestingly, two out of the three institutions started allocating to hedge funds with their own proprietary capital. Now comfortable with that experience, they are developing or planning to develop products for others in their respective countries.

U.S. SITUATION

California Public Employees Retirement System (CalPERS), a $168 billion public pension plan, announced in August 1999 that it would invest up to $2 billion of its assets (i.e., 5 percent of its actively managed U.S. stock investment) in hybrid strategies. Hybrid strategies include, among other things, hedge funds, market neutral funds, arbitrage funds, and corporate governance funds (those that seek to improve returns by influencing company management). At CalPERS, these investments are considered part of the U.S. equity allocation rather than its alternative investment weighting. In November 2000, CalPERS said they intended to devote $1 billion to hedge funds.

CalPERS's actions added credibility to the hedge fund community as an investment for other pension boards. With the largest U.S. pension plan making an allocation, others became interested. For example, in May 2000, Public School Teachers' Pension and Retirement Fund of Chicago announced its interest in adding $600 million to its hedge funds and emerging managers program. This fund increased its commitment to alternatives to 4 percent of the total fund.

Another example is New York State Teachers Retirement System. The $91 billion fund indicated it, too, is researching the concept and would invest as much as $1 billion in the sector. An allocation to several managers is being investigated.

The $1.4 billion Oklahoma Firefighters' Retirement System announced plans to allocate $100 million to hedge funds. It was reported that Pequot Capital, Capital Works, and Weiss Peck Greer would each receive a $33.3 million allocation.[2]

Meanwhile, the $5.7 billion Louisiana State Employees Retirement System is seeking an event-driven manager for a $50 million allocation.[3]

The long-term objectives of these institutions are to achieve higher absolute returns and diversify from traditional investments such as stocks and bonds, especially if they are wary about the volatile stock market. An increasing number of institutions do not expect the stock market to return 15 percent per year over the long term. The attractions of hedge funds lie in their historically high returns and their potential for a lower correlation of returns with traditional stock and bond management, reducing the overall volatility of an institution's total portfolio.

Institutions have also been increasingly examining the bond portion of their portfolios. In many cases, that asset class receives about a 30 percent allocation. Such low returns for such a large portion of the portfolios are diverting some interest to explore other investment possibilities, including alternative investments. (See Table 18.2.)

Preferred Strategies

Many of the institutions are allocating to a market neutral strategy such as long/short, convertible arbitrage, or merger arbitrage that is expected to deliver 1 percent to 1.5 percent a month. Some feel comfortable taking a market neutral fund of funds approach.

Others use an overlay approach. For example, they may overlay market neutral equity long/short strategy with S&P 500 futures, creating an enhanced index strategy.

Portable alpha is the concept that describes a product being structured around market neutral hedge funds while using a futures overlay benchmark. For example, if using the strategy with an overlay of S&P 500 futures, the pension plan gets a return that exceeds the S&P 500. The client can pick whatever futures contract as a benchmark one prefers. The concept is referred to as portable alpha since the client decides which asset class can receive the excess return and can change that decision each year, thus making it portable.

CASE STUDY INTERVIEW: CalPERS

CalPERS has been involved in hedge funds since about mid-1999. Mark Anson, senior principal investment officer, says that less than 1 percent of the $168 billion in assets is committed to hedge fund managers. For there to be any increase, board approval is needed.

In February 2000, CalPERS had allocated a $125 million investment to Abacus Partners. And in August 1999, CalPERS had allocated about $300 million to Pivotal Partners Fund, a San Francisco–based fund that invests in computer-related technology companies. Pivotal's two founders used to manage money for CalPERS before they started their hedge fund in 1998.[4] About $900 million had already been committed to three corporate governance funds.

CalPERS's objective is to invest in hedge funds on an opportunistic basis. "I use hedge funds not to hedge but rather to expand my investment opportunity set," says Anson. He is looking for managers

Table 18.2 Sampling of Institutions Using or Considering Hedge Funds

Aegon
AIG (American International Group)
Ameritech
BP Amoco
British Coal Staff Superannuation Scheme
California Public Employees Retirement System
Commerzbank
Conseco Corp.
Daido Life Insurance Company
DuPont
Eastman Kodak
General Motors
Helvetia Patria
IBM
Louisiana Firefighters
Louisiana State Employees Retirement System
McKinsey Consulting
Merck
Mineworkers' Pension Scheme
Nabisco
Nestlé
New York State Teachers Retirement System
Oklahoma Firefighter's Retirement System
R. J. Reynolds
San Antonio Police & Fire
Sumitomo Life
Swiss Life Insurance Company
Tokio Marine and Fire
US West
VEF (SwissAir pilots' pension fund)
Viacom
Virginia Retirement System
Weyerhaeuser
Winterthur Insurance Company
Zurich City Workers
Zurich Insurance

who target a particular sector or segment that isn't covered in the portfolio. They are meant to fill gaps in the portfolio. He says the objectives have been met.

Reflecting upon good and bad experiences with managers, Anson says good experiences are those managers who know exactly what their competitive advantage is and how to exploit it.

Bad experiences include managers who are unable to explain in simple terms what they do. "A hedge fund manager that cannot explain to me his investment objective in a precise format will fall to the bottom of my pile. If he can't explain to me his investment objective in clear and precise terms, then I question whether he can implement an investment strategy in a clear and precise manner."

Other bad experiences with managers involve those who believe they can charge outrageous fees as a matter of entitlement. "One hedge fund manager said to me: 'We charge 3 percent and 30 percent because that is the only way we can keep our assets under management down to several billion.' This manager went to the bottom of my pile," said Anson.

CalPERS is interested in crossover or hybrid funds that contain a component of private equity and an equity long/short program within a targeted sector or segment. Many of these crossover funds come from the private equity sector and target a specific industry such as the Internet, media, or communications.

CalPERS will consider new hedge fund managers if they have been successful in other venues of investing such as private equity, says Anson.

What about a fund of funds? Anson says it is a valuable product for portable alpha but it is an unfinished product. "It is unfinished because I must decide when, where, and how to apply it to my portfolio."

CalPERS does not use a consultant to allocate to hedge funds but does use Wilshire Associates for due diligence regarding selected managers.

Transparency is a critical issue for CalPERS for two reasons. First, hedge funds use trading programs and strategies that are very different from the traditional long-only investments to which most institutions are accustomed. Second, says Anson, given the unique skill-based nature of hedge fund investing, you cannot add the risks of one hedge fund manager onto another. Hedge fund strategies map risks differently from each other. As a result, it is difficult to summarize the risks of a pool of hedge fund managers in a comprehensive manner. Transparency would go a long way to resolving this issue, concludes Anson.

JAPANESE ACTIVITY

Japanese institutions are increasingly allocating to hedge funds due to lack of investment opportunity in a very low interest rate environment, and a negative carry problem. At the time of the stock market bubble, life insurance companies raised money from mutual fund investors, promising very attractive returns. As interest rates fell sharply, negative carry occurred.[5] To fill the gap, some Japanese insurance companies are investing in hedge funds.

It is estimated that those institutional allocations are about $6 billion and are expected to grow three to four times in the next four years. One example is Sumitomo Life, which announced its intent to invest 5 percent of its $220 billion assets in hedge funds. Sumitomo Life is the most active insurance company in hedge funds.[6] It is believed that the current allocation is less than 1 percent or about $2.2 billion. Sumitomo's fund of funds—it had allocated to about 10 U.S. and European fund management companies which in turn invested in hedge funds— has assets of ¥100 billion ($911 million) with the expectation that it will grow to ¥350 to ¥400 billion ($3.2 billion to $3.7 billion). The goals are to return 5 to 7 percent over LIBOR for yen interest rates, to diversify the company's investment mix, and to improve returns through diversified sources.[7]

Daido Life Insurance Company, jointly with Mitsubishi Corp., set up a ¥10 billion fund to invest in U.S. and European managers. About 5 percent of the assets goes to alternative investments.

In a bid to diversify its portfolio and raise returns, Tokio Marine & Fire Insurance Co. plans to expand alternative investing to include private equity and hedge funds to ¥100 billion ($911 million) in four years.[8]

Many of the Japanese institutions view alternative investments as a fixed income substitute. The institutions are looking for a low-risk, low-volatility product that has a simple strategy and is transparent.

Meanwhile, Japanese trading companies are also setting up products for their Japanese institutional clients. For example, Nikko Securities launched a 12-manager fund of funds that hopes to raise ¥20 billion; the minimum investment is ¥100 million ($925,000). Nissho Iwai America Corp., a subsidiary of Nissho Iwai Corp., will open an internal fund of funds to outside investors in early 2001. The fund allocates to about 15 managers but excludes global macro, mortgage-backed securities, sector funds, emerging markets, and short sellers.

ITOCHU Capital recently introduced three products for Japanese institutions. Columbus Trust is a diversified fund of funds; Fujiyama Trust is a fund of funds that focuses on managers who trade mostly in Japanese markets; and Dynamic Selective Trust, a feeder fund, among other things combines existing funds of funds and selects single managers.

CASE STUDY INTERVIEW: LARGE JAPANESE INSTITUTION

This large Japanese institution has been allocating to hedge funds since 1996. Initially, it had allocated to a large fixed income manager. Performance was good in 1996 and 1997. And at the end of 1997, it redeemed.

The institution wanted to continue with a hedge fund program and decided to take the fund of funds route for its next step. The institution feels the fund of funds approach works best for it since the fund of funds manager closely watches the positions, leverage, allocations, and types of investments. Due to time zone differences as well as the complexity of the information required, it is difficult for the institution to run such a program from Japan. It went to an established large fund of funds that had an existing relationship elsewhere in the institution.

The institution's objective was conservative—medium-term return in the mid-teens with medium risk. The main purpose was to have the assets noncorrelated to the Japanese market where the institution has considerable exposure. The allocation represents about 1 to 2 percent of the institution's total assets.

The program, which has stayed relatively the same size for the four years, currently allocates to 30 managers. The institution wants diversification of strategies and among strategies. Significant strategy allocations are given to market neutral, market timing, and event-driven areas. Not included in the portfolio are private placements, distressed, high-yield bonds, emerging markets, or managed futures. The portfolio is reviewed twice a year for reallocation. About 25 managers have been terminated over the years for not living up to performance expectations.

While the fund of funds manager makes recommendations on the hiring and firing of managers, the final decision lies with the institution. The institution's criteria for hiring include at least a two-to-three-year track record and the ability to redeem out of a fund in less than a year. And before investing, representatives will meet the manager and the key people. In their organization, seven people are involved in the process—two of them are located in the United States, and one is in the United Kingdom. By locating people overseas, the institution can gain easy access to managers and information. Most of the managers are based in the United States and Europe. Some of the managers receiving allocations include the superstar managers interviewed in the book.

The program did well in 1997, 1999, and 2000; 1998 was a down year for hedge funds in general and for this portfolio as well. The main benefit has been a smoothed portfolio and noncorrelation to Japanese exposure. The institution is very comfortable with this approach, and discussions are taking place to double the size.

Going forward, this Japanese institution would like to see more disclosure in general. In venture capital, it is used to so much information and would like to see the same with hedge funds. It would also like to know who the other investors are and see a more detailed portfolio. In general, the institution believes the fees are reasonable.

As one of the large users of hedge funds in Japan, this institution sees growing interest in Japan for this product not only from financial institutions but also from pensions and wealthy individuals. While the negative performance of 1998 hurt, general interest is increasing. In the future, this large Japanese institution may consider distributing hedge funds to retail Japanese markets.

EUROPEAN ACTIVITY

Recent reports indicate strong activity is taking place in Germany, especially among insurance companies. Many require a guarantee, but they are willing to lock up assets for as long as 10 years.[9] Publicly held companies and pension plans are also active, while the banks are lagging.

Recent examples of Swiss institutions allocating to hedge funds are Nestlé's $4.1 billion Swiss pension fund. VEF, the SwissAir pilots' pension fund, allocated $30 million in October 1999. Many of the large Swiss insurance companies have also started to allocate to hedge funds, such as Winterthur, Helvetia Patria, Zurich Insurance, and Swiss Life. The Swiss institutions are generally comfortable with hedge funds since Swiss private banks have been allocating proprietary bank capital to hedge funds for many years.

More entities are educating themselves. One example is the public employees pension fund in Zurich. European sources report Versicherungskasse der Stadt Zurich (VSZ) is seeking a manager to invest 2.5 percent of its assets, or SFR300 million ($176 million), in hedge funds.[10]

CMT Pension Trustee Services, which manages a $16.4 billion for the British Coal Staff Superannuation Scheme and the Mineworkers' Pension Scheme, has been asked by the trustees of both pension funds to prepare a research paper on alternative investments. It was reported that each entity was considering investing as much as 2 percent of its respective assets.

CASE STUDY INTERVIEW: SWISS LIFE INSURANCE COMPANY

Until 1987 Swiss Life Insurance Company had only about 2 to 3 percent of its portfolio in equities; the maximum allowed was 5 percent. Swiss pension law changed in 1985 to allow pension schemes to invest up to 50 percent in equities. Due to this change, the investment regulations for life insurance companies in Switzerland have been adapted in the same way. Fred Siegrist, head of investment strategy and risk management of the Swiss Life Group, said that equity allocation at the company increased to about 20 percent up to the mid-1990s. That was a comfortable amount considering its free reserves as a mutual company and the obligation to cover the liabilities at all times. Furthermore, local life insurance competitors limited equity allocations to 20 to 25 percent for the same reasons.

As time went on, Siegrist says they thought about the next step they could take in diversifying the company's portfolio. Looking toward the United States, they started to consider alternative investment strategies, especially hedge funds and private equity. In 1997, they made their first allocation to a fund of funds product launched in Switzerland. It was one of the first hedge fund of funds structured as a holding company and quoted at the Swiss Stock Exchange. Later in the same year, first investments were made in private equity fund of funds. Swiss Life decided to invest up to 5 percent in alternative investments of its portfolio over the next three years. The company is managing over CHF120 billion ($70 billion) in policyholders' money.

In taking its next step in 1998, Swiss Life took a stake at RMF Group and created a joint venture, the Swiss Life Hedge Fund Partners. This new company would manage all Swiss Life's money in hedge funds and sell products also to external clients. RMF, an alternative investment firm in Pfäffikon, developed a multistrategy portfolio allocating to five different styles: equity hedged, event driven, global macro, relative value, and managed futures. Today, the portfolio has about 90 different managers. RMF helped determine the mix of strategies as well as which managers to use in each strategy. Siegrist says that after the Long-Term Capital Management incident in 1998, this diversified portfolio and the approach chosen helped to convince the board of directors of Swiss Life to stay in hedge fund investments, even if the investments have been performing under par at that time.

In June 1998, Swiss Life allocated $300 million. Swiss Life's objectives were a net return of 10 to 12 percent per year, an annual standard deviation of 5 to 6 percent, and a correlation to the stock market (S&P 500) of 0.03 to 0.40.

Siegrist says that since inception over $1.3 billion has been invested and the objectives has been met. The actual annualized return has been 11.7 percent, with a standard deviation of 5.4 percent and a correlation of 0.32. Over the past 12 months, the return has been 13.9 percent, standard deviation 4.0 percent, and correlation of 0.2 percent.

Further products were implemented in 2000, such as collateralized debt obligation and high-yield investments. By the end of September 2000, Swiss Life had invested over $2.5 billion in these asset categories.

In the future, Swiss Life will use managed accounts rather than funds as much as it can. This enables it to have more transparency and better-managed risk. In the funds, the lock-up periods are not flexible. With managed accounts, the management team can react quickly if the manager doesn't meet the set criteria or is performing badly.

In 1999, Swiss Life took another step. Swiss Life Hedge Fund Partners launched a new product. Here the client can invest in one of the previously mentioned five styles through a fund, can combine them together to fit specific needs, or can choose a combination of the styles decided by Swiss Life Hedge Fund Partners. Every style fund is composed of 15 to 20 managers.

Swiss Life's relationship with RMF is a joint venture, and the two firms work closely together. Swiss Life currently has seven people in Swiss Life Hedge Fund Partners and is looking for more. RMF has developed from 20 people in 1998 to 90 people today.

Siegrist also says that Swiss Life is moving from being a pure life insurance company to being a financial service provider for long-term savings. "We want to be a big player in alternative investments in Europe, in hedge funds and private equity as well," adds Siegrist.

19

SIGNIFICANT ENDOWMENT PRESENCE CONTINUES

In the United States, endowments have been the most active institutional group allocating to hedge funds. This is largely due to investment committee members who are already familiar with the concept as high-net-worth investors. Endowments and foundations have a history of moving into new types of investments quicker than pension funds.

NACUBO, the National Association of College and University Business Officers, started to include hedge funds in its endowment survey in 1994. At that time, the average endowment allocation to hedge funds was 0.4 percent. By 1999, 104 U.S. colleges and endowments out of the 508 participating allocated to hedge funds. (See Table 19.1.) The average allocation had grown to 2.3 percent, which equated to $3.9 billion. Public universities allocated an average 2.1 percent, while private schools allocated about 6 percent of their portfolios average.[1]

A large variation exists in the percent allocation by the individual colleges. For example, Yeshiva University in New York City allocates 42 percent of its endowment to hedge funds. Others allocating over 20 percent include Bowdoin College (27 percent), Denison University (27 percent), Reed College (26 percent), Clark University (25 percent), Alfred University (25 percent), King's College (24 percent), Wheaton College (24 percent), and Oberlin College (20 percent). Some other colleges make no allocation whatsoever to hedge funds.[2]

Table 19.1   Sampling of Endowments Allocating to Hedge Funds in 1999

Alfred University	Furman University	Ohio Wesleyan	University of
Amherst College	George Washington	University	Michigan
Berea College	University	Pacific School of	University of North
Boston University	Georgia Institute of	Religion	Carolina
Bowdoin College	Technology	Pennsylvania State	University of Oregon
Carleton College	Grand Valley State	University	University of
Carnegie Mellon	University	Pepperdine	Pittsburgh
University	Hamilton College	University	University of
Case Western	Hamline University	Pitzer College	Rochester
Reserve	Hampton University	Pomona College	University of San
University	Haverford College	Randolph-Macon	Diego
Chatham College	Hollins University	College	University of
Christian Theological	Illinois Institute of	Reed College	Southern
Seminary	Technology	Regis College	California
Clark University	Juilliard School	Rensselaer	University of the
Clarkson University	Kenyon College	Polytechnic	South
Colby College	King's College	Institute	University of Texas
Colgate University	Lafayette College	Rhodes College	University of Tulsa
Colleges of the	La Salle University	Saint John's	University of
Seneca	Lesley College	University (MD)	Washington
College of William	Lycoming College	Saint Louis	University of
and Mary	McGill University	University	Wisconsin
College of Wooster	Michigan State	San Diego University	Vassar College
Colorado State	University	Seattle University	Wake Forest
University	Middlebury College	Southern Methodist	University
Cranbrook Education	Mills College	University	Washington and Lee
Community	Mount Holyoke	State University of	University
Davidson College	College	New York—Stony	Wesleyan University
Denison University	New School for	Brook Foundation	Western Methodist
Dickinson College	Social Research	Thomas Jefferson	Wheaton College
Doane College	New York University	University	(MA)
Emory University	Northeastern	Trinity College (CT)	Williams College
Fairfield University	University	Tulane University	Woods Hole
Fordham University	Norwich University	University of	Oceanographic
Franklin and	Oakland University	California	Institute
Marshall College	Oberlin College	University of Iowa	Yeshiva University

Source: NACUBO 2000.

The most commonly allocated hedge funds in 1999 (in order) were Tiger Management, Everest Capital, Pequot, Maverick Capital, Och-Ziff, Highfields Capital, Kingdon Capital, and Omega Advisors. According to the NACUBO study, some of the frequently allocated funds of funds are Commonfund, Blackstone, and Torrey.[3]

When Robertson's Tiger Management announced on March 31, 2000, that it was liquidating, this meant that a number of endowments would have to reallocate assets. A quick sampling showed that a great percentage of the endowment money in Tiger stayed within the hedge fund industry. For example, the $256 million endowment at the University of the South in Sewanee, Tennessee, announced that it was looking at six to eight hedge funds for the $15 million it had liquidated/withdrawn from Robertson.[4] The University of North Carolina (UNC) said it continually rebalanced while Robertson was going through this difficult performance so that by the time he had retired the allocation was down to 3 percent. It had gradually increased allocations to other managers.

Increasingly in 2000, more U.S. endowments became involved in hedge funds as they want to reduce dependence on market-related securities. For example, in March, the University of Tennessee, Knoxville, announced its first foray into hedge funds by hiring Commonfund to manage $20 million. Texas A&M University's foundation announced it was more than tripling its hedge fund holding to 10 percent within 18 months.[5]

Louisiana State University Agricultural and Mechanical College said it was looking to make a 5 to 10 percent or $11 million to $22 million allocation to hedge funds later in 2000—its first foray.[6]

CASE STUDIES

I talked with four endowments to get their perspectives of the hedge fund industry. What were their objectives? Did their experiences live up to expectations? What types of strategies and managers did they use? Did they prefer superstar managers? Had they fired any managers—and if so, why? Did the endowments make their own decisions or did they rely on consultants? Did a fund of funds approach fit into their picture? What would they like see changed in the hedge fund industry?

I wanted a variety of perspectives on the issues. The University of North Carolina at Chapel Hill endowment represents the large public university that is quite sophisticated and experienced in hedge funds. The $1.1 billion endowment has been allocating to hedge funds since 1990 and has consistently allocated about 30 percent to hedge funds through 20 managers. Stanford Management Company, which invests Stanford University's $8 billion, represents a private institution that has been involved with hedge funds for quite a while. Stanford, which began its first hedge fund allocation in 1990, currently allocates to 18 managers.

Vassar College, a private school with an endowment of $675 million, started its hedge fund program in 1992 and allocates about 11 percent of its portfolio to five hedge fund managers. Wesleyan University, a private institution with an endowment of $580 million, began allocating to hedge funds in 1998 and currently allocates about 10 percent through seven managers.

Despite the differences among these endowments, some similarities existed.

Similarities

Growing Sophistication
Three of the four endowments had recently gone through reassessments of their investment and allocation processes, and significant changes had been made. Generally, they wanted to build a more professional investment office and enhance the quality of the investment fund program. Among other things, this included improving performance, adding alternative investments, moving toward equities, and moving away from fixed income. Major staff changes were made.

Objectives
While the specific objective and benchmarks differed, the general goals were the same: enhance returns, reduce risk, and provide diversification.

Significant Allocation
All the endowments allocated at least 10 percent to hedge funds.

Positive Experience
The endowments were quite pleased with their hedge fund experience and found that their goals were being met. The year 2000 was especially telling for them. While the traditional equity managers were having problems, the hedge funds did quite well. Return patterns were different from returns of traditional equities, and volatility had also been reduced.

In-House Research/Use of Consultants
While three of the four endowments used a consultant as a sounding board and a source for reports, all did their research and due diligence in-house.

Firing Managers
Performance was not a reason to fire a manager. The general consensus was that managers would be fired only if they did not adhere to their stated strategies, did something unexpected, or were not actually the type of manager they described themselves as.

Dislike of the Term
While the endowments were happy with their hedge fund experience, they universally did not like or use the term "hedge fund," because it was a generic term that evolved over time to describe many different unrelated styles of trading. Wesleyan and Stanford preferred "absolute return," while UNC used the term "marketable securities."

Fees
The endowments did not feel that fees were too high, but a preference existed for hurdle rates. A manager who did worse than the hurdle shouldn't get paid, while one whose return was above the hurdle should get a higher percentage.

Differences

Number of Managers Used
The University of North Carolina (UNC) takes the view that to protect itself against single-manager disasters, potential fraud, or adverse situa-

tions, it needs to allocate to many managers. It currently allocates to 20. Stanford University currently allocates to 18. In contrast, Wesleyan University allocates to seven managers, while Vassar College currently allocates to five.

Strategies Used

One endowment focused on absolute return strategies where they earn premium for providing liquidity to the market with regard to illiquid investments—market neutral, event arbitrage, fixed income arbitrage, and distressed.

The other three endowments used various strategies. In each of these three cases, equity long/short was a preferred strategy. Interestingly, none of the same managers were used in this category.

The various other strategies used by the three endowments included multistrategy, fund of funds, global macro/opportunistic equity, event arbitrage, distressed, and absolute return.

Fund of Funds

Only one of the four endowments was a proponent of the fund of funds approach, as one of its five allocations was to a fund of funds. Due to some internal problems it had on rebalancing, the endowment felt the fund of funds route for its core investments could make sense and impose some discipline.

Benchmarks

No uniformity existed on the benchmarks used to evaluate returns. For example, UNC used the Russell 3000 and MSCI EAFE (Morgan Stanley Capital International Europe, Australasia, Far East index) to evaluate long/short hedge fund managers. It used the MSCI World Index to measure opportunistic hedge fund managers and inflation plus 8 percent for absolute return managers.

On the other hand, Vassar College used a flat 13 percent benchmark, and Wesleyan University, while not yet certain of the benchmark to use, compared managers against their peers.

Rebalancing

The University of North Carolina and Vassar College both had allocations to Tiger Management. Their experiences in that situation were different. While UNC evaluates managers quarterly, the endowment is continuously rebalancing; it is a fluid environment. As Tiger was having its problems, UNC's allocation had dwindled as the endowment had gradually increased allocations to other managers.

Vassar seemed to have difficulty reallocating assets. While a decision had been made to fire the manager, the investment committee did not act quickly enough, and performance was affected. Rebalancing was agreed upon in principle but not enforced, perhaps due to consensus decision making by committee.

Stanford University had a challenging 1998. In hindsight it would have had less assets allocated to hedge funds and would have added more at the end of 1998. They realize that by taking a contrarian approach, they would do better (i.e., add money to managers after a decline, when things look the darkest).

Stanford rebalances all the time, increasing allocations to managers when the spreads are widest.

New Managers
There is a growing acceptance of allocating to new managers. A big plus is the new manager having worked at a well-known and well-respected hedge fund prior to spinning off and starting his or her own fund. One endowment, however, required a five-year track record to see how the manager did in various economic cycles.

U.S. Managers
One of the four endowments is actively searching for European managers. The others are satisfied with U.S. managers and note that many of these trade globally.

Transparency
Transparency was not a concern for two of the endowments, as the endowments felt they were getting the information they needed—quarterly data on performance, exposure, leverage, and principal trades. They acknowledged they didn't need detailed information on a daily basis.

One endowment wanted a good third-party risk-reporting system, and also felt the larger and more established managers were not the most transparent. Only a subset sent regular risk reports detailing exposure and leverage.

GOING FORWARD

One complaint regarding the hedge fund industry was that managers needed to provide products that meet investors' needs—consistent returns, lower volatility, and lower correlation to traditional products. Managers need to get to know clients and understand their needs rather than just sell product.

Another suggestion was claw-backs (i.e., having the manager vest in his or her carry over time so that it might take three years to be vested). It was felt this would further align the manager's and the investor's interests.

CASE STUDY INTERVIEW: UNIVERSITY OF NORTH CAROLINA AT CHAPEL HILL

The $1.1 billion endowment fund at the University of North Carolina at Chapel Hill was one of the early adopters of alternative investments, including hedge funds. A strong endowment fund board composed of investment professionals helped map out a plan for including alternatives into the traditional core portfolio. With respect to hedge funds, it was Julian Robertson's decision in 1990 to step down from the board so he could manage some of UNC's assets. Robertson, a North Carolina native, a UNC graduate, and a board member, believed that he could add more value to the fund by managing a portion of the assets directly rather than just serving as a member of the board. The university was fortunate that Robertson made this decision, as UNC profited during the next decade by having a portion of the endowment funds invested with Tiger Management, says Mark Yusko, chief investment officer.

Hedge funds continued to play a role at the endowment over time, and other funds were added by the board to complement the Tiger investment. The endowment grew rapidly during the 1990s and the need for the development of a professional investment office, akin to the Yale or Stanford model, to help manage the increasing complexity of the investment program drove the board to search for a chief investment officer in the fall of 1997.

That search led to South Bend where Yusko had helped build the investment program at his alma mater, Notre Dame, since 1993. Yusko arrived at UNC in January 1998 with a set of goals laid out by the endowment board to build a professional investment office and help the board enhance the quality of the investment fund program. The first step was to adopt a new strategic investment policy in May, including adding more alternative investments, a higher concentration on equities, and less reliance on fixed income. UNC also wanted to be more aggressive in hiring emerging managers. By the fall of 1998, the first major portfolio changes were made to begin the realignment of the fund to the new investment policy.

UNC's allocation to marketable alternatives (hedge fund type products) has remained fairly constant at 30 percent since 1998. One unique feature of the UNC program is the ban on the use of the "h" word. As mentioned earlier, UNC does not use the hedge fund label, primarily because it is a generic phrase that has evolved over time to describe many different unrelated styles of trading. Yusko also emphasizes that UNC does not see hedge funds, or marketable alternative managers, as an asset class but as a style, or strategy, of gaining exposure to specific asset classes like equities or bonds.

One of UNC's portfolio management themes is that it likes to have multiple manager relationships in each asset class and be well diversified in each segment of the portfolio. The investment staff does their own independent due diligence on all managers and is very thorough in their evaluation prior to manager selection. Across the marketable alternatives portfolio, UNC allocates funds to more than 20 managers in three general categories—long/short, opportunistic equity, and absolute return.

Long/short managers are long-biased and can focus on either U.S. or non-U.S. equities. There are multiple managers in this category, including firms such as Feirstein Capital, Raptor Fund, and Boyer Allan.

The opportunistic equity category includes many different types of funds. All use the long/short model, but are not necessarily long-biased, and are global in nature; and the category includes nonequity managers as well as equity managers. There are multiple mangers in this category, including Maverick and previously Tiger prior to liquidation of the fund. In fact, as mentioned earlier, by the time Robertson wound down Tiger in March 2000, UNC's allocation had dwindled to 3 percent as it had gradually increased allocations to other managers.

Absolute return, the third category, includes lower-volatility strategies such as event arbitrage, relative value, and distressed managers. This segment has the highest number of individual managers, as diversification by style and strategy is very important within this group. Citadel, Satellite, and Oak Tree are examples of managers in the absolute return segment. UNC has a 10 percent strategic allocation target for absolute return and a 10 percent strategic target for opportunistic equity. No strategic target exists for long/short managers as they are added to the U.S. and international equity portfolios to provide hedged exposure and access to superior investment management talent.

Yusko says UNC is constantly adding and deleting managers over time. It is a fluid environment. "We don't do searches in the traditional mode. We are always doing searches." To manage the steady stream of manager meetings, Yusko has assembled an investment team over the past two years including six investment professionals, two operations professionals, and two support staff. UNC uses Cambridge Associates as a sounding board on manager issues; however, the consultant is just one of a number of resources utilized to find, evaluate, and select the best of breed managers for the portfolio. The investment staff does most of the analytical and due diligence work internally. Yusko and his group then make recommendations to the investment fund board, which has ultimate decision-making authority for portfolio changes.

Performance Is a Symptom

Yusko feels that performance alone is not a reason to hire or fire a manager. Performance is a symptom of something else, perhaps the need for a change in the organization or a change in strategy.

So when does a manager get terminated? Usually when he or she does things differently than expected, or perhaps when they are more aggressive or more leveraged than they said they would be.

Yusko acknowledges that managers will go through tough periods. If the manager is doing what he or she is supposed to be doing, UNC will keep the manager and look to the next portion of the investment cycle when that strategy will be in favor. The team will allow a manager to continue to be a part of the portfolio team until the strategy doesn't make sense or there are significant organizational changes.

UNC's rebalancing philosophy is to sell on strength and buy on weakness. While all the managers are evaluated quarterly, rebalancing does not necessarily occur quarterly, but rather when compelling opportunities arise.

Pleased with Results

UNC's objectives for the inclusion of alternatives, and in particular marketable alternatives, are return enhancement and diversification benefits for the overall portfolio.

Yusko says UNC has been pleased with the results. For the long/short strategies, UNC uses the Russell 3000 index as a benchmark for U.S. stocks and MSCI EAFE (Morgan Stanley Capital International Europe, Australasia Far East index) for international stocks. For opportunistic equity managers, UNC uses a global benchmark, the MSCI World Index. For absolute return strategies, UNC uses a 8 percent real return (i.e., inflation plus 8 percent).

Yusko happily pointed to performance in 2000. "For the first six months of 2000, it has been a difficult period for traditional investments. We are pleased with how the marketable alternative strategies have done—especially absolute return managers. They are up about 14 percent for the first half of the year."

Relationships, Relationships, Relationships

UNC backs managers early in their careers. "We look for those firms which don't have $1 billion of assets under management and/or a five-year track record. . . . It is all a relationship game." Yusko says that the best and brightest managers also refer to him the names of others they think highly of. "Whereas in real estate, you hear location, location, location. Here, it is relationships, relationships, relationships."

Funnel Theory of Management

Yusko has developed what he calls a funnel theory of management. It is the law of natural selection—he wants to fish at the end of the funnel for the best and brightest managers. He wants to know which managers are coming out of the Soros organization or Citadel, for example. Strong firms produce strong managers, and talented people eventually want a shot at running their own shop. History shows that emerging managers from strong organizations produce stellar results for those intrepid investors who back the firms early on in their life cycle.

The theory is that managers will start at a big institution after school. Then, they may move to a boutique firm. In search of a larger piece of profits, they may go off on their own. And then eventually, they will start a hedge fund. With a hedge fund, they manage their own money along with their investors'. Under this environment, they have the right incentive: to perform to get the best results rather than just gathering assets and generating management fees. It is a funnel-shaped movement and the best managers end up at the end of the funnel.

UNC is currently very interested in European managers. The endowment has allocated to Boyer Allan and has looked at many other managers. The plan is to hire a few more in the next few months.

Does Yusko see any difference between the U.S. and European managers? He sees Europe as having more opportunity since the environment is less competitive. "The European equity markets are like the U.S. markets were 10 years ago." Yusko also observes that the stigma against entrepreneurship and being a hedge fund manager are gone in Europe.

Yusko recalls how he happened to be at Marshall Wace's new offices in London when they were just starting to open for business in November 1997. That day, Yusko sat with Paul and Ian on boxes and talked about when they might get to $100 million under management. Today, Marshall Wace has over $2 billion in assets and is closed to new business.

Yusko believes that a manager who is going to make it, has to be adept at more than one thing and has to be multiskilled. For example, from 1983 through 1990, technology managers had a very difficult time making money on the long side. Yet from 1990 to mid-2000, technology had been a great place to be.

Black Eyes

Have the recent hedge fund scandals hurt UNC's appetite for hedge funds? Yusko feels the hedge fund industry has had a fast pace of growth. There have been tremendous opportunities and some setbacks.

He admits that the financial press, focusing on the negative stories, has made his allocation job more difficult in terms of making board members comfortable with strategies that are portrayed as risky. It means he has to constantly educate the board and manage risk in the overall portfolio. He wonders why the press doesn't highlight the great performance, both in terms of high returns and in many cases low volatility, particularly on the downside, that some of the managers generate.

Alluding to Long-Term Capital Management as an example, he highlights how the label "hedge fund" hurt other managers that were nothing like LTCM. "One manager sneezes and everyone catches a cold." He also emphasizes that one of the reasons UNC has many managers with smaller allocations is to prevent such single-manager disasters as well as to protect against the potential impact that fraud or other adverse situations can have on a portfolio with oversized positions.

At the Cusp of Something Momentous

Surprisingly perhaps, Yusko prefers longer lock-ups. The expectation is to hire a manager and develop a long-term working relationship, and a relationship takes time to build and judge. To have immediate liquidity and a short lock-up doesn't make sense; it is counterintuitive. He prefers to get lower fees in exchange for longer lock-ups.

Yusko is not a zealot for lower fees but he does believe in hurdle rates. A manager who does worse than the hurdle shouldn't get paid. One who does better than the hurdle should get a higher percentage so that the total compensation is equivalent to the standard 1 percent management and 20 percent incentive fee model with higher upside potential for truly superior performance.

Yusko feels the transparency issue has been overblown. If you can't fire a manager on a daily basis, why do you feel the need to see the data daily? It's a waste of time, concludes Yusko. "It's like letting your teenager take the car. If you don't trust him, don't give him the keys. But you don't have to go on every ride with him." For some managers, Yusko will look for monthly information, but generally it is quarterly data on performance, exposure, leverage, and principal trades.

Yusko feels that the hedge fund industry is at the cusp of something very momentous. A confluence of events—unprecedented valuations in traditional investments, unprecedented migration of managers out of traditional management firms into hedge funds, and institutions' desire to capture gains of a bull market without giving up upside potential— presents a huge opportunity for the hedge fund industry to become more institutionalized.

Yusko sees the big issue for the industry as migrating toward being more solution-oriented rather than product-oriented. The days of "if you build it, they will come" are gone. Yusko feels the hedge fund industry needs to create products and services to meet institutions' desire for consistent returns, lower volatility, and lower correlation to traditional products. Managers must get to know clients and understand their needs. They should build products and services to fit those needs rather than just being a product vendor.

Yusko observes that some of the newer hedge fund managers are more client-oriented than the established firms. They hire client service people and operations managers early on and recognize that the true value in an organization is in the people and the relationships.

Yusko feels the industry is actually undercapitalized and expects a staggering amount of pension, endowment, and foundation assets eventually to enter.

CASE STUDY INTERVIEW: STANFORD UNIVERSITY

Stanford Management Company, which invests Stanford University's $8 billion endowment, began exploring alternative investment opportunities in the late 1980s. The goal was to achieve returns close to long-term equity returns, diversify the overall portfolio, and achieve a better reward/risk ratio. The endowment made its first distressed securities investment in 1990, and a few years later it made a risk arbitrage allocation.

Anne Casscells, chief investment officer at Stanford, says the two initial managers are still in the portfolio. In addition, the endowment has allocated to 16 others over the 10-year period. About 10 percent of the overall portfolio is allocated to hedge fund strategies; this allocation has been relatively stable over time. The goal is to make about 1 percent per month and to have standard deviation like bonds.

"The theme among our allocations is to invest in activities where you derive fundamental return for providing liquidity to the market, where you earn a premium for being invested in illiquid investments," says Casscells.

With this theme in mind, about 25 percent of the portfolio is allocated to market neutral strategies, another 30 percent to event arbitrage, 25 percent to fixed-income arbitrage, 15 percent to distressed securities, 3 percent to convertible arbitrage, and the remaining percentage allocated to various other strategies such as global tactical asset allocation, emerging markets, and currencies. Casscells refers to these as absolute return strategies. These strategies should make money regardless of whether stocks and bonds or rising or falling, excluding periods of liquidity crisis.

In these areas, the skillful manager will add value to the upside and reduce risk. She makes the analogy between these managers and underwriting insurance. Good underwriting of risks helps trim losses in difficult markets.

Selection Criteria

The selection, monitoring, and rebalancing of managers is done internally. There are eight people in the investment area. More than one person meets with a manager. And the allocations are approved by the senior staff, which meets weekly.

What are the selection criteria? Casscells says that a five-year track record is attractive. "It is important for them to have experience as an independent firm in difficult markets such as during 1994 and 1998." She observes that many of the managers who worked at investment banks during these difficult times were not independent. They personally did not receive the extreme margin calls. It is for this reason that she prefers managers with longer track records.

To date, all the managers they've allocated to have been U.S.-based since there are few non-U.S. managers in these categories. Nevertheless, most of the managers they allocate do trade on a global basis. For example, in market neutral, a number of the managers cover the United Kingdom and Europe. In the fixed income arbitrage category, G-7 and G-11 countries are included. Merger arbitrage managers trade in Europe. Distressed, however, has not yet successfully expanded outside the United States. This may be due to the more challenging bankruptcy systems abroad.

On the issue of asset size, Stanford prefers that the managers not be too large because it is often difficult to deploy lots of assets. Stanford also prefers that managers do not go substantially outside their specialty. Casscells observes that those managers that got hurt in 1998 in merger arbitrage were those who were new to the game. She also prefers that a manager's assets do not grow too rapidly.

The most important element is the manager's quality and character. The manager should be bright, exceptionally motivated, not arrogant, and humble enough to respect the markets, as well as honest and trustworthy.

Rebalancing

Casscells says that in convertible arbitrage and merger arbitrage, Stanford adds to managers when the spreads are wide. "We think about it all the time. While we meet with managers quarterly, there is no formal rebalancing period."

Stanford has terminated only a few managers. In one case, a fixed income manager was directional, not an arbitrageur. In another case, a manager strayed from his stated mandate. And in another instance, the manager had trouble sticking with his strategy and flip-flopped so much that he missed a great opportunity.

Casscells says Stanford has been pleased overall with the hedge fund allocations. The year 1998 was challenging. In hindsight, they should have had less money allocated and added more later.

"You can make more money if you take a contrarian view and add money to managers after a decline," she says. "November 1998 was a great time to invest in fixed-income arbitrage. Even though it is psychologically hard to do, you should add assets when things look the darkest." Stanford did add to the fixed income allocation after 1998.

Casscells says that at that time, Stanford also started its exposure to convertible arbitrage. She notes how convertible arbitrage is a great example of providing a premium for an investor providing liquidity in an illiquid area. She observes how it doesn't have a natural home and seems to have problems every four years when liquidity dies.

Have the publicized blow-ups had any impact on the hedge fund allocation? "The blow-ups do cause us to reexamine the program and make sure we are satisfied with our due diligence and monitoring. We want to avoid situations like Long-Term Capital Management, which was not transparent, had its interests misaligned with investors', and strayed outside their core areas of expertise."

Ideal World

In an ideal world, Casscells would like the managers to have a hurdle rate of either Treasury bills or LIBOR. Once they achieved that rate, then they would get their stated incentive fees. Most of the market neutral managers they use have a hurdle rate. Some fixed income arbitrageurs do, but most event arbitrageurs do not.

She would also prefer that the managers be vested in their carry over time so that their interests were better aligned with those of the investor. This is also referred to as a claw-back. For example, under current practice, if the manager earns $100 of carry in year one and then has a loss in year two, the manager does not lose any of the carry. But if only one-third of the carry were vested each year, the manager would participate alongside investors in losses as well as gains for the unvested portion.

Ideally, she would also like more transparency of positions or to have a good third-party risk-reporting system. Some managers will give good transparency on positions but often they are not the most successful or established managers.

Most managers will talk about their portfolios. A few will even mail it to investors. A subset of fixed income managers send out regular risk reports that detail the exposure and leverage.

CASE STUDY INTERVIEW: VASSAR COLLEGE

Vassar College has been allocating to hedge funds since 1992. While the percentage has gradually increased over the years, Jay Yoder, director of investments,* says since 1995 the allocation has been in the double digits. It currently stands at about 11 percent. Alternative investments overall—including hedge funds, venture capital, buyouts, real estate, and energy—totaled 29 percent of the $675 million endowment as of June 30, 2000.

In 1993, the endowment was invested with only two hedge funds. By 1999, it had five allocations. The college wants exposure to different strategies and has allocated to one growth equity long/short manager (Tupelo); two multistrategy funds—one having a high return/high risk

---

*Since the interview took place in July 2000, Yoder has left Vassar College and is now at the Smith College endowment.

profile (Everest Capital) and the other having a moderate return/risk profile (Elliott Associates' Westgate); a global macro manager (Tiger Management); and a managed futures fund of funds (Commodities Corp.). As the portfolio gets larger, the college intends to diversify further.

Vassar's rationale for using hedge funds is to both enhance returns and reduce risk. The benchmark is a flat 13 percent. Since inception, July 1, 1992, until the end of the first quarter 2000, the annualized return has been on target at 12.9 percent. "Obviously, we would have liked to have done better, but we did match our benchmark," says Yoder. He is pleased that returns have not been strongly correlated to the U.S. stock market.

Vassar underwent a major change in philosophy at the start of 1996. Rather than just be considered an alternative to equities, hedge funds were now considered a separate asset class. Initially, hedge funds were used as a pure equity alternative to reduce overall portfolio volatility.

Rebalancing Problems

Tiger Management was Vassar's second manager allocation made in early 1993. Because of strong returns, the college's initial allocation to Tiger of $11 million (3.9 percent of the portfolio) grew to $39 million (7.5 percent of the portfolio) in early 1998. After that time, though, Tiger struggled. In early 2000, the investment committee decided to fire Tiger because of recent poor returns. The firm closed, however, before any action could be taken. Nevertheless, Yoder says that Robertson earned an average annual return of 14 percent per year for the college over that entire seven-year period.

Yoder emphasizes that by not rigorously rebalancing among its hedge fund managers (including Tiger), the endowment hasn't done as well as it should have. "The endowment should have taken money off the table when profits had been made and added to funds' allocations following poor periods," says Yoder. While Yoder often recommended rebalancing, and even succeeded in writing a rebalancing rule into the policy, the investment committee often proved unable to remove money from those managers who had recently done well or add to those whose recent performance was below expectations. "Committees usually require consensus decision making, which by definition cannot be contrarian," observes Yoder. Vassar's committee, which includes both members of the board of trustees and nonmember investment professionals, typically meets quarterly. Yoder puts together the agenda and makes recommendations, but the committee makes all final decisions.

Yoder says that no two investment committees operate the same way. Typically the players include an in-house staff, a committee, and a consultant. Some endowments rely heavily on the consultant, while others have the consultant serve largely as an extension of staff.

Considering a Fund of Funds for Core Holdings

In finding a solution to their problem, Vassar is considering a fund of funds approach for its core holdings. The rationale is that if the committee has little confidence that they can select a good hedge fund and religiously rebalance their holdings, a fund of funds may be a better approach.

Would they consider a consultant? Yoder believes that many consultants are generalists who don't necessarily have any more experience than Vassar does. In recent years, Vassar has largely conducted its own searches and hasn't relied heavily on a consultant.

Views on the Industry

Yoder does not perceive hedge fund managers' fees as a problem. He feels transparency is getting better. It is critical to know the managers' strategies and main exposures, but an investor doesn't need to have detailed information on a daily basis.

CASE STUDY INTERVIEW: WESLEYAN UNIVERSITY

In the 1960s, Wesleyan University in Middletown, Connecticut, had one of the top endowments in its peer group regarding size on a per-student basis. In the late 1960s, Wesleyan sold one of its publications, *My Weekly Reader*, and received a huge inflow of cash. The endowment doubled. As a result, it spent too much, gifts from donors dried up, and a very conservative investment strategy was followed. Within years, the endowment was at the bottom of its peer group in terms of size on a per-student basis.

In 1998, the endowment rewrote the investment policy. The goal was to improve performance; the focus turned toward asset allocation. The endowment looked at the return/risk trade-off with regard to its long time horizon and diversification. It realized it could reduce risk and short-term volatility and enhance return potential.

The broad asset allocation target was 75 to 80 percent for equities and 15 to 25 percent for fixed income. Within equities, there was a 30 percent target for alternative investments, 15 percent for international equities, and 10 percent for absolute return strategies, says Thomas Kannam, director of investments. Kannam arrived at Wesleyan from Dartmouth's endowment in 1998.

Wesleyan started allocating to hedge funds in 1998. (Absolute return is the term Wesleyan uses.) The objectives were to achieve diversification, enhance returns, and reduce risk.

The $580 million endowment allocated to seven hedge funds representing different styles that are uncorrelated to broad stock market exposure. Each of the seven groups were given an initial $5 million allocation. Since that time, three of the seven funds have received additional allocation. The styles receiving allocations were event arbitrage, distressed, U.S. long/short, Japan long/short, and macro.

Managers who've received additional assets include Peter Schoenfeld Asset Management. Kannam says the manager does a lot of European merger arbitrage deals which he likes. Cerberus International, which focuses on distressed, also received additional assets. The Black Bear Fund (U.S. long/short) is the third manager receiving a larger allocation.

The 1999 NACUBO survey indicates Wesleyan also allocates to Rosehill, RS Investment Management, and SCI Capital Management.

Kannam says the endowment had met with Tiger Management but passed because the firm was so big. Kannam does believe that size impacts strategies, and looks at size carefully, especially if a manager is over $1 billion.

Wesleyan does its research and manager due diligence internally. While it is a base client of Cambridge Consulting and gets those reports, Wesleyan does hedge fund analysis in-house. The in-house team includes Kannam himself, an investment professional, an analyst, and two support people.

Similarly, Wesleyan is not so keen on taking a fund of funds route at this time. "We've built a portfolio and want to see how it goes. We can always do a fund of funds later, if it is appropriate," says Kannam. "We do feel we can do it directly on our own."

Usually Wesleyan will start with a specific strategy in mind. From that point, it will then search out specific managers. Kannam says they look at all managers, including new ones. "We look for the best we can find. Whether it is hedge funds or private equity, we are willing to consider new managers, especially if they are spin-offs from a larger well-known hedge fund manager," says Kannam. "They are hungry when they start out and want to build a reputation." Kannam says they also look for teams that have worked together elsewhere.

Wesleyan is happy with how the absolute return plan is working out. "While the traditional equity managers have been down [in 2000], the hedge fund managers have been up." Risk has been lowered, and returns are different than those of traditional equities.

"We haven't yet perfected a benchmark in evaluating the managers," says Kannam. Currently, Wesleyan looks at the peer universe as well as achieving a multiple of T-bills. The endowment believes in rebalancing.

Wesleyan has not yet fired a manager. The main reason for terminating a manager would be for failing to adhere to his or her stated style or strategies—for example, if the manager says he doesn't use leverage and he does.

Kannam says they are trying to get the Wesleyan board to look at the seven hedge fund managers as a subportfolio rather than individually. One of the long/short managers has been volatile. While he did the best of the seven in 1999, he is doing the worst in 2000.

Kannam feels the staff and committee relationship at Wesleyan works well because the large investment committee has divided itself into small groups. The staff makes recommendations, and the overall board tends to defer to the small committee group.

What would Wesleyan like to see changed about the hedge fund industry? Kannam says he would like to see more information and transparency. He expects that fees will eventually be pressured lower but believes that you get what you pay for and doesn't have a problem with the current fee structure.

PART FOUR

Moving Forward

20

WHERE THE HEDGE FUND INDUSTRY IS HEADED

The hedge fund is at an exciting crossroads. The number of new funds being started and diversity of hedge fund managers' styles are at a peak. At the same time, institutional interest and allocations are at an all-time high.

The year 2000 served as an interesting litmus test of whom the top hedge fund managers are. With the Dow Jones Industrial Average, S&P 500, and Nasdaq dropping 5.6 percent, 9.4 percent, and 39.7 percent respectively, the true hedge fund managers showed their colors. Those managers that were not truly hedged or did not have adequate risk controls fell by the wayside.

In this watershed environment, changes need to be made for the hedge fund industry to continue to grow and prosper in the long term. These changes need to be made both from the manager as well as the investor point of view.

Cultures are different between the hedge fund community and the institutional community; an acknowledgement of that will go a long way in working out a mutually beneficial compromise. In some instances, most hedge funds managers' objectives are absolute return whereas institutions are used to relative performance and benchmarks. Another issue is that most hedge fund managers prefer using a fund structure to avoid regulation. Most institutions prefer separate accounts so they have more transparency.

Transparency is an area that needs work. Hedge funds use trading programs and strategies that are very different from the traditional long-only investments to which most institutions are accustomed. Risks differ for the various hedge fund strategies. As a result, it is difficult to summarize the risks of a pool of hedge fund managers in a comprehensive manner. Transparency would go a long way to resolving this issue for institutions. Furthermore, institutions that are experienced in venture capital are used to receiving investment details and would like to see the same practice with hedge funds. Institutions are interested in knowing what other investors are involved—or at least the types of other investors.

Institutions are becoming more knowledgeable and experienced in hedge funds. Many feel comfortable enough to focus on strategies outside of market neutral or to delegate assets to a strategy other than fund of funds. Some are allocating to new managers or non-U.S. managers. Many are focusing on specific strategies. Institutions are not concerned that fees are too high but generally prefer hurdle rates. This is a feature they will continue to push for.

Some institutions are requesting that managers understand their needs and customize innovative product to meet their needs rather than just sell them ready-made product. The institutions want consistent returns, lower volatility, and lower correlation to traditional investments. Along these lines, managers need to be more client-oriented. Investor relations appears to be an area that many hedge funds have not placed emphasis on.

Manager capacity and size will continue to be an unresolved issue as the top managers grow even more as institutional assets flow in. Managers need to be cautious as they grow; they need to continually measure and quantify the impact of increased size on performance. Their top priority should be delivering superior performance through various market conditions—not being the largest hedge fund in order to collect the most fees.

Investors need to continue their strong due diligence efforts to avoid the blow-ups and problems that have occurred. One main issue is determining when a manager has reached his or her capacity. Too many assets could hurt a manager's performance. And if the institution does allocate to a mega-manager, it needs to find out who actually is managing its assets—is it the main portfolio manager or a subportfolio manager? The experience of each needs to be considered. And if it is the latter, is the subportfolio manager qualified and as experienced as the main manager?

Managers need to make technology their friend (i.e., to harness the flow of technology) to give them an edge. As some of the strategies become more complex and global, only those managers with technological capability will be able to take advantage of the complexity. A bifurcation by manager skill and capabilities will take place.

And the hedge fund firms need to succeed in perpetuating their firms. Team structures and culture need to be instilled so that the next generation at these elite firms can take over and maintain the work that preceded them.

Endnotes

1 The Watershed Events of 2000

1. MAR/Hedge International Conference on Hedge Funds, October 12, 1998.
2. *New York Times*, "A Tiger Fights to Redeem His Old Roar," December 19, 1999, page 1.
3. MAR/Hedge International Conference on Hedge Funds, October 12, 1998.
4. Ibid.
5. *Business Week*, "The World's Best Money Manager—What You Can Learn from Julian Robertson," November 12, 1990.
6. Ibid.
7. *Business Week*, "Wall Street's Best Kept Secret," November/December 1990.
8. *Wall Street Journal*, "Tiger Funds Go Prowling for a Partner," June 30, 1997.
9. Ibid.
10. *News & Observer*, Raleigh, North Carolina, April 2, 2000, page E1.
11. *Wall Street Journal*, "Tiger Makes It Official: Hedge Funds Will Shut Down," Gregory Zuckerman and Paul Beckett, March 31, 2000.
12. *Wall Street Journal*, "George Soros Alters His Style, Making a Role for Son Robert," June 16, 1000, page C1.
13. CNN, "One More Soros Farewell," June 9, 2000.
14. *MAR/Hedge*, "New Soros Manager Trades Mostly Currencies," September 2000, page 3.
15. *Wall Street Journal*, "How the Soros Funds Lost Game of Chicken versus Technology Stocks," May 22, 2000, page 1.
16. Ibid.
17. Ibid.

18. George Soros, *Soros on Soros: Staying Ahead of the Curve* (New York: John Wiley & Sons, 1995), page 40.

19. Robert Slater, *Soros: The Life, Times and Trading Secrets of the World's Greatest Investor* (Burr Ridge, IL and New York, NY: Irwin, 1996), page 71.

20. Ibid., page 74.

21. Ibid., page 85.

22. Ibid., page 90.

23. *Soros on Soros*, page 63.

24. Ibid., page 28.

25. George Soros, *The Alchemy of Finance* (New York: John Wiley & Sons, 1987), page 13.

26. Slater, page 18.

27. *Soros on Soros*, page 28.

28. Slater, page 29.

29. *The Alchemy of Finance*, page 15.

30. *Soros on Soros*, page 10.

31. *MAR/Hedge*, "Decision-Making at Its Best," October 1996, page 10.

32. *Soros on Soros*, page 11.

33. Ibid. pages 11–12.

34. Ibid., page 59.

35. Ibid., page 65.

36. Ibid., page 68.

37. Ibid. pages 69–70.

38. Ibid., page 10.

39. Ibid., page 12.

40. *USA Today*, "Super Traders Throw Tradition Out Window," James Kim, page 5B.

41. *New York Times*, "House Panel Given a Lesson in Hedge Funds," April 14, 1994, page D1.

42. "Malaysia Mahathir Scolds US Allowing Soros Speculation," Dow Jones News Service, August 22, 1997.

43. *Soros on Soros*, page 247.

44. Ibid., page 212.

45. Ibid., page 237.

46. Ibid., page 246.

47. *Wall Street Journal*, "Soros to Appoint a CEO after Firm's Chaotic Year," August 10, 1999, page C1.

48. Ibid.

49. *Time*, "Turning Dollars into Change," William Shawcross, September 1, 1997, page 49.

50. *Time*, "The New Philanthropists," July 24, 2000, page 50.
51. Jack Schwager, *Market Wizards: Interviews with Top Traders* (New York: Simon & Schuster, 1989), page 193.
52. *Money*, September 22, 1987, page 32.
53. *Wall Street Journal*, "Steinhardt to Close His $2.6 Billion Funds," Laura Jereski, page 11.
54. *Wall Street Journal*, "Odyssey Is Dissolving $3 Billion Firm," January 13, 1997, page B4.

2   Unofficial Reasons for Retirement

1. *Wall Street Journal*, "Tiger Funds Go Prowling for a Partner," Laura Jereski, June 30, 1997, page 11.
2. CNNfn, "Another Soros Goodbye," June 2, 2000.
3. *MAR/Hedge*, "Turning Point—Asset Size versus Performance," June 1994, page 6.
4. John Bogle, *Common Sense on Mutual Funds* (New York: John Wiley & Sons, 1999), page 99.
5. Ibid., page 100.
6. Ibid., page 264.
7. Ibid., page 168.
8. Fraser Seitel, Emerald Partners, Infovest21 Conference, June 8, 2000.
9. *Wall Street Journal*, "Steinhardt to Shutter His Hedge Fund," October 12, 1995, page C1.
10. Robert Slater, *Soros: The Life, Times and Trading Secrets of the World's Greatest Investor* (Burr Ridge, IL and New York, NY: Irwin, 1996), page 155.
11. Ibid., page 156
12. *Wall Street Journal*, "George Soros Alters His Style, Making a Role for Son Robert," June 16, 2000, page C1.
13. Ibid.
14. *MAR/Hedge* median benchmarks, www.marhedge.com.

3   Overview of the Hedge Fund Industry

1. *MAR/Hedge*, "Good News—and Bad—for Hedge Funds," October 1999, page 1.
2. *MAR/Hedge*, "Hedge Fund Fever Comes to Europe," February 1998, page 1.
3. Infovest21 Conference, September 7, 2000, New York City.
4. *MAR/Hedge*, March 1999, page 44.
5. *MAR/Hedge*, June 2000, page 39.

6. *MAR/Hedge*, January 2001.

7. *MAR/Hedge*, September 1998, page 44.

8. *MAR/Hedge*, Web site, www.marhedge.com, January 2001.

9. Ted Caldwell, *Look Out Mountain Hedge Fund Review*, "Selected Reprints from 1996."

10. *New York Times*, "After a Fund's Fall Is Wall Street Wiser?" Roger Lowenstein, September 17, 2000.

11. Roger Lowenstein, *When Genius Fails* (New York: Random House, 2000), page 146.

12. Ibid., page 191.

13. *Wall Street Journal*, "Long-Term Capital Chief Acknowledges Flawed Tactics," August 21, 2000, page C1.

14. Ibid., pages 113–114.

15. Ibid., pages 95–96.

16. Ibid., page 113.

17. Ibid., pages 127–129.

18. Robert Schulman, Tremont Advisers, MAR/Hedge International Conference, October, 1998.

5   Lee Ainslie, Maverick Capital

1. Annual Partners Meeting 2000, Pierre Hotel, New York City, October 19, 2000.

2. Ibid.

6   Leon Cooperman, Omega Advisors, Inc.

1. *New York Times*, "On the Defensive, Wamaco's Chief Executive Plays Aggressively," June 7, 2000, page 1.

8   John Henry, John W. Henry & Co.

1. Managed Futures Association, Chicago, Illinois, July 13, 1995.

2. *Time*, "A Hedgie Bets on Baseball," April 26, 1999, page 56.

3. *Miami Herald*, "John Henry, an Unusual American Success Story," January 31, 1999.

10   Bruce Kovner, Caxton Corporation

1. *Wall Street Journal* "A $100M Man Finally Gets Attention, Much to His Chagrin," October 11, 1991, page 1.

2. Jack Schwager, *Market Wizards: Interviews with Top Traders* (New York: Simon & Schuster, 1989), pages 53–54.
3. *Wall Street Journal*, "A $100M Man Finally Gets Attention, Much to His Chagrin," October 11, 1991, page 1.
4. *Forbes*, "Trust Busters," June 2, 1997, page 146.
5. *Washington Post*, "Illustrated Bible Is Everest for Artist; American Barry Moser Said the Spiritual Project Provided the Challenge of a Lifetime," August 7, 1999.

13 Paul Singer, Elliott Associates

1. Infovest21 Conference, June 8, 2000.

15 S. Donald Sussman, Paloma Partners

1. *Barron's*, "Unhappy Returns," March 29, 1999, page 18.

16 David Tepper, Appaloosa Management

1. *Institutional Investor*, "The Rise and Fall of Michael Smirlock," December 1, 1998.

18 Institutional Interest

1. *Wall Street Journal*, "Investors Get Invitation to Come Mix with Rockefellers," March 1, 2000, page C1.
2. *HedgeWorld*, "Oklahoma Firefighters Retirement System May Alter Hedge Fund Mix," September 7, 2000.
3. *HedgeWorld*, "LA Looks to Place $50M in Event Strategy Fund," September 22, 2000.
4. *Wall Street Journal Europe*, "CalPERS Gets Nod for $11M Investment," September 22, 1999.
5. Hiroto Satomi, ITOCHU, Infovest21 Conference, June 8, 2000.
6. Ibid.
7. *Nikkei Finance Daily*, "Sumitomo Life to Boost Substitution Investing," May 17, 2000.
8. *Nihon Keizai Shimbun*, "Tokio Marine and Fire to Expand Alternative Investments," July 3, 2000.
9. John O'Hara, Commodities Corp./Goldman Sachs, Infovest21 Conference, June 8, 2000.
10. *MAR/Hedge*, "Zurich Pension Plots Alternative Investment," September 2000, page 10.

19 Significant Endowment Presence Continues

1. NACUBO, Endowment Study, prepared by Cambridge Associates, Washington, DC, 2000.
2. Ibid.
3. Ibid.
4. *HedgeWorld*, "University of South Looking for New Hedge Fund Home for Its Tiger Dollars," June 16, 2000.
5. *HedgeWorld*, "Texas A&M Triples Hedge Fund Holdings," August 21, 2000.
6. *Alternative Investment News*, "LA College Looks to Investing in Hedge Funds," September 2000, page 1.

Index